EAST END TO WEST END

The role that paid the mortgage!

EAST WEST
END to END
JOHN CAIRNEY

First steps in an
Autobiographical Journal

MAINSTREAM
PUBLISHING

British Library Cataloguing in Publication Data

Cairney, John
    East end to West end.
    1. Acting. – Personal observations
    I. Title
    792.028'0924

    ISBN 1-85158-175-8

Typeset in 11 on 12pt New Baskerville by
Blackpool Typesetting Services Ltd, Blackpool
Printed in Great Britain by Billings & Sons, Worcester.

FOR MY CHILDREN
JENNIFER, ALISON, LESLEY, JANE
and
JONATHAN

WE ADVANCE IN years somewhat in the manner of an invading army in a foreign land. The age we have reached we hold but as an outpost. We still keep open our communication with the rear and the first beginnings of our march. There is our true base, and not only the beginning, but also the perennial spring of all our faculties, where familiar things become the shadow shapes of memory, and where we can return, upon occasions, to the still-enchanted forests of our childhood.

Robert Louis Stevenson
from 'Virginibus Puerisque', 1878.

PROLOGUE

What is the first thing you can remember? I mean, the very first thing that comes into your head? Don't force it. Don't try to think of something. Just close your eyes for a moment and let the picture come into your mind.

In January 1981 I was being interviewed on a Sydney radio station by a charming woman called Carolyn Jones. She was a good interviewer in that she genuinely talked to her guests; even more, she listened. She made the interview a conversation, and in the course of ours she and I had got to talking about early memories, and I suddenly said to her, 'What is your very earliest memory?'

She answered with hardly a hesitation, 'Lying under a jacaranda tree and looking up to the sky. I must have been in my pram.' She went on to talk about the scene quite beautifully. 'What's yours?' she asked.

'My earliest memory?' I said. Like her, I tried not to think of it too much, but I hardly needed to. 'A stone wall,' I answered. I saw it at once, as soon as she asked. It was just there. Maybe it had been there all the time. A wall, a grey, stone wall, running at my right-hand side for as long as I can see. I don't know it it's a high wall or not, but I know I can't see over it, and I wonder what lies behind it?

Later that night, while having a meal in the Chinese quarter with the programme secretary, Maggie Dallmyer, and her husband, I learned that calls had come in to the show from all over Sydney about people's first memories. And had apparently led to some funny incidents Down Under – fair dinkum!

One man rang in to say he was putting up wallpaper and was at the top of the ladder at full stretch to the ceiling when he found himself listening to what we were saying. He patted the wallpaper in place then came down to turn up the volume on his little 'tranny', but before he could climb up the ladder again, the roll he had been sticking slowly unrolled, bringing with it the roll beside that and the roll beside that and so on, until he could only watch his morning's work peel off the wall – all for a bloomin' radio show.

A wife rang in with a story about her husband. He had said goodbye to her as usual at the front door before going off to work. Normally, she said, she stood in the doorway in her housecoat and waited until he had got the car out of the garage and down the drive, then she would nip out, close the garage door, and run back in. That morning however, he seemed a long time getting out into the main stream of traffic. She closed the garage door, and hurried back to her front door and, glancing back, saw that he was still there. From her kitchen window, she looked out again and saw him slump over the wheel. 'My God, he's had a heart attack!' She rushed out again and down to the car. She was in such panic that she'd forgotten she'd taken off her housecoat and was standing at the driver's window in her nightie! She wrenched open the door but her husband's hand was immediately raised for her to be quiet. He was fiddling over the radio controls and saying, 'Listen to this Scotch guy. He's on about the first thing he can remember.'

Nostalgia for a tenement

It's a sordid, derelict waste land now
Where not even weeds will grow
But I did! On that very spot
Many years ago.
For here once stood a building
Proud and clean and neat.
Now there's no trace
Of that special place
In the rubble at my feet.
But I can still remember
What this street was –
Once upon a time . . .

JOHN Cairney, my grandfather, is the beginning of my story, and in name at least is also the end of it. He is the alpha and omega of Cairney lore, the keystone of my family wall.

Like many west of Scotland Scots, John Cairney was really more of an Irishman. John's father, James Cairney or Cairns, settled with Sarah Devine or Divine in the Lanarkshire coal-mining communities east of Glasgow in the middle of the last century. Like so many thousands more, they were refugees from the Irish potato famine of 1845. They just got on the first boat they could get from Donegal and got off where it landed them. Mine landed in Glasgow and made their way to Coatbridge.

Parish records show that John Cairney was, in point of fact, christened John McKearny at Old Monklands parish, his brother Edward was Edward Kernes, brother James was Kerney and another brother Tom was Carney, as were the four sisters, but as far as the family is concerned the name is Cairney. The name is not Irish at all, but Scots, and is a variation of a place called Cairnie in Kincardineshire, near Keith, which is up Aberdeen way. Cairnie granite is quarried there: 'a silver stone with natural lustre, which dulls if over polished. Is impervious to inclement weather, but is brittle and breaks easily.' Abercairney, Invercairney, Cairney-mount and Cairneyhill also occur down the east coast to the north shores of the Forth, so a Cairney must have been around at some time. Family hearsay, which is a lot more dependable than parish records anyway, insists that a John Cairnie walked south from there when Victoria was crowned. Whether he did or not, we can't be certain now, but we like to believe it.

What we do know is that John Cairney, my paternal grandfather, was eighteen and living with his father and mother in Bargeddie, a mining village between Coatbridge and Baillieston, in 1878. He was a collier, like his father, and like every other man he knew. He also played the pipes – Scottish bagpipes. Young John was a very good piper. He had the pinkie, you see: both his little fingers were curved, the easier to curl round the stops in the chanter. John the Piper, he was called, and after his shifts at the coal face he played at dances, social occasions, weddings and the like. An imposing figure he must have made – not in kilts, but in a suit as befits a Lowlander – in a black suit, starched collar, and a Stewart tartan tie. He also had the beginnings of what was to be later a luxuriant moustache. A favourite with the girls, too, was John. Especially with one – the Baillieston police sergeant's daughter.

Theirs couldn't have been the easiest of courtships. He was a poor white-trash Catholic, and she the daughter of a policeman, Protestant, Masonic/Orange Order ascendancy. Protestant reaction to Catholics in Scotland has always been extreme, but at that time was particularly rabid. The Irish had flooded into Glasgow and its environs, much as the Pakistanis and Asians were to do a hundred years later, and feeling against them was just as bigoted and unreasonable, and therefore extra-vehement. The present and ridiculous Rangers and Celtic divide in the city is proof that virulent traditions die hard. Certainly, their path of true love did not run too smoothly and it all came to a head on the night of the police dance.

As was the custom, soloists were hired for the dancing for a couple of shillings. John was the piper that night, but the only problem was that because of his shift at the Barrachnie pit, John couldn't walk home to Bargeddie in his pit clothes, wash and change into his suit, and get out again to catch a tram to the Masonic Hall for the dance in time to pipe in the top table. It was the sergeant who suggested that, since John had to walk past the Baillieston police station on his way to the pit for seven o'clock that morning, he could leave his suit, shirt and new black boots along with his pipe-box at the desk and collect them at six o'clock that night on the way home. He could clean up and change at the police house and walk round to the hall with the sergeant in good time for 7.30 p.m. when the guests would be assembled. This seemed a sensible plan. So, on the morning of the dance John handed in at the front door of the police station his wooden box containing his precious pipes, his best boots in a brown bag and his suit on a hanger. The sergeant himself came to the door in a long-sleeved vest and trousers with braces dangling. John had never seen him out of uniform before and was a little taken aback. But the good sergeant only grinned from a face half-shaven, the white lather thick on one side, and taking the things in, placed them in the hallway.

John returned that evening as arranged and knocked at the door, leaving a black knuckle print on the white woodwork. He tried to rub it off, but that only made it worse. He was covered in a film of soot from his cloth cap to his steel-toed working boots. His hands and face might have been black, his eyes and lips red, but the whites of his eyes were sparkling, and his heart was high with hopes for the evening. He had never been in such a fine house as the sergeant's. And he would see Margaret, the sergeant's daughter, again. The grin on his grimy face vanished as he found himself staring, not at the expected sergeant, but at the sergeant's wife, a tall, overbearing woman who was by no means reasonable. John didn't like her, and she certainly didn't like John. Furthermore, she didn't like Catholics or miners or pipers and would he clear himself off from her clean front door forthwith! John stammered some-thing about the sergeant. The sergeant was busy. And the daughter? She would thank him to see no more of her daughter. It was not her wish she should marry beneath her. John thought he heard crying from inside. He found himself getting very angry, but he kept his temper. He had to wash and change for the dance.

'Not here you won't!' he was told firmly.

'But the dance –'

'The dance is in the hall,' retorted a pair of pursed lips.

'But the sergeant said –'

'Whit the sergeant said is nae concern o' mine. He disna wear his stripes in the hoose.'

That's for sure, thought John. 'OK, Missus. If ye'll just hand me oot my pipes there. Here, I'll get them –' He made to enter but she stopped him with a screech.

'Don't you dare come in my hoose wi' your dirt!'

John would have pushed past her to get his things, but the door was opened from the inside and Margaret was holding his box.

'Here are your pipes, John,' she said shyly.

'Thanks.'

He was as embarrassed as she was. He took the box, trying not to smudge her hand with his sooty fingers. He looked at her, already in her blue frock for the dance. She was very beautiful, he thought, but he noticed her eyes were red.

'And what about this suit here?' interjected the mother.

'You can keep it, Missus. You might need it. You obviously wear the breeks here!'

13

He gave a last look at the girl, who was now half-hidden by the door. He wanted to say something, but couldn't. He only shrugged and turned away. As he did so, he heard the mother going on at the daughter. The door shut hard behind him.

He walked away quickly, because he walked angrily. He walked blindly past the police station, past the Miners' Institute at the edge of the village, past the tram terminus at Coatdyke, all the time cursing his fury at policemen, and especially policemen's wives. He hardly noticed that he'd walked past his own house. He was still angry, and still in his pit clothes, still walking, as darkness began to fall, but he only lit the oil-lamp fixed to his cloth cap and kept on walking, angrily, relentlessly. Night gradually closed in around his marching figure, and he was beginning to feel a little foolish by now but still he didn't stop. He was faltering now, and no longer angry. Just sad. He had loved that girl. He thought . . . Ach, what was the use? He wasn't their type, their class. What was he after all; just another ordinary miner who could sing a bit and play the pipes. What was so special about that? He wondered how the dance had gone. Who had they got in his place? How had she looked in that blue frock? Who had she danced with? There'd be talk. Oh aye, there'd be talk. Now that it was dark and he was tired and hungry, he felt a bit stupid. Where the hell was he?

A farmer on a milk cart found him, lying flat on a grass verge fast asleep, his head on his box, his miner's lamp shining up into the early morning sky.

'I thought ye was a darkie lyin' there wi' a light shinin' oot yer heid!' the old farmer told him when they'd got in the house.

'I'm a miner,' said John.

'There's nae mines aboot these pairts.'

'I'm a piper tae.'

'I wondered aboot the box.'

John was given a chance to wash and then tucked into a big breakfast. The old man also gave him a change of clothes. 'Ye canna gae aboot wi dirt on yer back like that.'

'But I can't –'

'Of coorse ye can. They're my son's. He's not much older than ye are yersel'. But he'll no' be needin' them noo.'

'Why is that?'

'He's awa' at the university in Edinburgh.'

'Is that right?'

'Aye,' said the old farmer proudly, 'he is that. Here, eat up that milk there. It cam fae a guid coo.'

14

'Aye.'

There was silence for a bit before the farmer spoke again. 'Is it trouble then?'

'Whit?'

'Running' awa' in pit claes wi' a pipe box.'

'No' really,' mumbled John. 'I juist took a notion.'

'A notion for whit?'

'Tae jine the army.'

Till that moment, John had never thought that he was going to join the army! It was the first thing that had come into his head. Well, what the hell? He couldn't go back home – not now – or could he? What would his father say? And his mother would murder him! There was no turning back now.

'Aye, ye'll be for Perth then. That's where the Black Watch is.'

'Aye, Perth,' said John. The Black Watch! Why not?

And that's how John Cairney joined the army.

Before that day was over he had swopped the farmer's son's tweeds and moleskins for the kilt and red tunic of the Royal Highland Regiment or the Black Watch, also known as Pontius Pilate's Bodyguard. On nothing more than a whim, he had accepted the Queen's Shilling and enlisted as a bandsman for no less than seven years with three in the reserves – or he could sign on for twenty-one and qualify for a pension.

'Seven'll dae fine,' John told the sergeant-major.

'Very good, my lad. Sign your name here if ye can write.'

'I can write.' And he signed his name.

'Very good,' said the sergeant-major again. 'So ye're a piper, eh? Very good. We'll soon have ye blawin' a braw tune.'

And so John Cairney became, not only a piper in a band, but a soldier of the Queen.

Within the year, he was in the pipe band that led General Roberts into Kabul at the end of the Afghanistan war, then found himself at Kandahar playing during dinner on the verandah of the officers' mess. Quite a change for a lad who'd never been further than Glasgow, and then it was only to the St Andrew's Halls with his father to hear Gladstone speak on the Fenians and Irish Reform. Funnily enough, he remembered Gladstone saying that there would come a time everybody would get a university education.

'We'll never see it, son,' his father had said on the tram journey back from the big city. John thought of the farmer's son.

John was a fully-fledged second-row piper in the regimental band by the time they were posted to India where he met Colonel

15

Kitchener. Maybe that's when he – John, I mean – started to grow a moustache. His next posting was to Egypt through the new Suez Canal, opened less than ten years before. Then the tour of duty was up and he came home by way of Gibraltar and the Bay of Biscay. And all because he 'took a notion' to walk one day to Perth! The boy-bandsman was now a soldier piper and the moustache was now thick on his handsome, tanned face as he came ashore at Glasgow Meadowbank Quay, a tall figure in red tunic and green kilt, with his pack on his back, a rolled bag on his shoulder and his pipes in their box. The battalion were dismissed on the quayside, and John made his own way through the docks and into Argyle Street at Partick.

It was 1890, he had money in his pocket for the first time in his life and he had shaken hands with General Roberts.

Now it was time to get home again. He looked for a tram that would take him to Drumpark, outside Coatbridge, where his parents now lived. First, though, he would have a cup of tea. He would have preferred a dram, but better not to go into the house with drink on his breath. He found a little tea-room and went in. He was served by a very striking little red-head with a strong Irish accent.

'So you're from auld Ireland then?' he asked her as she cleared the table.

'No, I'm from Smith Street.'

'Where's that?'

'In Hillhead.'

'Is that in Glasgow?'

'Is it daft ye are? Of course it is.'

'It's a big place, Glasgow.'

'Will ye be wantin' more tea?'

'Sure, I will,' said John, and he had another cup – and another. Till the place was closing and he had missed the last tram to Coatbridge.

'Can I walk ye to your street, Miss?'

'What, with all this gear an' all? And you full o' tea. Ye'll need a cart.'

'I'll manage,' said John cheerfully.

'Here, let me carry your box at least,' said Ellen. 'In the name – what's it ye have in it?'

'My pipes.' John grinned as he watched the girl struggle.

'Is it lead they're made of?'

'Naw,' said John. 'Silver and gold and ivory from the East.'

16

'D'ye say so?' said the colleen, wide-eyed.

'Naw. I was only kiddin'. I bought them from Chisolm's at Glasgow Cross. Here, let me.' He swung them up easily and they made their way into the gas-lit streets. 'Where's this Smith Street then?'

And that's how my grandfather met my grandmother, Ellen McLaughlin.

They were married within the year at St Bridget's, Baillieston, and on a June morning moved into a miner's cottage in Buchanan Street. Their first child was a boy, and they called him John, but he died in infancy. The next child was also a son, so they called him John too. But he died as a baby. The next child was called James. By this time the South African War had broken out, and John was called to the regiment again. It's not known if Field Marshal Roberts had asked for him personally, but John went out anyway, as a pipe-major for General Kitchener.

'Don't get yerself killed now,' my grandmother had said.

'Don't worry, Ellen,' replied my grandfather. 'No' even the Boers would shoot a piper!'

Ladysmith could not have been more relieved than was my gran when her John came marching home again just over a year later, this time not in the red tunic but in the new khaki – but the kilt was the same. Some things must never change.

Life no doubt resumed as easily as it was predictable for a miner's family: down the pit and up again all week, a long lie-in on a Sunday, and only births, weddings and funerals to break the monotony. The difference was that John was now a piper in his prime, and he was given a job on the surface by the bosses, so that his lungs could be spared. His two young sons, however, James and Edward, now with him at Barachnie, were not so lucky. James, named for his old Irish grandfather, was first into the miner's cage as soon as he left school, followed by Edward, who was named for his uncle. My uncles had been clever at school, especially James, particularly in mathematics. The headmaster of the primary school, Mr McGregor, as well as Canon Horgan (referred to by James as 'Canon Fodder') both made determined efforts to keep the boys at school – at least to secondary level, even to the university in Glasgow. They were convinced that James would win the scholarship. But it was hopeless. John and Ellen now had four children in the house and another one would be born the following year. It was a lot of mouths to feed on little more than a pound a week. The boys' pittances were needed. So the older boys did not go up to St Pat's, Coatbridge, after all, but down the mine. Which was a pity for all concerned, as James was already a great footballer, and the school team could have done with him, and Eddie had a lovely tenor voice, which would have been an asset to any school choir. All the Cairney boys could sing. The only trouble was that they were all tenors so they all had to learn to harmonise!

So two mere wee boys had to swallow their ambitions along with the coal dust. But they never quite lost all their academic leanings. James would take a book on the calculus to the coal face, and at break-time sit with his back to the seam and work out problems. Eddie's reading was a dictionary, and he would sit opposite his big brother, learning new words in order to catch him out. But he rarely did.

So their years of youth passed, and with them their parents' happy and productive marriage. Another sister, Sarah, was born to join Mary and Tom, and the burgeoning Cairneys had to squeeze up a bit in their little miner's cottage. The older ones used to stay with their various aunts to relieve the dormitory pressure at home. And when John himself was away on piping business or at the championships, Gran would take the two youngest in beside her. If it was poor, at least it was cosy.

Then the First World War happened, and nothing, anywhere, was ever quite the same again. Grandad Cairney was forty-eight and head of quite a big family. Ellen, the third girl, now made the team up to six. But John was fit and strong, and insisted that the army take him back. It was thought, however, he should serve this time as a piping instructor, rather than as a front-line soldier, and though quite indignant at this, he agreed and, once more, was in uniform. A rather portlier figure this time, but Gran was happy. John did see some action, however, but it was only at Maryhill Barracks in Glasgow, where as a sergeant he was constantly separating his large Black Watch Highlanders from the ferocious little Glaswegians who made up the Highland Light Infantry. The latter were very poor soldiers but inveterate fighters, and the former, though slow to anger, were formidable when roused, so the officers and NCOs of each regiment had their hands full. And these men still had to see a German. Grandfather did get to France. I think he must have written to Kitchener! He got as far as Paris. From what I hear, it was a very different sort of action he saw there. The kind not mentioned in despatches!

He was home again in 1918, and in the following year was given the honour of leading the massed pipe bands in the Victory Parade from George Square to the Glasgow Green. The whole of

18

Baillieston was delighted for him! The route to be taken was from a general muster on the Glasgow Green then a march up the High Street along George Street and into the Square, round the Square and the same route back to the Green for the stand-down and dispersal. James and Eddie waited there with ten-year-old Tom to see their father come in leading the parade. The boys were proud of their marching, pipe-major father in his kilt and bonnet with the plume. To Tom, the youngest, he was still a god, a hero figure – as every father should be to a ten-year-old son. Tom was determined that when he grew up, he would be a piper too. The little boy looked forward to going home in the tram afterwards with his father and big brothers, and to carrying the pipe-box, which his father always let him do. And he'd promised to buy ice-cream wafers from the Italian man with the barrow. That was the best bit.

The day of the parade was very hot, and the crowds sweltered in the afternoon heat. The lemonade and ice-cream men were kept busy, and the fresh supplies were constantly being called up. These were delivered in huge lemonade lorries and one of these lorries was having a hard time making its way to the Square via North Frederick Street, which was a very steep incline from Parliamentary Road down to George Square. The driver was taking it very gingerly through the crowded street, when the overladen lorry lurched foward out of control. The brakes had given out. The driver jumped clear – people screamed – and the lorry careered down the rest of the hill. People got quickly out of its way, and the lorry, now with all the force of a juggernaut, smashed into the parade as it passed in the Square at that very moment, ploughing straight into the front line of the pipe band – killing John Cairney instantly.

The funeral was a big occasion in Baillieston. People couldn't remember a bigger turn-out for anybody. The MP was there, the Colonel of the Black Watch, the provosts of Glasgow, Coatbridge and Airdie, all the priests, the Church of Scotland minister and the Salvation Army choir. Gran stayed at home with her three daughters and baby son, Philip, but the boys walked with the men to the graveside. Tom was supposed to play his boy's pipes at the grave, but he couldn't do so for crying. A man from the police band stood in as Tom ran to his brothers. It was in all the newspapers. It was almost laughable – the irony of it. Here was a man who had walked to Perth, climbed the rocky foothills of Afghanistan, sweated on the plains of India, sweltered on the sands of Egypt, survived the Bay of Biscay in a troopship, not to mention the whole of the First World War and dangerous years down a pit, and then was knocked down by a lemonade lorry! So ended the eventful life of John McKearney or Kerny or Kernes or Carney, but known to me as the John Cairney, my father's father and my grandfather. A fund was instituted for Gran and her seven children, and it was enough to set her up in a newsagents sited opposite the Baillieston police station.

As always, whatever happens life goes on, although it was still capable of a few surprises – even shocks. They say troubles come in threes, and the next sadness for the Cairneys was the illness of daughter Mary, the one who played the piano. She was the quiet one, and when she married John McGovern, who was even quieter, they both seemed to fade into a distance of their own, emerging only to produce a couple of quiet sons. Mary played the piano beautifully. Goodness knows how they could ever afford to buy one, but there it was in the bedroom, pale mahogany with candle-holders. She would sit and play for hours, when she was well enough. Then suddenly the music stopped. Mary had slipped away. She had been like a wraith for most of her life, but now in death she took on real ghost substance. Her husband said very little. He was always a quiet man. He just got quieter.

The third trouble was not long in coming. At that time, pit ponies were employed to pull the coal-bogies up the gradients under-ground, and although it wasn't his job, James made a point of feeding the little animals now and then. He also fed the rats, so that they would give him peace to eat his 'piece' and read his book by the light of his lamp. If he threw something into a corner the rats would scurry after it and leave him alone. Sometimes he and Eddie would switch off their lamps and in the absolute blackness listen to the rats' squeak and try to judge how far away they were. The Cairney brothers were early into radar! One break-time, James was standing at the foot of one of the gradients. He had just released one of the ponies from its traces, and was feeding the little animal, when the bogie it had been pulling was suddenly knocked along by another bogie and it came rolling down towards them. Eddie shouted to his brother to get out of the way, but James tried to get the pony out of the way instead, and the steel bogie, gathering speed, caught the young man on his bare back and broke his spine. But he had saved the pony. Uncle James would spend the rest of his life as an invalid. Paralysed. Except for his hands and arms. And all for the sake of a blind pit pony.

With Jim in London, 1959

The brothers rigged up a system of pulleys and wires at his direction, so that he could work away at his various bedside projects, keeping his hands and his mind busy, and help keep his mind off himself. Twenty-two years of age and everything to live for: about to sign for Celtic, doing a correspondence course on electricity and wireless, engaged to a very nice girl, the pride of the Legion of Mary. The irony was that James and she were about to be married when he left the pits to become a football player. It was all so unreasonable, so unfair. Celtic sent him all the books he wanted and paid for the rest of the correspondence course. They said he might even get a degree by post.

'Aye,' James said wryly, 'the *Sunday Post!*'

His girl visited for a long time, but eventually her visits became fewer and fewer and then stopped. The next thing they heard was that she'd gone to be a nun.

If James could no longer go out in the world, it seemed as if the world now came to him. A mirror was fixed up which let him see out into the street, and at the street door another one was angled to let the outside people see in. Everyone knew about James' mirror, and no one would pass that door without at least passing the time of day. When he was tired he would just turn his mirror off, so to speak. His remarkableness was now shown to the full. They still speak yet in the family of the circle round the bed nearly every night for singing, or stories or cards, and endless discussions. Canon Horgan would engage James in debate adjudicated by Mr McGregor, with Eddie listening and nodding, and young Tom practising with two fingers on Mary's old piano which was now in James' room with all his instruments and books. It was from a book that he made a 'Cat's Whisker' – the first wireless to come to Baillieston. It caused a sensation, and even interfered with the regular card-school! From another book, he built an aeroplane, a bi-plane, with a real little engine and a propeller. It could really fly, and made regular purring flights into the curtains, till one day somebody left the window open!

It's not known when Uncle James slept, or if he ever did. He did all his reading through the night, and seemed to be busy all day. He never seemed to be tired or depressed. He had always a joke and a quip for every situation, and a word for everybody. Maybe that was part of his act, a kind of latent hysteria perhaps, underneath the calm. It must have been hard for him, despite his brainpower and his sense of humour. It takes character to be an invalid, and not a little bit of acting. He survived like this for ten years; then one morning when Gran came in with his tea he was lying smiling up at her – dead.

Gran Cairney moved her survivors up the road to a new one-storey building put up by the Baillieston Co-op. She was given the keys which had, tied to them with twine, a brown cardboard label on which was written in a spidery hand: Mrs Ellen Cairney. No 38f. 2 apt. Dwelling. The Widow Cairney had taken possession, and in doing so, revealed her true colours. She was a tower of strength to her fatherless brood, and ruled them as if with her steel poker. Not yet sixty, she was in the prime of her fighting Irish fitness, and laid about her freely when required to.

Her only weakness was my father, who was now twenty. To be twenty in the twenties was supposed to be in heaven. Well, it could be said around then that my dad was having a helluva time to himself. It was not a time to be serious. With his pudding-bowl hairstyle in a razor-sharp centre parting, his ears sticking out like tail-planes above a high-buttoned collar, he was the natty young gent of the period, even to the extent of a Norfolk jacket and spats over two-toned shoes. By this time, he had learned to play the banjo and ukelele, and was the recognised life and soul of any party. Even then, he was known to enjoy a drink. In order to finance his hectic social life, he was not above dipping his hand into his mother's shop till. If anyone else had done that, she would have cut their hand off, but Tom was special in her eyes. He was the piper. He was his father's son. It was certainly true that he had an uncanny manual musical skill. Whatever the instrument he took up – pipes, violin, piano, guitar, banjo, uke – he could play them all, and was self-taught.

Uncle Eddie, since the loss of his hero-brother, retreated into himself more and more, and to his gramophone records of operatic tenors. He would sit for hours winding up the horn gramophone by the handle, and singing to Caruso, McCormack, Gigli and the others. Everyone teased him about not being married. Uncle Eddie said there was time enough for such drastic action.

And 'drastic' might be exactly to the word to describe the marital action taken by Ellen, the youngest and prettiest daughter, when she took everyone by surprise by falling in love with a Protestant! Andrew Swan was a big, bluff, hearty, good-natured man, who loved Ellen Cairney as much as she loved him, but Gran Cairney proved unexpectedly intractable. If Ellen persisted with this match, she would be shown the door, and her name never mentioned again. It was the other side of the police wife's coin. And it was heads or

tails who was the worse offender: the sergeant's wife for not allowing John Cairney to court her daughter, or John Cairney's wife for
not allowing her daughter to be courted by a Protestant plumber.
She was marrying a good man who had a good business and was
popular in the village, but the doughty Irish mother saw no further
than a dreaded mixed marriage. She hadn't even met Andrew, but
that made no difference. Her daughter would go to hell if she
married that man, and that was the end of it, and she could go to
hell if she went ahead with it.

Things came to a head when the red-headed mother faced the
red-headed daughter, four angry eyes locked in an impasse. Neither
would give way and Ellen left to join her Andrew and make her own
family just down the road and round the corner, never to be
mentioned in her mother's house again. And she wasn't. It seems
silly now, but it was a life or death matter then, and Gran Cairney
was convinced she'd consigned her youngest girl to hell. I don't
think she ever forgave herself. By now she was nearly inured to
trouble and misfortune in her family – and they talk of the luck of
the Irish!

So, with the stoicism bred from hard experience, she gave a hitch
of her long white apron, rolled up the sleeves of her black blouse
and got on with the business of working-class survival. Fortunately,
her other daughter, Sarah, was that commodity much needed in
every large family – a saint – who contented herself looking after
the house while Gran looked after the shop. Sarah knew she would
join her husband-to-be, now in Canada, as soon as he had saved up
enough dollars to send her fare. Philip, the youngest, was already
showing signs of becoming an even better footballer than his big
brother James. Not only were Celtic asking about him, but Mother-
well too, and an English team called Middlesbrough, but Ellen
wouldn't hear of her boy leaving home, and Philip, in his easy-going
way, wasn't all that bothered either. He was the only child not to
have known his father, but sister Sarah spoiled him as much as
Gran spoiled Tom. Between both women, both boys were virtually
waited upon.

Eddie could only shake his head. 'You're just wasting those boys,'
he would tell his womenfolk, then light up his pipe and go back to
his operatic records and his biographies. Eddie must have had a
tough time trying to find a quiet corner in that house.

Philip was by far the most relaxed of all the children. He was
happy enough to keep himself to himself playing 'headers' with a
tennis ball against the garage door, or 'keepie-uppie' with the

bigger 'tanner-ba' on the back green as long as there was light. He knew what he was going to be, and was happy enough to wait for his day to come.

It was Tom, my father, Tom, the piper's son, who was the hyper-active Cairney and the cause of most rumpuses in that fatherless household. He never seemed to be able to hold a job for long, and at that time jobs were hard to get, but Gran Cairney refused to be deterred. Being friendly with Mrs Connolly, she was able to influence Mr Connolly, the local transport and haulage contractor, and Tom was now working for him as a lorry driver. That was another strange twist of the Cairney fate – John Cairney's son, Tom, as a lorry driver. Not that it mattered, he was rarely in the driver's cabin. With his mate, and fellow-driver, Tam Smith, he was nearly always to be found in a card-school somewhere playing for money, or playing any of his many instruments for whoever would listen, or just lying behind a hayrick on Cameron's farm smoking a stolen cigarette. My father was Baillieston's Huckleberry Finn, and Tam Smith his Tom Sawyer.

Tom Cairney, however, was just as smart as his two big brothers had been, although there was a lazy, wilful streak in him, almost a weakness. Eddie had wanted him to be sent to music college, but to Tom that seemed too much like work. He had been given, in full measure, all his father's charm, and had no qualms about twisting his mother and sisters round his finger. His instrumental skill and pleasant light singing voice gave him the kind of social cachet that his father had enjoyed a generation before with the pipes. It was only a question of which woman was going to grab him. Mary Coyle did.

She was one of the same kind of Irish brood as he was, but with a difference. She was a city girl, he was a country boy. She lived in the East End, in Shettleston. They each came from seven of a family, but where the four Cairney brothers had three sisters between them, the four Coyle sisters had three brothers between them. And where the Cairneys were sandy-haired, choleric, volatile, big-eared and brilliant, the Coyles were taciturn, saturnine and uniformly handsome. Black-haired, black-eyed, pale-skinned and lithe, the girls – Sarah, Grace, Mary and Bridie – perfectly complemented their three brooding brothers – John, Hugh and young James, who was much less Brontë-like and perhaps most like the outgoing Cairneys in temperament and personality.

Unlike the Cairney house, there were few books in the Coyle home, though plenty of magazines. They had a gramophone too, but their records were all dance music, and Paul Wightman playing 'When Day is Done' and lots of early Bing Crosby. No opera here. Certainly no bagpipes, although young James Coyle had a drum-kit in the garden shed. The only real musical taste the two families had in common was for lugubrious Irish songs, preferably sung by Count John McCormack.

No two families were less alike. Where Grandfather John Cairney had been large, genial and overt, Grandfather John Coyle was monosyllabic, so as almost to be mute. Where the Cairney children had worshipped their father, the Coyles almost went in fear of theirs. He ruled his family the way he ruled his railway repair gang. With a crowbar! Yet one wondered what secret grief contained the man, or perhaps it was only that he lacked the Cairney gift of tongues! John Coyle was always behind his wall.

But if their father was austere, the Coyle family were more than compensated by the tall, graceful figure of their junoesque mother, Agnes O'Neil Coyle from Warrenpoint, County Down. 'The Little Flour' my father called her. She was always baking! Where little Gran Cairney was sharp and spiky and all elbows, large Granny Coyle, on the other hand, was ample, soft-bosomed and radiated calm. She did much to compensate her children for their dour father. Perhaps she was the only one who understood his shyness. Granny Coyle found all her happiness in her baking, her children and her church duties at St Mark's. She was truly a Mother Superior in every sense of the word.

She was just the kind of mother my mother needed, as I believe that Mary Coyle, her fourth child, and third daughter, was something of a spitfire when young. So much so, she had been sent to Ireland to work on her father's cousin's farm to cool her down with some hard work, but Mary ran away within weeks and arrived back in her own house one evening in bare feet and with someone else's coat. She had made her own way back, and wouldn't say how she did it – and she was only sixteen. Old John blustered, but his little Mary Elizabeth remained firm, and nothing more was said. She was mad crazy on dancing – ballroom dancing. She was a good dancer, and given her flashing looks and good figure, she was a very popular partner with the boys, as she curved her way through her teenage years. Dancing was all the rage then and every club hall, social and institute had its weekly dance. One favourite venue was the Miners' Institute at Baillieston. The miners themselves had just built that hall and the young men had laid the most modern floor: 'a rare flair', as Glaswegians called it. It became the mecca for all the ballroom dancers for miles around, and my mother was one of a party of girls who came out regularly in the No 15 tram on a Saturday night for 'the dancin'' at the Baillieston 'Stute, as it was popularly known.

One winter's evening when 'the snow lay on the ground', the Baillieston boys created an icy path leading from the tram lines to the door of the dance hall. They covered it with a light film of snow, so that when the girls jumped down from the tram, most of them slipped and slid all the way down to the pavement, where the Baillieston boys were waiting for a glimpse of stocking or something just as shocking. My mother was there that night with her older sister, Sarah, and both of them made the posterior journey down the path to much shrieking and laughter from the watching boys. Mary landed with her flailing legs about her blushing face, only being stopped by a dandy figure who stood above her, arms akimbo, laughing down at her confusion. She was all ready to give him a piece of her considerable tongue when her eye caught the spats he was wearing under his Oxford bags. It was now her turn to laugh and his to blush. He turned quickly away, but as he did so, he slipped on the ice and fell on his bags, with much loss of male dignity. She helped him up nevertheless, and after some thawing out around the institute stove, they danced the rest of the night together.

The next week he took her to the pictures in Glasgow to see and hear, for the first time, Al Jolson in *The Singing Fool*. While they stood in the queue at the Coliseum, he proposed to her. He swore for years he was only making conversation, but she called his bluff, and married they were before the next summer was out. Nine months later, to the day, almost to the hour, I arrived.

It was 1930, a Sunday in February. Around lunch-time, or dinner-time as they would have called it, in Gran Cairney's at 38f Buchanan Street, the men had just come back from last Mass, and my mother was struggling with me in the back room.

'Bear down,' Gran Cairney kept calling.

'There, there,' said old Dr Gracie.

From all the various doors in the building came the smells of Sunday roasts and the sounds of Sunday talk, but from that small back room came the strong stench of fear and the sounds of heavy labour. Meanwhile, down in the Boy's Guild Hall, which also served as a changing-room for the scratch games of football, my father sat

27

playing cards with his friends, while his young brother, Phil, waited on the doorstep at 38f, ready to act as runner as soon as the big event materialised. Since he was the athlete, it was thought he would be the quickest in fetching my father to the scene of the crime! But I was a long time in coming. Maybe I had a premonition of what was to come. Which was more than my poor mother had, such was the innocence of between-the-war Catholic girls from working-class families. My mother was encouraged in her ignorance of the facts of life by well-intentioned parents and relatives, who thought that such knowledge would only get her into trouble. Therefore it must have come as a shock to find out what really happened at a birth. Especially where she was prominently involved! As Dr Gracie, in wing collar and dark morning jacket, tried to reassure her, and Gran was holding her down, muttering to herself in Gaelic, poor young Mary retreated further and further from what she said were the doctor's 'sore fingers' and fell on to the floor – where I was born.

I am sure my young mother was both surprised and relieved.

'And what are you going to call your boy, Mrs Cairney?' enquired the doctor kindly.

'John, of course,' snapped my gran without being asked.

'John,' said my mother meekly.

'John Cairney,' added Gran quietly.

There appeared to be no complications, and Gran and various aunts, mother and son were soon sitting up prettily awaiting visitors, the first of whom should have been the proud father. Uncle Phil ran at full speed to fetch his brother Tom but the new father had a winning hand and would not leave the table – even for me.

As another Cairney, and another John, I was the apple, not only of my mother's eye, but also of my gran's. Perhaps it was only because I was another John Cairney, but I gather that Gran Cairney doted on me. But I had eyes only for the bread bin! An ordinary, white enamel, square-shaped bread bin with a removable lid on top and B–R–E–A–D etched out in large black letters on the front of it. The B had a chip out of it, as if it really had wanted to be a P instead of a B. As a baby, no matter whose arms I was in, I would crane and twist and turn till I was facing that bread bin, and would howl the place down till I did. Whenever I cried for any normal, infant reason, the call would go out for the bread bin, and it would be plonked directly in my eye-line, at which, for some mysterious reason, I would immediately be quiet. No one could understand

28

why. The link between a baby and a bread bin is not one that is immediately obvious.

I was just over a year old when my parents moved into a home of their own, a tenement flat in Parkhead. Brother Jim was expected and arrived a few months later. By which time, the Cairneys were established with their two beds, sideboard, table and four chairs, at No 20 Williamson Street, Parkhead, Glasgow E1. This was a ground floor, street-facing, room and kitchen and brother Jim was born there. We were the full extent of the new Cairneys. When my sister, Agnes, was born in the regulation eighteen months after Jim, we moved upstairs, second landing on the right. Poor little Agnes died of meningitis at nine months, and my mother had no more children. Not because she couldn't – she wouldn't. I don't think she ever really recovered from the catastrophe of her baby daughter's death.

My only memory of my sister is seeing Dad carrying a little white coffin down the stairs towards me. I had to press back against the stair window to let him pass by.

Like every child, I was given to play acting. I was right into religion at five years of age. I was forever celebrating Mass against the sink at home, draped in a velour tablecloth with a vase as a chalice and forcing toddler Jim to be my altar-boy. I made up my own Latin, and used to drive my mother mad as she had to push me aside to get in and fill the kettle or a dinner pot. And I would grumble like mad about having my 'service' disrupted. Jim would take the chance to disappear again. Generally, into the shoe-cupboard.

My finest performance was reserved, however, for my First Communion Day, 5th December, 1935. The tradition in Glasgow was that after breakfast in the school with classmates, we were given a holiday, but first of all we had to have the mandatory photo taken by the professional photographer in his studio.

Our local photographic studio for all occasions was Jerome's at Bridgeton Cross and I was duly taken there. I behaved perfectly and all went well, but coming home again the trouble started. Since my mother thought I looked so smart in my white silk blouse and black velvet trousers under a smart grey coat and with black patent leather shoes and white socks, she decided to take me out to Baillieston to show me off. I must have been especially full of grace that morning, for no sooner had we settled in our seats in the lower deck than I had my good coat off and was heading up the gangway to the driver's door where I turned and solemnly, and very loudly, with exaggerated gesture, began to make a very deliberate sign of the cross intoning, 'In the Name of the Father, and of the Son, and of the Holy Ghost . . .' I then invited everyone to say their prayers. 'Our Father, Who art in Heaven, hallowed be Thy Name, Thy kingdom come . . .'

Most people laughed, my mother tried to hide. One old woman joined in. My mother had me off that tram at the very next stop. And there we were, stranded on the pavement on the Shettleston Road, my mother trying to get me into that little grey coat again, and me, full of tears and frustration at being cut off so early in my public ministry! Meantime, the tramful of pagans went hurtling on to Airdrie.

My mother was more cautious with me in public after that. She used to keep a scarf handy, and if it looked as if I were becoming too voluble, or impolite in the volume of my candid comment, she would put the scarf round my neck and pull – tightly. An attack of mumps soon after was more effective in silencing me. And if I got it, Jim got it. So both of us had scarves on!

We were also both in Belvedere Hospital with scarlet fever at one point. I was given a post office van and remember pressing the bright, red cold metal against my brow. I must have enjoyed my first-ever stay in hospital because when I came home I insisted on my mother going about with a white tea-towel on her head so that she'd look like a nurse!

I have only the happiest memories of my early schooldays. Apparently, on my first day I caused some consternation in the infant class by not wanting to go home at the end of the first day. It took the combined efforts of my mother, Mrs McGowan, the infant mistress, the janitor and a macaroon bar before I'd leave.

Elba Lane School, a wooden U-shape of cream and tan bungalows set round a tarmac playground facing the brick wall of Adam's scrapyard, was not only my first school, but the occasion of my first sin. It was 1937, Coronation year, and the bunting was still up everywhere in red, white and blue streamers. I was seven, which meant I was technically within the age of reason, according to theologians, so I have no excuse. As in all Glasgow schools, the sexes were rigidly kept apart, girls on one side of the class, boys on the other. In our respective sides, we sat two by two, as if in the Ark, sharing a desk, the same bench seat and an inkwell. My companion in that year, though not my best friend as the girls say, was an easy-going little East Ender with a taste in cream buns, Pat Breslin. He brought two in every day. His father worked in the City Bakeries, so it was either a taste he was born with, or which he was helped to develop. It was a taste denied me, however, for Pat never, on any day, offered me as much as a lick of one of his overloaded cream buns. I felt deprived, frustrated and one day I took the matter into my own hands.

He was on what we called Milk Duty one morning. That is, he took round the little half-pint bottles and distributed them, with a straw, round the rest of the class. We would then sit and sip them at our desks. For some children there, it was their first meal of the day. The poorer children got free milk, but we paid a halfpenny for ours. This morning, Pat was longer than usual for some reason, and I yielded to temptation. The two buns were sitting on his desk awaiting his return. I sat staring at them, and then, in a wonderful, exhilarating spasm of guilt I swept one up into my mouth and had it swallowed by the time he came back. A small riot followed. I acted out my total innocence defiantly. Even though there was probably flour all round my mouth and a blob of cream on the end of my nose! But there was nothing he, or even the teacher, could do about it now. No cat could have felt more content. Pat brought only one bun to school after that.

Then the guilt set in. As Catholics, we're trained early in guilt. It is almost a concomitant pleasure to any sin. No sin worth its salt could be properly enjoyed unless it carried its full quota of guilt. But by the end of that day, mine was hurting. Should I own up to Pat, should I tell the teacher, my mother, the priest? It was agonising. I had to make amends somehow. I couldn't buy him a cream bun. That would be admitting the crime. Besides, I had no money. When I got my Saturday sixpence from Dad at the end of that week, I had my plan. I bought a little bar of Fry's chocolate and ran with it to the church. Going right down to the altar rail, I placed it under the statue of Our Lady with the Infant Jesus. 'That's for the Baby Jesus,' I whispered.

I looked at the chocolate lying there – pristine, untouched by a child's hand. I looked round. Only the usual old women in black. I reached out and quickly snapped the little chocolate bar in two. 'My mammy said too much sweeties is bad for ye.' And I ran up the aisle with a half in my hand and out into the Saturday sun. I knew Our Lady would understand. As long as Baby Jesus enjoyed it. He must have done because it wasn't on the rail when I went to Communion the next morning.

A thirties childhood was mostly spent outside, and for an East End Glaswegian that meant in the streets. There was plenty to do. Apart from the football, there was roller-skating on the asphalt, guidies and girds, leavie-o, kick-the-can, moshie and all the other esoteric pastimes. Everybody knew by a sort of street-osmosis when it was time to move on to the next thing. A peculiarly city game, however, if only for the boys, was what was called 'hudgies'. This was the practice of jumping on the tail of a lorry as it stopped by the traffic lights at the junction of Springfield Road and London Road. You were then carried along London Road to the next lights at Carmyle. The trick was to jump off at these lights and get a lorry back. Even if you didn't it wasn't too far to walk back. If by chance you missed the lights at Carmyle, you had another chance at Mount Vernon. After that, it was the great unknown, but that's how I got to visit Edinburgh for the first time!

I caught this lorry one afternoon at the lights on our corner. Traffic wasn't nearly as heavy then, and I had no trouble getting on the back of this big, open, empty lorry. But I missed the lights at Carmyle. What's more, I missed them at Mount Vernon, or else that lunatic driver went through a red. For he was a lunatic, or a cruel bastard. He must have seen this idiot eight-year-old clinging to his tail-board as he hurtled along the London Road. But he didn't stop. He didn't stop at Uddingston, or Newhouse, or Harthill or Bathgate, while I clung on eagerly, then anxiously, then frantically. I pulled myself up over the tail, on to the boards of the back, and crawled behind some tarpaulin to try and get some shelter from the wind as that maniac hurtled that lorry along the Edinburgh road. He didn't stop till we had reached Princes Street!

I was frozen with cold and terror as he came round and dragged me off. He was laughing his head off as he pulled me on to the pavement; taking my shoulder, he wheeled me round to face the way we had come. 'Glesca's that wey, son. Here (he gave me a threepenny bit), that'll get ye hauf-wey there! Unless ye want tae try an' get another hudgie back?' Still laughing, he climbed up into his cabin and drove off, leaving me tearful on the strange Edinburgh pavement.

But as I looked up I saw the castle. Wow! A real castle in a street? I was absolutely stunned. What a sight it was: Edinburgh Castle rising out of the Princes Street Gardens. It was a fantastic wonderland to a Glasgow keelie. Without hesitation, and with no thought now of my predicament, I headed straight for it. I had to get in to that place. I didn't know then that you had to go in from the

Esplanade on the Royal Mile. To me the only obvious way was to climb the wall from the Gardens. In doing so, I skinned my knee badly, and lost that driver's threepenny bit. I came slowly down from the ramparts realising that I couldn't take Edinburgh Castle all on my own. I was only eight. It started to get darker and I made my way back to Princes Street, with its foreign maroon trams. I was starving and now that all the excitement was wearing off, I suddenly became what I was – a lost and frightened little Glasgow boy all alone in Edinburgh.

I started to cry standing under the statue of a man on a horse. Nobody took the slightest notice. I tried to stop a couple of women, but they both brushed me aside. I started to howl. I must have made quite a noise for a policeman appeared and he took me along to the police box where I blubbed out my tale. A tail of a lorry ride! The Edinburgh policeman could not have been kinder. He gave me tea, and put his tunic round me while he went on the telephone. I had only a shirt and short trousers on and sannies. I was glad of the tunic. It was still warm. He then took me for a bag of chips and walked with me to the bus station while I ate them and put me on a blue bus. Then he had a word with the conductor, gave me a salute, and a bar of chocolate, and sauntered off. I gave him a wave from the platform as we drove off. The conductor let me sit at the place reserved for luggage. It was lovely and warm, and I fell asleep. It had been quite a day.

I was wakened as we were coming in to Glasgow and the conductor said, 'I wis tae let ye aff here.'

I didn't know where I was. And I got frightened again. 'But I don't live here,' I said.

'Too bad, son. But ye get aff here. They're expectin' ye.'

I was put off at Tobago Street police station, off the London Road. The bus had actually passed our own street. The conductor pointed to the door I had to go in, then the bus drove off. I went fearfully into the police station. There was a sergeant at the desk – and there was Dad in the waiting-room.

'*Dad!*' I flew at him, and leapt into his arms.

'Sign here, sir,' I heard the sergeant say.

Even though I was a city boy, a Glasgow keelie as I said, the country connections with Baillieston were still maintained by way of a No 15 from Parkhead Cross. We caught this tram every Sunday after eleven o'clock Mass at St Michael's, so as to arrive at Gran Cairney's in time for the traditional family Sunday dinner after the twelve o'clock Mass at St Bridget's. This Sunday institution, followed by tea at the other gran's on the way home, was to provide the bed-rock on which all my childhood security was based and provide the armature on which I would hang most of my boyhood experience.

Aunties, with talk of babies and nappies, and recipes and knitting patterns and other, unmentionable things, whispered or mouthed silently across the table. We children soon learned to lip read! And cheery uncles, with red faces over starched white collars, some still wearing their caps on in the house, some with moustaches that caught in the soup – soup you could stand your fork in. And not only family, strangers came too. Friends who were visiting, and friends of friends. Even the man who came for the Sunday church collection! All packing into those two rooms, jostling for room to sit among the rosewood furniture, or spilling on to the outside landing, to lean against the railings in the sun. What crowds there were round that kitchen table waiting for the main course: succulent stewing steak, with floury potatoes and green veggies that were really green. And 'soor dook' and creamy milk to drink or what seemed vats of strong, sweet tea in huge teapots. What feasts. And the dumplings, vast 'cloutie' or cloth dumplings replete with currents, raisins, and wee silver threepenny bits! Enough to pay the whole family's tram fare home that night.

Nearly everybody lived within easy tram-travelling distance of each other before the war. The private car was a rare luxury. Mr McKinlay, the coalman in the next close, had the only one in our street. It was years before the next one appeared. Till then, everybody, in Glasgow at least, lived their lives on tram lines. Blue buses were only used when you had to really travel: Balloch, or Stirling or Edinburgh. Trains were for the impossible journeys: Aberdeen or London or Stranraer for the Irish boat. Everywhere, and everything else, was by tram. Or the 'caur' as we called it. Rattling and trundling along on gleaming rails that snaked the huge city in a kind of steel cobweb, the tram car was everything to the Glaswegian: the perambulator carrying the new baby home, the tumbril carrying the schoolboy to an exam, the carriage taking the city Cinders to the ballroom where her pimply prince awaits, having come just as far in another tram, which had another colour, another number. It was a shopping basket for wifies in shawls, a removal van for newly-weds, a wagon for the football warrior, an ambulance for Saturday drunks, and for us on a Sunday, a douce charabanc for all the family. Sparking under high wires, guided by gauntleted drivers in peaked caps, grim as granite, controlled by conductors who were part-time Corporation employees and full-time comedians, the caur noisily threaded its way through the patchwork of city streets, giving its colour to the greyness on either side of it. To travel by tram car was, in every sense, to be transported. You knew where you were with a tram. You were on rails, you see.

And after the Sunday walk along the new road to admire the asphalt, you came back with your uncles to find all the dishes cleared away and the best tablecloth laid on which tea was served – quite daintily too, for the adults, while the children played and squabbled outside. We were called in and lined up and given a biscuit and a coin and a quart bottle of soup to carry, sealed with silver paper secured by an elastic band. I remember how hot it was on my short-trousered legs sitting on the car on our way home.

This was via our other gran's where we had yet another meal, a kind of high tea, at dusk, and left from there at nightfall with yet another cache of small coins given us by yet more uncles and aunts, and now carrying, in addition to the soup, a batch of Granny Coyle's newly baked treacle scones, still steaming under a tea-towel. It was always a very tired quartet of Cairneys which finally mounted the two flights of stone stairs to our flat in Williamson Street every Sunday night. Jim and I had hardly time to count our hoard of pennies and threepenny bits before we were asleep in the room bed and, through the wall, our parents in the kitchen bed quietly argued about some incident in their day. Then the popping sound as the gas-mantle was turned off and darkness and silence fell on a tenement. Another Sunday had been survived. They were nearly always the same, these Sundays, until one Sunday in September which was very different: Sunday, 3rd September, 1939.

We didn't go to either gran's that day, but instead, like everybody else in the country, we sat in our own house, listening to the battery wireless, and to the voice of a man called Chamberlain talking to us all from London: '... no such undertaking has been received and consequently, I have to tell you that this country is at war with Germany.'

'Does that mean us, Dad?'

'Sure does, son.'

'Whit'll we dae noo?' asked my mother.

'Put the kettle on,' said Dad.

Thanks to a piping contact, Ned Keegans (who actually was a side drummer), Dad was given a place at the furnaces in Beardmores, the local steel works, providing he agreed to coach the works band and play for the army cadets. Anything for a job, so Dad took it. He found furnace work harder than he bargained for, so he wangled himself a union post and spent most of his shifts 'in meetings'. He was no fool was my old man.

He was now thirty years of age, and in danger of becoming an elderly dandy, but the war came just in time for him, and since he was just too old to be conscripted at the outset, and still young enough to enjoy wearing a uniform, he joined the Fire Service. He said his experience at the furnaces made him a natural 'fire' man. My mother, who had only worked in Coats' thread works for a very short time between leaving school and marrying, was drafted to the Echo radio factory in Rutherglen to make electric switches. She didn't mind. I think she enjoyed the company of all the women. She made friends there whom she kept for the rest of her life, Lena Aniello and Jean McGregor and others. She also learned to smoke. But that was later. Meantime, she was anxious for her two boys. She was only twenty-eight, but looked younger. She always did.

The outbreak of war affected everybody's lives. Wars do. Uncle Phil, the youngest Cairney, had been about to become a professional footballer the year before, but he was badly burned in an accident at Hinshelwood's paint factory in the Gallowgate and couldn't leave for Middlesbrough when he was supposed to. He was brought home from the factory in an ambulance and I have a picture of him sitting in Uncle Eddie's big chair at 38f looking like the invisible man, swathed in bandages from head to feet, and only those light, bright blue Cairney eyes peering out. A young girl was with him. A laughing girl from Newbank, Glasgow, called Mary Preston. Theirs was to be a war-time wedding. Uncle Phil was young and strong and fit and he recovered well.

At any rate, he could still run. I was staying at Buchanan Street around that time, and getting some row about something from Gran Cairney. It must have been serious, or she was in the right, for I took great offence, and rose from the table, and ran away. It was morning, and I just had short trousers on and bare feet. But I was out that door in a jiffy, down the outside stair and out round the front and into the street. I ran as fast as my bare feet could take me and roughly in the direction of Glasgow, but in no time I heard the same pit-pat of bare feet behind me. It was Uncle Phil, still in his pyjama jacket, but with braces flying behind his trousers, and he was gaining on me with every stride. I was always able to run, and now I was going really fast. But so was he. I felt a hand on my hair, and I was dragged to a halt. Still holding me by the hair he had me, in no time, up before Gran again. 'Ye never finished your toast,' was all she said.

Uncle Phil was called up almost right away, and never got to sign for Middlesbrough. Jim and I were evacuated. Like a million other city urchins we were plucked from the familiar streets, and in a special train from Whitby Street Station, Parkhead, we were 'evacuated' with the rest of St Michael's Primary for 'the duration of hostilities'. In some cases, this was only until the next weekend! Most survived till Christmas and a few never came back at all. Our train-load of little East Enders finished up at a tiny railway station 'Somewhere in Scotland' as they said then. It could have been Mars for all we knew. The only sign we saw said GENTLEMEN. One of the smaller girls thought it said Bethlehem!

There was a sharp smell in the air. We soon learned it was fresh air. Coming as we did from our city smells of soot and smoke and gas and chips and damp stonework, it was unnerving to suddenly smell country smells – like wild flowers and wet grass and all the thousand scents of soil. We were the invaders, a children's army, gas-mask crusaders, gas-light pale, grimy with street dust and already street-wise to the adult world. But these were a different kind of adult: real country folk, with centuries of natural quiet behind them. But not for long. We were all on the Home Front now. The posters on the station platform said:

CHILDREN ARE SAFER IN THE COUNTRY.
LEAVE THEM THERE.

We were left all right. A long line on the grey flagstones, waiting with our teachers. Some of the tiny ones were already crying, even though they had their mothers with them. I felt like crying myself when I thought of my own mother. 'Don't get separated,' she had said.

I wonder how she had felt that morning, giving her two children away to complete strangers, not knowing if, or when, she would see us again. She was told not to worry, we would be all right, and anyway, didn't she know there was a war on? I pulled Jim, smart in his new Burberry raincoat, a bit nearer me, and he dropped his little brown case and everybody could see his new slippers, new pyjamas, new toothbrush – and his old football boots!

'Keep still, you Cairney boys!' said a teacher's voice.

Strange teachers – not Miss Callaghan or Miss Mulligan from St Michael's. I wished they were. We would have felt safer. We checked our gas-masks in their cardboard boxes. Jim and I had sweets in ours – just in case. I knew we would eat them before the Germans got us. One boy had his pet mouse in his! We then checked the name-tags pinned to our lapels, just to remind ourselves of who we were. We felt like parcels, being posted to people who didn't really want them. The foster-parents, those mothers and fathers by government order. Strangers who had to become instant family. It was like being up for sale: 'Bring all your second-hand children here! Every one a bargain! Only slightly used. Two careful owners since birth.'

It was a bit of a risk all round. But we were to remember there was a war on! A funny war it seemed to me. The 'Phoney War' they called it. I wonder who we'll get, I thought. I wonder who'll get us? Jim and I were lucky. We were selected by Sir Malcolm and Lady Campbell of Westerkirk, Dumfriesshire, and, to the envy of all our classmates, we were swept away by Sir Malcolm in his big Armstrong-Siddley. I was only sorry it wasn't 'Bluebird'!

Like Winston Churchill and most of the Second World War generals, I started keeping a war diary. Mine seemed entirely composed of headlines culled from the four-page newspapers of the time. Things like the entry for 9 April 1940: HITLER INVADES DENMARK! The only difference for 10 April was: HITLER INVADES NORWAY!

A month later I had a feast:

GERMAN ARMOURED COLUMNS SWEEP THROUGH NETHERLANDS!
KING LEOPOLD SURRENDERS BELGIUM TO THE NAZIS!
BRITISH EXPEDITIONARY FORCE RETREATS FROM DUNKIRK!
CHAMBERLAIN RESIGNS – CHURCHILL LEADER OF NEW COALITION!

I never bothered with secondary news like: 'The Evacuation of Children from all Main Centres is Complete!'

Suddenly, Jim and I were living in a mansion with servants, and as many rooms as a tenement and with a garden as big as Tollcross Park. Catapulted in a day from a two-room and kitchen in Williamson Street to the guest wing of Westerkirk House somewhere in the

As a student 1950 – The Importance of Being Earnest?

rolling ease of rich Dumfriesshire. To the opulent grandeur of the private estate from the grubby warmth of our working-class warrens. It was my first glimpse of the good life lived by the landed gentry, and I loved it. It was a good life, and I took to it as if 'to the manor born'. I'm not so sure about Jim. He didn't ever say much. There was no doubt, the Cairney brothers were living a very privileged existence as guests, however temporary, of Sir Malcolm and Lady Campbell. It was not that they were extravagantly rich or anything, and I had no idea then he was a famous racing driver. Anybody who owned any kind of car then was famous as far as I was concerned! Thanks to the war, I was now part of that charming, and charmed, world of 'above stairs' as then revealed to a very 'downstairs' little boy. It was *Brideshead Revisited* by *No Mean City*! It was certainly very different, I can tell you.

Children are the most realistic of animals, and the most optimistic. They have to be. Having no past to speak of, and a limitless future, as far as they can see, they can freely indulge in the present, in whatever is happening *now*. Not that they are without their worries. Children have their problems too, and they are no less, just because they are on the small size. Speaking of animals, skinny dogs and terrifying cats had been exchanged for horses and cows and other alien beasts. The town had come to the country overnight, and both felt the shock. I think we evacuees were the first casualties of the Second World War. I soon realised how lucky Jim and I had been being billeted with the county set. I am sure there were a few tears before all the different bedtimes in all those other billets in attics and spare rooms, and also, so I heard, in outhouses and barns. There was a rumour someone had been billeted in a kennel. The dog must have been called up!

But some things didn't change. Even in the emergency conditions of sudden war-time, the social pecking order, as ordained by county rankings, still obtained. The local squire and his lady still got first pick of the intake. I'm sure Jim and I were chosen by Lady Campbell only because we were neatly dressed alike and wore schoolboy caps. The doctor's wife and the minister's wife got the next choice, the schoolteacher's the next, then the bank manager's, the local publican and so on, down to the outlying farm labourer's family who had to take whatever was left: generally, the roughest, toughest, scruffiest little brood, sullenly disreputable and sharing a common determination to get back to their beloved streets as soon as possible.

One old farmer landed just such a section in his little agricultural cottage. It took the two local policemen, a clutch of schoolteachers, the priest and an Alsatian dog to get them out again after only a couple of weeks and on to a Glasgow train.

'I've worked all my life with pigs,' said the old man, 'but I've never seen anything like those Dolans from Glasgow. I would sooner they had sent me the Germans!'

Like the Dolans, we imagined we had come to conquer the countryside, but in fact it was the countryside that conquered us. We were cowed by its stillness, overwhelmed by its greenness, dazzled by its colour. Everything was in colour – every possible shade of green with slashes of yellow, gouged with brown, flecked with red. Maybe it was Mars? Coming as we did from our city black and white, or more exactly monochrome grey, it was hard to cope with Technicolor! There was new awareness generally, and I was grateful to this funny-phoney war for opening my eyes and ears and senses to a whole new world. I was ten years old and a born-again sensualist.

There was no doubt that the Campbells had something. Class. All we had was working class. They were fascinated by us. They would have us come into the drawing-room after dinner, and say to their friends, 'Oh, do hear how they talk. It's so odd.' I wondered if they'd ever heard themselves? Our trump card was that we could sing. We weren't Uncle Eddie's nephews for nothing. So we scored, Jim and I, with our Ernest Lush boy soprano versions of songs like 'God Keep You Is My Prayer' and 'Sons of the Free'.

But just to live in a house like that! Ghostly bedrooms, with high, dark ceilings, bell ropes hanging at every fireplace, all linked to a row of numbered bells in the kitchen, high up on one wall. Thick, carpeted stairs you weren't supposed to slide down. Long, dark, mysterious corridors. The all-pervading smells of furniture polish mixing with cut flowers in the 'posh' part of the house and carbolic soap with disinfectant in the nether regions. There was a billiard-room, where you didn't need to pay to play, a library where you didn't need a ticket to take out a book, with steps on wheels which reached the highest shelves. I never saw any of the family come near the library. Certainly not Sir Malcolm, and not even Donald, his son, whom we saw once in his army officer's uniform. Another lovely place was the morning-room. Imagine, a room just for the morning. But it did get all the sun then.

I always thought it was the 'good morning-room', for we were only allowed in there to say 'good morning' to Lady Campbell. After school in the village, we had to go to our rooms and wait there

41

till dinner, to which we were summoned by the scary echo of the Oriental gong. Even when I was waiting for it, like any normal, hungry wee boy it still made me jump. Although we were always ready for it – face and hands washed, hair combed, fresh shirt, shoes shone – and all this just to eat! Still, it was worth it. I don't think Her Ladyship had ever heard of rationing, or if she had, the hard facts of the new austerity had certainly never percolated within the comfortable walls of Westerkirk House. Certainly, there were no tea coupons for her!

The dining table seemed at least a mile long. Tall glasses. Wine for the adults. Water for us. Starched dinner napkins in chunky silver rings. Candles, always slightly tilting. A battery of cutlery to have to work. 'Start from the outside and work your way in. Miss a course, miss an implement. And if in doubt about anything, take a sip of water – not from the finger bowl – and look around. Nothing in it. Good manners are nothing but good sense.' Lady Campbell's crammer course in the social graces was much appreciated by this little boy. What we didn't get from her we learned from Atwood, the butler, before he was called up for the air force. He was a two-faced so-and-so, Atwood. So polite to the guests at every serving, yet we could see him making faces and lifting his eyes to heaven behind their backs. He rarely spoke to us.

He was very autocratic in the kitchen. Which is the polite way of saying he was bad-tempered. He had a special trick of swearing out of the corner of his mouth. Especially if Elsie was around. Elsie was the day maid, a big, strapping girl who was waiting to go into the ATS. Her boyfriend was in forestry or something, and he often used to call at the house, or the back of it at least, in a van. This used to annoy Atwood, as I think he was fond of Elsie. Although you'd never think it, the way he used to talk to her. Adults are funny.

It was Elsie who used to bath us before she went off to meet her van driver. She did Jim and me together in the big bath in that freezing bathroom. The bath, with all its Victorian fittings, was enormous. It was certainly bigger than the jawbox at the sink in Williamson Street, where Jim and I were hosed down every night with cold Loch Katrine water from the swan-necked tap. Baths were once a week either at the steamie in Tollcross Road on a Friday night, or at the Shettleston Swimming Baths every Saturday morning. Now we could both lie full-length every night in our very own private bath, and look up admiringly at Elsie who was all hot and steaming herself. She used to give us the big sponge and leave the bathroom to prepare the beds while we washed 'Wee Willie' ourselves. I remember that Jim and I weren't very sure at first who or where 'Wee Willie' was!

When we didn't know something we tried to look as if we did until we had a chance to compare notes later.

'Why does she say "Wee Willie"?' asked Jim.

'Because she's shy,' I said.

'She's no' shy wi' the forestry man,' said Jim.

'How do you know?'

'We can hear them laughin'.'

There was no answer to that.

'D'ye think the forestry man has a "Wee Willie"?'

'Everybody has. Men, anyway.'

'I thought they had "Big Willies?"'

'Go to sleep, Jim.'

We could always arrive at some kind of fraternal consensus. At times, though, in that big house, among these secure and certain people, it was difficult not to be perplexed. It was often hard to adjust. You have to remember that Jim and I came from a long line of flat caps. All this wasn't supposed to have happened to us. But it did, and we had to cope. I think Lady C was rather surprised that we had manners, and could read, and might even venture an opinion, unasked. She used to tell us some nights of the long line from which she came. Did she imagine we were spontaneous? In bed, our mouths thick with toothpaste, we would lie and listen to the silence. There was nothing like that country silence. There was no traffic, you see, no trams. Some nights, when it was still like daylight, we would lie in our beds practising staying alive without breathing, while outside we could hear Elsie giggling with her forestry man. Downstairs, Sir Malcolm would strum the piano inexpertly, while Her Ladyship would sing French songs in her unexpectedly girlish voice.

I remembered I hadn't said my prayers – and my diary! I hadn't filled in my diary.

RUDOLF HESS LANDS IN EAGLESHAM. THE BATTLE OF BRITAIN BEGINS

Suddenly, on one summer's day we were home in Glasgow again. A man came in a car and told us to pack our cases. We were sitting at a jig-saw at the time, so it wasn't as if we'd done anything wrong. He told us to hurry, we had a train to catch. Nobody came to say goodbye. By this time, Elsie and Atwood had gone and Sir Malcolm was often away, but we never saw Lady Campbell, or her daughter, or Donald the son. We left as abruptly as we had come, and it was almost as if it had never been, that season we'd had in the mansion house. Still, as my father said when we got home again, there was no doubt it had given us both a bit of polish. 'Mansion Polish,' he added dryly.

At St Michael's again, I was reunited with Miss Susan Callaghan, my formidable primary teacher. I had gone to her as soon as I came out of kindergarten at Elba Lane and she saw me all the way to the qualifying examination, or what we would call today the 11-Plus, which determined your further education, either grammar or tech-nical, which for us meant St Mungo's Academy in the city or St Mark's Junior Secondary just along the road. Miss Callaghan was determined that all her pupils should go to the Academy, and heaven help us if we didn't make it. Even in a war, she had her priorities right.

She had a great thing about reading. She would make readers of us all. That way, we could learn everything for ourselves if we had to. If you can read, you can do anything was her view. And if you enjoyed reading, so much the better, for learning's a pleasure. Her love for books was only equalled by her hatred of comics – boys' papers particularly.

'Outmoded public school rubbish,' she would mutter. 'Dangerous class nonsense. Well, it's not for my class – boys or girls,' she would declare to all of us roundly. 'What will you have to do with that kind of life anyway? No, you'll never learn anything from a comic.'

Like every boy, Jim and I devoured comics. I got the *Hotspur*, and he got the *Wizard*, Tom Gibson got the *Adventure* and Tom Gray, the *Rover*. By swopping around, we each read them all in a matter of days, unknown to Miss Callaghan. That is, until one afternoon in the top primary class, where we now were, she asked us to stand up and give her a sentence concerning any famous man in history. Starting down at the front, she made her way round the class with the more or less predictable names predominating – Churchill, Stalin, de Gaulle, Roosevelt – even Hitler and Mussolini coming from the boys, and the Queen, Mrs Churchill, Mrs Roosevelt, and several 'My Mammy's' coming from the girls.

'No, Mary, there is no Mrs Hitler!'

When my turn came, I stood up at the back like the specky, wee swot I must have been then. I wore glasses till I was about ten, and must have looked every inch the wee professor.

'Right then, John, who is your famous man?'

'Napoleon Bonaparte was a famous man,' I announced, 'who was marooned on the island of Elba.'

'Come out here, John,' said Miss Callaghan.

'I went out to the front, wondering what I'd said wrong.

'Follow me,' she said.

I was taken into Miss Mulligan's class next door, and made to say it again – much to my embarrassment.

'You see, children,' said Miss Callaghan, when we got back to our own classroom, 'that's what comes of reading. Tell me, John,' she said, turning to me, 'where did you get a word like "marooned"?'

'From a comic, Miss.'

'Sit down, Cairney.'

SUNDAY, 7 DECEMBER 1941 – PEARL HARBOUR PRESIDENT ROOSEVELT BRINGS THE UNITED STATES INTO THE WAR

How could we lose now with Clark Gable, John Wayne and Gary Cooper on our side? Not to mention Mickey Mouse, Donald Duck, Trigger, Lassie and Rin Tin Tin! We returned from our rural exile just in time for the Clydebank blitz. We could see from our room window the red glow in the sky the night the Singer factory got it. It all came down to a simple matter of survival, which meant we all went down to the shelter.

For some it was the brick shelter in the public square, for others the Anderson shelter at the foot of the garden, or the Morrison shelter, built round the dining-table, the cellar, if you had one, or a cupboard under the stairs. Wherever it was, whenever the dreaded siren went, at whatever time of the day or night, that's where you went as fast as you could run, with your pyjamas under your siren suit, two pairs of stockings, long woollen scarf, gloves and a knitted balaclava helmet. You also carried a spare blanket and pillow, hot water bottle, Thermos and a bottle of something – if you could get it. Add to that, torches, candles, books and comics, an occasional Bible, sometimes a hymn book. Children brought their favourite toy, pensioners brought their favourite photo and nearly every mother sat with a tin box on her lap. It was never opened, but everyone knew it contained all the insurance policies, all the family's birth certificates, holiday photos and her marriage lines. Why did every wife bring her marriage certificate to the shelter? I suppose it was just in case – or rather, just in tin box! Every contingency was considered. The only thing you didn't allow for was that you would be killed in the shelter. Yet thousands were. Meantime, we waited for the all-clear. While we waited we had a singsong. When we weren't singing we were talking, and when the talk died down, we slept.

We boys slept last. For us, war was still a game. For the children of the blackout generation, it was all one great adventure. Peering out into the starry night, scissored by searchlights, probing with their light-fingers, silvering the tethered barrage balloons. Or listening for the drone of the Junkers and the Heinkels above the coughing of the 'ack-ack' guns. Cheering when a hit was made, seeing the plane burst into a Catherine-wheel of coloured flame, marvelling how a parachute survived the fire and opened in the glare of its own incendiary bombs, and fell silently, like a Red Sail in the Sunset, or in an eerie silhouette. Wondering what a German looked like. Then just as suddenly as it began, it would be quiet again. Hoping the raid would last all night, or at least until two in the morning. You see, if the all-clear went after midnight, we didn't go to school till the afternoon, but if it went after 2.00 a.m., we didn't go at all! So, on our shelter nights, around half past one in the morning, when even the dogs were sleeping (dogs always knew when it was safe to sleep), there was I, among a clutch of eager, schoolboy faces at the doorway, all turned skywards, shining with entreaty, 'Come on, Gerry, where are you?'

On our way to school next morning, we crept like snails among the ruins of the night before, getting in the way of the air-raid wardens and the rescue workers, and trying not to look at the occasional dead body you could see swelling up among the rubble. Keeping a sharp lookout for bits of shrapnel, especially with a number on it. And better still, a swastika. Although I must confess I never saw one. I never found anything interesting in bits of shrapnel, but it was a boy in my class, Bill Brady, who found a map, a German map in a leather folder, with every street in Glasgow on it, written in German, but with the English words underneath. An army officer came to the school and took it away.

After school, we collected waste paper in big, hessian sacks. We took any kind of paper, even old books, for recycling. I sold my school books several times. 'Please, Miss, I lost them in the air-raid!'

I made a point of going round all the Italian ice-cream shops, because there were always bits of broken chocolate and stuff like that at the bottom of the brown boxes, and, remember, sweets were rationed at the time. Many of the Tally ice-cream shops and fish and chip shops were closed and boarded up, because the Italians who owned them had been interned as aliens. It was daft to think that Mr Matteo, or Mr Travisari, or Mr Coia were spies. In any case, people didn't take Italy's part in the war very seriously. I mean who could be serious about somebody like Mussolini? We had known our Italians all our lives. They were as Glasgow as we were. They just had a different way of swearing, that was all. And yet they were all shipped off to places like the Isle of Man, some of them for years, in case they were dangerous spies. It was the same with the Jews. Just because they had German-sounding names.

Other days we collected beer bottles, jam jars, any old iron. There was even a market for rags, woollen rags. Nearly everything could be turned into a penny or a pound if you knew where to look and where to sell. The battered streets were a rich field for enterprise. A lot of fortunes were made in the blitz, I can tell you. Somebody with a van and what seemed like a uniform had only to turn up saying, 'Wanted for the war effort,' and they could virtually take what they liked from private property. Miles of iron railings disappeared never to be seen again. Expensive furniture was shipped away for safe-keeping never to be returned. It was business as usual! Thor, the god of war, helps those who help themselves.

Other days, when it was light enough, my pals and I would go down to the railway station to watch the troop trains leaving, but there was a bit too much kissing and cuddling and crying for us. So we'd carry on down to the docks at Broomielaw and count the battleships, camouflaged in green and blue, their guns under tarpaulins, the sailors with beards. We heard that one ship, full of explosives, was saved by a handful of men from the Glasgow Fire Brigade who went aboard when it was on fire. Had it gone up it would have taken half of the centre of Glasgow away with it, so they say. They also said that a land-mine had dropped on Dalmarnock power station, but hadn't gone off. It could go up at any time, so they said. The dare we used to play was to walk past the big, red brick wall as slowly as we could. I could do it, but I generally sprinted the final few yards. My nerve never ever lasted the full distance. After all, there was a bomb in there, so they said. And they were right. One afternoon, it did go up with a tremendous explosion, taking most of Allen Street opposite with it. And, of course, removing the big, red brick wall. When my pals and I heard, we gulped and said, 'Here, what if . . .?' How many times that was said in the war.

Everybody, sensibly, lived for the moment. Keep your chin up –
hang on – wait and see. A lot of war was a matter of waiting. Standing in line. That's when the British invented the queue. People
used to join every queue they saw. After all, people didn't queue
for nothing. Mrs Drurie in our street thought she was queuing for
oranges and ended up giving a pint of blood! Blood oranges?

When I think of blood, I think of Felix McKenna. He was a couple
of years older than I was, but smaller by a head. He was a brilliant
footballer, and sometimes the only way to get the ball from him, in
what were appropriately called our scratch games behind Strath-
clyde's football ground, was to kick him. Tommy Wharton, even
then a big boy, was our referee because he wasn't good enough to
play on either of the street sides. We must have given him good
practice, for he became a world-class football referee. It was he who
told Felix and me to settle our differences off the field and not on it.

'You can fight as much as you like after the game,' said big Tom.

'Sure,' said Felix, 'anytime.'

'Sure,' said I, my blood up, 'anytime.'

'Right,' said Felix. 'Where?'

'Anywhere,' I said, a little less forcefully, 'anytime you like.'

The gauntlet had been thrown, and picked up. Now it was only
a matter of fixing the details.

'I'll come up for ye efter your tea,' concluded Felix.

'Right,' I said bravely, but my mouth was already dry.

'Let's get on with the game then,' said Tom, and blew his whistle
for the re-start.

I could hardly take a mouthful of my tea. Jim looked sympathetic,
but ate up heartily. He was such a good football player, he didn't
need to foul as I did. Then I heard it. A knock at the door. My heart
rose to my mouth but the best part of a meat pie was already there.
I swallowed uncomfortably, and went to the door. Felix was standing there.

'Are ye comin' oot?'

'Aye,' I said huskily. 'I'll get my jacket.'

Felix and I walked along London Road to Westhorn Park, talking
about this and that – mostly football. He had been asked to sign for
Shettleston Juniors, but he was still too young. I said I wished I
could be signed for somebody, but he thought I'd make a better
manager. We talked like the best of pals, yet every step was bringing
us nearer the moment when we would try to punch lumps out of
each other. We picked a spot on the other side of the cycle track,
away from view.

'Fair or unfair?' asked Felix.

'Fair,' I muttered, making a mental note to be as unfair as I could if the chance came up.

We removed our jackets. Felix threw his down. I folded mine carefully. I was in no hurry.

'Come on,' I heard him growl.

'Right,' I said, rising. As I did so, I threw a punch right away, and got him on the ear.

He staggered back, holding it. 'Here, I hivna started,' he yelled.

'But I have,' I yelled, and charged.

The battle was engaged. I don't know how long we fought in that park in the early evening summer light, but I know I was getting more and more tired by the minute. I had the longer reach, but he was faster. But he was slowing. So was I. At one point we found ourselves leaning on each other, fists flapping uselessly behind the other's back.

'Do you quit?' I said, trying to keep the plea out of my voice.

'Never,' he whispered. I moved aside and he fell flat on his face.

I helped him up. 'You've got a black eye,' I told him.

'Have ye seen your nose?' he croaked.

I felt it. It was still there but it was warm with blood.

'I think I'd say it was a draw?' proposed Felix.

'Fair enough,' I agreed.

We shook hands on it, and collected our jackets. We shared an ice-cream wafer on the way home. Part of it we put on our wounds, the rest we ate. Honour was satisfied.

'What happened to you?' my mother asked.

'I fell,' I said.

'Oh, aye.'

She didn't say any more. Nor did Jim. But then, he never did. A Glasgow boyhood had its own code, its own rules. Not that anything was ever set down formally, but by some kind of tenement telegraphy you knew what you had to do in a given situation. I had been called out. I couldn't not answer. Felix and I became the best of friends after that. At least, I never fouled him again.

I took up cricket, and in my first game I was wicket-keeper. In the very first ball, the batsman, Tom Gibson, swung – and I had to have five stitches in my left eye just above the cornea! I was obviously not cut out to be a sportsman. I could run. I might have taken up athletics and joined Shettleston Harriers with Eddie Bannon; instead I ran second-best to Bobby Gibson in drawing Hurricanes and Spitfires on our school jotters on our desks, even on the backs of our hands like tattoos! It was our own Second Front.

NEW YEAR'S DAY 1942 – HITLER ATTACKS STALINGRAD 5,000 CANADIANS INVADE DIEPPE – 4,000 KILLED

Then, for some reason, it was decided to evacuate us again. Once more, the whole school was put on a train and this time, instead of travelling south, we went north. Well, north by north-west, to be exact, by way of Oban, Fort William, Pitlochry by very slow train and then via Queen's View by bus till we found ourselves passing through Kinloch Rannoch and coming upon a hill where stood our new war-time home: Dalchosnie Lodge. It was a stately shooting lodge of some pretension, the summer house in fact of the newly late Prime Minister, Neville Chamberlain. I loved it at first sight, this Edwardian pile under the pyramid of Mount Schiehallion. This time, Jim and I were two of ten boys from Glasgow taking up the dormitory accommodation now created out of the guest bedrooms. We were to be cared for by two young matrons, Mrs Boyd and Miss Deighan, who met us in the hall. They were not like our teachers at all. They were young, they were blonde and fair, and they were Protestants! They were as new and strange to us as we were to them. Another adventure was beginning.

The girls from St Michael's were at Temple Lodge, another big house nearby, and just along the road from that was the school-house, and its one schoolmaster, Mr Peter 'Three Eyes' (he had one in the back of his head!) McPherson. The Big Mac or Burning Pete, as we also called him, was a typical Highland dominie. He was not what one expected. A bespectacled, ink-stained Horatius, standing bravely on the bridge to better things, armed with the ambiguous, double-edged sword of knowledge – too little of it being dangerous, too much a burden – he fought off our pre-pubertal Philistinism and puerile apathy, somehow keeping open, at whatever cost, the rocky road to the imagination, that shadowy region given to startling illuminations or black darknesses. Mr McPherson, it was said, had to give up the ministry for his health, but we were the gainers for that. He was a born teacher, and, thanks to that cough of his, he had found his true vocation.

A whole hazy summer stretched ahead. We stole apples, and gathered strawberries and formed ourselves into a Scout Troop –

50

the 1st Dalchosnie. We also divided ourselves into opposite houses – Boyd and Deighan. The influence of all those public school comics again! There were the usual incidents and fights and runnings away. One of the boys, Donaldson I think his name was, was drowned in the loch. We weren't allowed swimming after that.

I made friends with John McDonald, the gamekeeper's son, and he helped me to build a stage for our concerts in the games room. Not that we made that stage ourselves. Everybody helped. I was only asked to paint scenes on the pelmet and back wall because I was good at drawing. It was my first ever contact with anything vaguely theatrical. That is, if one discounts the back-court concerts we had to take part in during the blackout days in Parkhead. Everybody had to do something when the chairs were brought out and set out facing the wash-house. My song was 'Bonnie Mary of Argyle' which I thought I sang quite well, until wee Felix said I sang like a lassie. That nearly started another rammy! Luckily the siren went and the concert party scattered. But it was a false alarm.

Thanks to Mr McPherson and his love of words, their use and their arrangement on a page, which he passed on to me (for this disease – *etymologia specifica* – is contagious!), I passed the examination for a scholarship to Breadalbane Academy, in Aberfeldy, at the start of the new term. I was on the evacuation move again – and my brother came too. He was as sad to leave Mrs Boyd as I was to leave Miss Deighan. Dear young Miss Deighan.

We were once again in another private house. Not a mansion this time, but a veritable castlette. Cluny House, it was called, and it was the ancestral home of the Earls of Cluny, traditional Jacobites who had supported Bonnie Prince Charlie in 1745. Our new host, the last surviving Earl, still living at the house then, looked old enough to us to have been at Culloden! He was a gentle, retiring, pink-faced old gentleman with a snow-cap of full hair and a fondness for playing Beethoven at full blast on his gramophone in the library. He also played the piano. Not songs you could sing though. He said his music was something called Chopin. He played it in a way that made it sound as if the piano were singing. He tried to teach me, but when I found that I couldn't play his Chopin after the first lesson I gave it up!

So, from a Sir, we had moved to a Lord. It would be Buckingham Palace next at this rate! Some people are born snobs, some achieve it, but there was no doubt that the Cairney brothers had it thrust upon them! Nor did we make any effort to resist. We

51

were being seduced by circumstances, and loving it. Experience can be a good teacher.

Schooldays now meant a bus ride every morning into Aberfeldy through the gilded bronze of a Highland autumn: a blaze of copper, gold and scarlet under a blue-green sky. Fir trees and heather, with the candle-flame of yellow gorse glinting like gold on the hills above the ribbon of slate-grey road. Only purple prose can do the scene justice! I was having my eyes opened, and I liked what I saw. It was great to be twelve. Old enough to know, and yet young enough to pretend that you don't. Big enough to take a knock, yet small enough to cry when it hurts; at an age when you can let your body run as fast and free as your imagination. Blissfully, apart from our schoolmiss crushes, we were still free of sex. There's a lot to be said for being twelve all your life!

Like children everywhere, we said our prayers every night. For our side, of course. Like German children did for theirs, I suppose. And the Italians. Though why the Italians should bother, I don't know. I mean, they had the Pope playing for them! Poor old God must have been in a quandary. All those innocents bombarding Him from all sides. As innocents, we couldn't take the war seriously, even when it was becoming more serious every day. It wasn't called a World War for nothing. Of course, as boys, we all knew about war. We'd read about it in books. We'd heard old men talk about 'Passion-dale' and 'Wypers' and 'Mons'. There was a man in our street had been gassed in the First World War, and Mrs Dow's son had been in Palestine, and weren't my grandfather Cairney's medals hung on the wall of the British Legion band-room? After all, we remembered. We helped to sell poppies every November, and we stood at attention when the bugler blew at eleven o'clock on 11th November every year for the two minutes' silence.

And yet the real war wasn't as real to us as the war we saw in the local village hall every Friday night with the land army girls and the Polish soldiers. War pictures like *In Which We Serve, Waterloo Road, Mrs Miniver, Dangerous Moonlight, What Price Glory?* Sixpence, I think. Walking home afterwards in the dark, under the pine trees, holding the hands of a land army girl and a Polish soldier. The rough, calloused hand of the girl, the smooth, gentle palm of the Polish soldier. Walking between them and singing loudly, just to show you weren't scared of the tree-trunk dark. But you were. In the film, only the baddies had got killed, but in the war, even the heroes were at risk. It was best not to think about it. So we didn't.

Better to think about tomorrow morning. Who knows? A letter

might come, a parcel even from our mother. I didn't think too much about my mother, but I sometimes worried about her. She was about thirty then, I suppose, looking like Joan Bennett, the film star in turban, clogs and blue overalls, going off on her war work to the radio factory. My father was now with the Ministry of Works in London. That was his war work. Ours was the evacuation. Everybody had to do their bit. Our mother was quite alone in Glasgow, like a lot of women then. The unwitting feminists of the forties: the piston-packin' mommas, many of them working for the first time in their lives, and doing a man's job at that – for a woman's wages. Not that my mother thought much about that. She liked getting out of the house.

One weekend she came up on a visit. She stayed at the Queen's Hotel, and we stayed with her. One on either side of her in the bed. It was great to have a soft, warm mother again. Before she went back, she treated us to a slap-up meal in the British Restaurant in Perth; snook, spam, chips and dried egg. And Camp coffee from a bottle. She also wangled an extra ration of sweets. I don't know how she managed it. Then she got on the train and we were taken back to Cluny House. Jim wouldn't stop crying in bed.

Never mind, it was another day tomorrow – even with a war on! Ordinary things still happened – even in a war. The seasons took their course. Birds came and went as they'd always done, taking little notice of fighter planes or barrage balloons. Flowers appeared on the earth as usual. After all, a seed had always known what a blackout was. Rationing had no effect at all on the colour of a rose. No one told nature there was a war on. I doubt if the cows and horses and sheep took much notice either. Nature knows more about the battle for survival than any boy growing up in a war. These thoughts were prompted by the fact that I spent most of my time at Breadalbane Academy freezing on the school allotments. It was 'Dig for Victory' and every square inch of the school grounds had been turned into a vegetable garden. I found that though my nose was red, my fingers were certainly not green. I approached the spade and the fork with all the enthusiasm of a townie, even though my horticultural partner was a kilted charmer called Fiona, whose voice was like tiny tinkling bells to my Glasgow ear. I did not like gardening. I didn't win a scholarship to end up weeding!

Churchill called this our finest hour. He should have seen this thirteen-year-old. He said we were living through history. I wish I had been aware of it. But then, even to live at all is to make a kind of history. We are all our own history, each and every one of us. Mine own took a swift turnabout then, for we were all returned to Glasgow. Once again, at hardly any notice. I wasn't sorry to leave the victorious digging, but I would miss the old Earl, and his Beethoven. He died that year.

When we got back to Glasgow the first thing I saw was the piano my parents had bought for me! It was standing in the room, our bedroom, where the dresser used to stand. I was amazed. Where did they get the money to buy a piano?

'That's war work for ye,' my mother said. 'Ye said in your letters ye liked that Chopin. So here ye are, ye can play it to your heart's content.'

But I didn't have the heart to tell her I hadn't carried on with the lessons at Cluny House, and that, anyway, it takes years to learn how to play Chopin. Chopsticks perhaps, Chopin – no. I did go for six-penny piano lessons to a lady in Westmuir Street, but the first thing I did as soon as I went in to her house was to ask if she wanted any messages. She always did. I had to go to the Co-op and kept giving my mother's number instead of the piano teacher's. 1-5-9-3-5. You can never forget it. I never did learn to play the piano. Mainly because I never practised.

'It's bad for my technique,' I told my mother.

'Oh, aye,' she said. But we kept the piano.

My new passion was drawing. I drew all the time. Even when I was sent to St Mark's School for a term, before the summer holidays. Thanks to Miss Callaghan and Mr McPherson, and their early good work, I had won a place at St Mungo's Academy and was due to start there in the autumn. In fact, I was very much in demand as a scholar. I could have gone to St Aloysius College for Boys, because I had started Latin at Aberfeldy, or I might have gone to St Joseph's, Dumfries, but I would have had to board there. I would have to risk becoming a Marist brother but my mother couldn't see me as that at all.

She couldn't see me as a Jesuit priest either. I had the chance to go to Stoneyhurst College in Lancashire but, according to her, that was just too far-fetched altogether to consider. Besides, it was in England. Our parish priest, Canon Durkin, was quite disappointed.

As a matter of fact, I did go to England that year, but it was to have a holiday with my father in Brixton, London. He was still there with the Ministry of Works. His job was to advise on which of the blitzed buildings were pulled down or shored up, and he had a whole gang of men under him. How my old dad became an expert on bombed buildings, I'll never know, but there he was asking if Jim and I could be sent down to him for a week. It was thought safer not to risk both of us, so I was posted like a parcel once again. I went down, in a blacked-out train, in a carriage full of merchant navy men who had disembarked at Greenock from the Atlantic convoys. Their conversation was enchantment for a wee boy: full of U-boats, and torpedoes, and fires at sea and lifeboats. Joseph Conrad had nothing on these men, in their roll-top jerseys and black duffel coats, talking of hair-raising things in the dim, quarter-light of that wartime railway carriage.

London was almost an anti-climax after the journey, but it was good to see Dad again. He used to give me half-a-crown every day and tell me to get lost till tea-time. I was out of that little house in Water Lane every morning like an eager little Marco Polo, taking the first tram up west, as the Londoners called it, and wandering around happily all day, seeing this and that, till it was time to go home again. And with quite a bit of change left! I was all alone all day in the metropolis, yet never for a moment did I feel lonely, fearful, threatened or any way less than absolutely thrilled to be there among all the crowds. I came home with quite a few of my half-crowns intact and spent most of the windfall on drawing pads and coloured crayons.

While at St Mark's for that term, I was adjudged to be such a menace in the woodwork class, and a positive danger to the other boys in my mishandling of saws, screwdrivers and such, that the teacher had me out at the big blackboard drawing my favourite wartime scenes for the entertainment of the would-be woodworkers. Naturally, my drawings now had moved from planes to ships at sea and U-boats. These chalk doodles were left on the board and were brought to the attention of the art master, who gave me extra coaching in the periods when I had proved lethal with a chisel. It was this teacher, Mr Robertson, who entered me for the Glasgow Schools Drawing Competition. I was glad to get the afternoon off in the pleasant surroundings of the Kelvingrove Art Gallery in Glasgow's West End. The idea was the pupils could draw anything of their choice in the gallery. There must have been hundreds of us there that day. I drew a koala bear on a tree trunk, and won a gold medal! Everybody was amazed, except perhaps Mr Robertson. I certainly was. And so was the attendant at the door of the gallery the day I went with my mother to collect the medal, because he wouldn't let us in!

'Ye must have the wrong card,' he kept saying.

My mother was getting more and more annoyed. 'But that's what he was sent,' she said.

'Well, there's been a mistake. A wee lad like that canna hiv number five. That's for golds.'

'But I got a gold,' I said.

'Ye whit? Is that right, Missus?'

'That's whit we've been tryin' to tell ye!'

'Well, I'll be . . . In ye go, son,' he said, taking my card.

What I remember best about that day was not the medal, or sitting in the front row with all the big children, or anything of the ceremony or the applause. No, it was going home in the tram afterwards – the 9 to Auchenshuggle. It was full and my mother and I were standing on the lower deck. A man got up. 'Here son, let your big sister sit here.'

My mother took his seat, positively glowing, making her look more beautiful than ever of course. I felt like handing that nice man my brand-new gold medal.

4 JUNE 1944 – FIFTH AND EIGHTH ARMIES ENTER ROME
5 JUNE 1944 – AMERICAN MARINES RECAPTURE THE PHILIPPINES
6 JUNE 1944 – D-DAY. ALLIED FORCES LAND IN NORMANDY

It was the turning-point. The war was nearly over.

I was now at St Mungo's Academy. It was a Marist establishment in Townhead, run by Marist brothers who were trained specifically to teach the brighter boys of the Catholic poor. Most of us were in the latter category. Because it was wartime, we were excused the usual blue blazers and caps, but our mothers were given a kind of transfer thing, which, when ironed on to whatever jacket we wore to school, would produce the Marist badge on the pocket in a neat, clear, white outline. At least it was supposed to. Some of the results I saw on boys' jackets suggested that the iron must have been stone-cold or else some mothers were influenced by the Dada art movement or the new Cubism. No wonder the boys had to use big hankies to obscure their top pocket! With clothing coupons scarce, they couldn't buy new jackets. Who needed uniforms anyway? We saw enough of them in the streets: Yankees, Canadians, Australians, New Zealanders, South Africans, Gurkhas, Poles, Norwegians, Free French. They were all around Glasgow at some time or another,

As "Snake" in "The School for Scandal" the Wilson Barrett Company
His Majesty's Theatre, Aberdeen,
my professional debut proper! Monday 1 June 1953

coming from ships, going on trains. You couldn't forget there was a war on.

Rationing was still strict, and things were still scarce. People tended to hoard. Especially Gran Cairney in Baillieston. She kept packets of tea in Uncle Eddie's gramophone, well away from the eyes of the food inspector. And tins of everything in the straw basket under the wall bed in the kitchen. She kept them so long that some of the labels peeled off. She used to shake the tins at her one good ear and guess the contents. It made for some interesting meals, but 'waste not, want not' was her motto. She squinted up at life with all the gritty cynicism of the under-privileged. 'Those who have get more, and those who have not, just do without.' Another favourite saying of hers often directed at her grandson was, 'Give your tongue a rest, and your head'll have a holiday.'

They don't make them like Gran Cairney any more. Having survived the First World War, Gran always held that they shouldn't have started the Second until all the old folk were gone! She started to put pound notes in the collection plate on a Sunday, which the pass keepers kept returning to her. It was a sign that her mind was going. My father was sent for. He took me to see Gran in the old folks' home. She was in bed, crouched in a foetal position, sucking her thumb. When I reached out my hand to greet her, she started to suck mine. I can still feel her warm, hard little gums. My father turned and walked out, but I let my little gran suck my thumb, till a nurse came and gently pulled it out. This was how Gran Cairney ended. With a thumb in her mouth.

4 FEBRUARY 1945 – THE YALTA CONFERENCE

As Churchill remarked: 'Better "jaw-jaw" than "war-war"!'

Gran Cairney's youngest son, my Uncle Phil, was demobbed from the Black Watch, and they gave him only the second suit of long trousers he'd had in his life. He had been in the Eighth Army and was at El Alamein with Monty. Just the two of them, Monty and my Uncle Phil! He walked through the whole of Tobruk without firing a shot, he said. He fired his rifle into the sand. Otherwise it might have gone off and killed somebody! He always marched behind the piper, he told Jim and me. 'I mean,' he said, 'no' even the Germans would shoot a piper.' Just what my grandfather had said. He'd walked all the way from Cairo, across the top of Africa, over to Sicily, up the wellington boot of Italy until he was wounded on the River Po. 'Imagine bein' wounded on the Po!' he laughed.

Lots of men were like Uncle Phil. Men with deep tans, as if they'd been on holiday. As many of them had – certainly not all. Men with beards or with their heads shaved. Tibetan monks in utility suits. Men with unspoken things at the back of their eyes, who would wake up screaming in the night for years to come. Men with yellow faces in bright blue uniforms, others in dark glasses, getting used to a white cane. Helped by thin-lipped wives, followed by children who were embarrassed by a stranger they had to learn to call Father. When my own father came back from London after the war was over, I thought my mother was very shy with him. For some it was hard to remember what it had been like before the war. For some it was hard to pick up threads that had snapped or just worn away.

1 MAY – ADOLF HITLER DIES IN BERLIN BUNKER
7 MAY – GERMANY SURRENDERS. ADMIRAL DOENITZ
CONCEDES DEFEAT
8 MAY – V E DAY

The bells were ringing, the flags were flying, and the bunting from the Coronation of eight years before was up again in its red, white and blue. Bonfires were lit, and there was singing and dancing in the streets. I found myself in White Street, Partick, in the West End of Glasgow. I've no idea how I got so far away from Parkhead that night. East End to West End is the longest journey you can take in any city. I just followed the fires and, without thinking, I had crossed the whole of Glasgow – east end to west end – and found myself, alone among complete strangers, singing lustily with them in the blaze of the street-fire.

The war was officially over, but somehow we knew things would never be the same again. The pre-war world of footballers in long shorts, black and white films, big bands and dancing, the Cowal Games, the Empire Exhibition, cigarette cards, and Brooklands motor-racing was already old-fashioned and dated. Innocence and optimism were now replaced by cynicism and austerity. A new kind of post-war caution was already growing up. Or was it just that I was? I was fifteen and a schoolboy, but I could feel it. Something was missing. The wartime camaraderie was gone. Everything would now get back to what it was. 'Normal service will now be resumed' as they used to say on the wireless. Would it? All I knew, even as a boy, was that we had had something then. For, once in a blackout, we had seen clearly that life was too important ever to be taken seriously.

VE Day plus one and I was back behind my school desk again – and within a week I was in trouble. My first headmaster at St Mungo's, Brother Germanus, was as Irish as both my grans. He was a genial little leprechaun, who lost something of his geniality when an essay of mine was brought to his attention. I was then in my second year and under the quirky tutelage of Mr Bennett, the English master. For me, he was in the direct line from Miss Callaghan and the Big Mac. He had their same way with a subject that made it always interesting, and their same love of vocabulary. But where Miss Callaghan concentrated on reading words, and Burning Pete on writing them, 'Billy' Bennett's emphasis was in speaking them.

'You'll never get out of your ghettos unless you can talk.' He made us stand up and talk in English, not always easy for a Glaswegian, and when we wrote, he encouraged us to go as far as we could in ideas and subject matter. 'It's the new approach we want, not dreary description. Speculate, don't pontificate.'

That's what got me into trouble with Brother Germanus. I wrote an essay about Mary Magdalen's following Jesus out into the desert during his forty-day fast, and my wild speculation about how they passed the time scandalised my headmaster. He took the pages on to the balcony of the school and publicly tore them up. Pupils were scrambling for them at playtime. I had quite a notoriety for a few days. I didn't know that I had unwittingly stumbled on the plot of *Jesus Christ, Superstar*!

Being at a boys' school, and being one of two brothers, it was hard for me to get to know girls. The nearest I got were female cousins and they were always with female aunties. At sixteen, girls were a delightful mystery to me. I wondered, for instance, why I never met any by themselves. They always went about in pairs. Did you ever notice that? A tall one with a short one, a blonde with a brunette, a beauty with a – well, plainer one. They had it all worked out. But then we went around in gangs or packs ourselves. It was all part of the pubertal ritual, I suppose.

Summer evenings in the park, seeming to wander aimlessly, yet following a prescribed orbit that would land you, at some point, face to face with the giggling girls, just where they wanted you to meet them. You found yourself shouting in your two-tone voice, much louder than you needed. Sauntering casually, yet breathing hard. And what a nuisance being a young teenager was. Searching the mirror every morning for pimples and blackheads. Trying to control sudden, and violent, perspiration. Your hands were clumsy, your feet were too big, yours shoes were shabby, your collar always turned up, and why were people always looking at you? And whispering, 'it's just a stage he's at.' Then they would wink, and nod knowingly – and laugh. And in any crowd, or in somebody's house, whenever there was a lull in the conversation, or an unexpected silence, that's when your tummy would rumble – or worse!

And there was the strange ceremony of visiting sick girls. I can think of three such young ladies in my youth: the girl Kelly, the girl Brady, the girl Murphy, all Irish-Catholic, all good friends, and all bedridden with tuberculosis, endemic in Glasgow just after the war. It was a sickness that made them look ethereally lovely, but you couldn't help noticing the dark shadows under their eyes. Yet they were our age, and at different times I remember being with a crowd in their council-house or tenement bedrooms, the mothers bringing tea and toast in, sometimes cake, and the atmosphere more of a laughing party than a sick visit. Then one day you were told not to come up that night, and generally a few weeks later, you were at the funeral.

It's a very fine line indeed between what you remember, or think you remember, and what really happened. But we're allowed to remember so that we can keep the past alive, or parts of it at least, so that we can cope with today, and prepare for tomorrow. Everybody has a memory of some kind. An incident, a happening, an event, distanced by time, but sweetened by it too. It's a sad and happy feeling – nostalgia, they call it.

The city lights were switched on again and I saw a neon sign for the first time. I thought it all very extravagant and wasteful, till I got used to it. Maybe that's what attracted me to the dance-hall as I got older. The local palais. For me, it was in Dennistoun; sometimes it was the Barrowland Ballroom, even the Plaza at Eglinton Toll, but every district had one. Dark as a dungeon, hot as a sauna, opulent as any cinema, but much more erotic, the dance-hall was the Mecca for the Glasgow Casanova to meet his fate – inside of course. How crowded it always was, the dancing then, or the jiggin' as it was more colloquially called. A swirling circus, shoulder to shoulder, breaking off at corners to show off a fancy step – or jive – despite the notice, prominently displayed: NO JITTERBUGGING!

How you loved it all – the thick pile of the foyer carpet, the luxury of the coloured lights, the Hollywood feel of the chairs and divans

61

around the floor. And on the stand, the band – all looking so foreign; well at least, un-Glasgow. But with very Glasgow names – Billy McGregor and his Gaybirds. The blast of noise they made in unison, the sweet moan of their quiet strains, the husky throb of the saxophone, the sexy squeal of the clarinet, the pounding of drums. Even the singers had a show biz mystique, that might only have been make-up and lights, but they were all of another world – an under-world. Or was it a dream world?

Pressing your partner as close to you as she will allow; but she knows how to use her elbows. You're sweating with all the freedom of pre-deodorant days and she's drenched in California Poppy. Her hair is tight under a head-scarf, or piled high like an ice-cream cone. Pretty lips smeared with beetroot juice, coal dust in her eyes, no stockings – but leg tan with an eyebrow-pencil line painted on by her sister. She was nearly always a wee smasher, a doll, a city Cinderella looking for a fella, but so off-hand you'd never guess. Pair-bonded in a syncopated rhythm, making the right move every time but always keeping you guessing. A circular trance just as long as a dance, and you're jettisoned as quickly as you were taken up. You watch, as with another, older partner, she cuts a swathe through the mêlée, curving a smooth parabola among the twinkling legs.

But in the oiled slipway of a very smooth slow foxtrot when the lights go down as low as they dare, you can be anyone you like: James Mason, or Stewart Granger or Cesar Romero. Your petite partner becomes Betty Grable or Veronica Lake. The only thing you couldn't be was yourself. And what a relief that was.

And if you were lucky, you got a lumber: companion to see home. If you were luckier still, she lived within walking distance, or at least a last tram away. Otherwise it was a taxi. An investment not always worth it. And a long walk home from Kirkintilloch or Rutherglen. But you never know – this could be your night. So out you go, out of the lights, out of the warm, into the damp air of the street, hugging her round the waist, as high as you dare, tingling with the touch of your thumb under her breast. You feel something hard and wonder what it is. Trying it on in the taxi until you find she's got the *Sunday Post* down her bra. You don't know whether to give her a hug or read the Broons! To reassure her you offer her your last fag and even though she doesn't smoke she takes it, and coughs all the way to her house. Her mother's waiting up for her, although sometimes it is her father who answers the door and she scuttles in quick under his arm, and the door slams in your face. You see yourself in the letter-box and just before it begins to mist up, you curl your lip at your own reflection and snarl just like Humphrey Bogart. 'Here's looking at you, kid!'

Then the door suddenly opens and the father's standing there. 'Well?' he bellows.

'Oh . . . I couldn't be better . . . sir. Uh . . . goodnight, Mr . . .' And you turn and run to the safety of the street and the outside world.

Suddenly it's a long way back and you've no idea where you are. You don't know what time it is. You've run out of fags. Your feet are sore in your new shoes, and you turn up your coat collar as its starts to rain again. You're angry, frustrated, disappointed and miserable. But you're young. Your step quickens and you start to whistle. What the hell. There's always next Saturday. Anyway, you never really fancied her. It was her pal you were after! You can't wait to tell your mates all about it tomorrow. And you kick a can the whole length of the street and run all the rest of the way home. But just before you sleep, you can't help having a soft thought for someone, even though you wouldn't dare say a word to their face.

But every Saturday night, however spent, leads inevitably to Sunday mornings and what Sunday mornings they were. Easing open leaden eyelids, squinting against the sunlight, white bright behind the paper blinds, feeling the heat on your face, the awful taste in your mouth. You try to swallow to take it away. Seeing the dust in the rays of the sun, following its reflections along the ceiling, down the doors of the rosewood wardrobe watching the pattern it makes on the carpet, where a shoe lies on its side, on top of last night's *Sporting Pink* and its already forgotten football results. Your new tie, still proud of its immaculate Windsor knot, is looped over the handle of the dressing-table drawer, and the trousers of your best suit sway by their braces from the top of the half-open door, like a man who's been hanged. And you realise you've still got your best shirt on! You can see your other shoe for some reason on the top of the piano, and you close your eyes again with a groan to the litter of the night before, as seen in the harsh glare of the morning after.

But then you remember it's Sunday, and you stretch your full length in the bed, while, outside in the street, the Salvation Army band already mustered in its circle – banners flying, trombones shining, faces smiling under peaked caps and ribboned bonnets, tambourines held high – makes its tuneful appeal to the Lord and a wall of curtained windows. From far away you can hear the rattle of a distant lawnmower, and, nearer, the noise of the Boys Brigade

63

on parade, the chatter of cyclists gathering for their weekend run, the buzz of a pair of anglers checking their rods, and the footstep of a solitary golfer – all part of your street's Sunday morning. Through the wall you can hear the drone of a wireless, and your mother, nagging at your father to get up. You twitch your nose at the Sunday smell of frying, square sausages and you find yourself smiling.

My schooldays were rapidly coming to an end. I found I was spending more time in the Argyle Cinema than in my fourth-year studies, and, apart from art and English, I took no interest whatsoever in the syllabus. I was getting into very serious training to become a layabout. I had won another drawing competition medal, and on the strength of a very strong recommendation from two art teachers and a hastily got-together portfolio, I was accepted as a student (provisional, at first, because of my age) at the Glasgow Art School. For a time I had a whole new surge of enthusiasm and the cold winter of 1947 found me hot with excitement for my new career in commercial art and lithography. But I found myself weighed down again by the dull demands of routine tuition. I could never let myself go and freely express my ideas as I thought an artist should. I kept forgetting, of course, that I wasn't really an artist. I was only an artist-in-training. A putative painter, perhaps? I only lasted a couple of terms at Hill Street. I got a chance to do some studies in the life class and was so appalled at the ugly sight of my very first nude that I behaved outrageously in class, and for some reason I can't remember, ended up in a fight with fellow-student, who probably was telling me to be quiet. I was so nervous about the whole incident that I was quite impudent to Harry Barnes, the vice-principal, and he expelled me on the spot – all for an old, couldn't-care-less, professional nude.

I began to worry that I had a Ruskin-like attitude to female nudity. I remembered, only a few months before, I persuaded a young nurse in Menteith Row, opposite the People's Palace, to remove all her clothes, garment by garment, while I talked to her. And when she stood there, in front of the gas fire, her hands by her sides, her toes curling on the thin carpet, I could only sit in the armchair staring at her pubic hair. I was absolutely paralysed – and mute.

'Satisfied?' she said at length.

I nodded. Another pause.

'I'm freezin',' she said.

I bent down and lifted up the white panties and handed them to her.

'Ta,' she said.

I then gave her the bra, and other items, one by one, and so, garment by garment, she dressed again. The only difference was that this time, she did all the talking. When she was fully clothed, she stood in front of me, in the same position on the carpet beside the fire, but this time its flame was burning very low. I knew how it felt.

'Fancy a cup o' tea?' she asked.

'No, thanks. I think I'll – '

'Aye, you'll have school in the mornin'.'

That was the final indignity. She was very understanding, this little Glasgow nurse, but she was way beyond me. When she let me out on to the landing, and softly closed the door, I could only slink down the stairs and out into London Road, crimson with mortification and embarrassment.

I took my time walking home and it must have been well into the early hours before I got to my own door. I opened the letter-box and felt for the key. It wasn't there! I whistled through the aperture, which was the usual signal for Jim to get up and let me in. I'd be glad to get to my bed. It was cold standing out on that landing. 'Come on, Jim,' I said to myself, folding my arms.

I put my face to the letter-box again to meet not Jim, but my mother's angry eyes flashing back at me.

'I hope ye don't think I'm lettin' ye in?' she was saying.

'Aw, come on, Mother, I'm freezin' here,' I moaned.

'Serve ye right, freeze away. You an' your gallivantin' till a' oors. Well, ye can just stey oot, if ye cannae be in at a decent time.'

'But Mother –'

'Away tae hell!'

And the flap closed in my face. I stood back, angry and miserable. As if I hadn't gone through enough tonight. What could I do now? I went down to the outside lavatory on the window landing and, inserting my thumb in the lock, I opened it. Every tenement boy was able to do that. I sat on the seat in the dark. At least I was out of the draught. I glanced up at the window, and I had an idea. If I could still manage it, that is. I stood on the wooden seat and prised open the little window. For years, I had stood on that seat gazing out in the direction of the River Clyde where I could always see the *Queen Mary* berthed by the dockside, and behind her the Cheviots and beyond that England. Actually what I was really looking at was the structure of the Springfield wire works superimposed on the second floor of Riverside School further superimposed on the funnels of Dalmarnock power station, behind which were the Cathkin Braes and beyond them lay Newton Mearns, which was England as far as I was concerned. But to a little boy between the wars, it was the *Queen Mary*!

But now I was a big boy and it was a question of whether I could get out of that little lavatory window. I could, with a bit of a squeeze, and, crouched on the sill, I reached out for the rhone pipe running vertically beside our window, but it was just out of reach. I now couldn't go back easily, and it was a bit of a risk going forward, but I had no option. Muttering a prayer, I lunged for the pipe and grabbed it with both hands, praying that it wouldn't come away from the wall with my weight, as I was now several hundred feet above the asphalt back court. I dragged myself up to our window-sill and somehow raised myself up to standing position, managing at the same time to kick over a scrubbing brush, but avoiding the bowl, which was also there covered by a saucer. I forgot that the window-sill was also my mother's fridge! The paper blind was down but, luckily for me, the window was always kept open slightly, so I was able to lower the top sash enough for me to lean in and pull up the lower one till I got it up enough for me to clamber through.

Suddenly, the paper blind shot up with a whirr and a sweeping brush head caught me full in the chest and almost had me out of the window again. It was my mother wielding the broom like a spear! I grabbed the handle and pushed from my side as my mother vigorously pushed from hers – and remember we were two storeys up! I got my feet in the sink, right into a basin of cold water, with something soaking in it, dishes crashed on to the linoleum, I yelled at my mother to stop pushing, she yelled at me to get back where I came from, them Jim rushed in and flew at me thinking I was a burglar! It was some time before order was restored, but eventually Mother was placated, and I was allowed in. It had not been my night.

I met Mary Theresa McFarlane in Tollcross Park. She was taking her big black dog for a walk, and I was playing football with the boys. The ball went among the trees and I went to get it. I found it under the same tree which Terry's dog had decided to make natural use of. Terry tried to call the dog away, but it already had its leg up.

66

'Mind my ball!' I called to it.

'I'm sorry,' said Terry.

'Don't mention it,' I said. 'I needed a breather anyway.'

The dog took its time. So did I. Terry McFarlane was an attractive young girl, with lithe leanness that suggested the good athlete she was. We made conversation, and I made a date to see her the next night – without the dog.

'Come on!' Shouts came from the football players.

I went back to the game, astonished at my audacity, but looking forward to seeing the girl again. We had arranged to meet at the Maukinfauld Road entrance to the park as she lived nearby in Pitcairn Street. Would she turn up?

She did. We walked. We talked. She was secretary to the editor of the local paper, the *Eastern Standard*.

'What do you do?' she said.

'This and that.'

'Sounds interesting. Where do you do this and that?'

'Here and there.'

'Now and then, I suppose.'

We both laughed, and from then on we were the best of friends. For the first time, I felt easy with a girl. It was almost like being with a real person. I liked this pert young lady with the dark eyes and the wide smile. I could talk to her, and she seemed to listen. I told her I had left school, and was supposed to be at the art school, but I didn't go too often.

'What do you do then? No, don't answer that.'

But I was serious this time. I told her I didn't know what I was going to do. I hadn't made up my mind.

'Considering the offers, is that it?'

'You could put it like that,' I said, 'except that I haven't had any offers. Not yet, anyway.'

'What do you want to do?'

'To tell you the truth I don't know.' And I didn't. And out it all came in a rush: I was going to be a priest, a religious brother, an English teacher, an art teacher, but not all at once!

'You don't look like a teacher to me.'

'What do I look like?'

'A priest, I think.'

'OK. I'll be a priest if you'll be a nun.'

'Not on your life. I've seen enough o' nuns.'

So Mary Theresa and I got to know each other. She said she was a member of St Michael's Youth Club in Dervaig Street and played badminton there. She was going there the next night. Why didn't I come along?

'Not on your life. I've seen enough of youth clubs.'

It was getting dark and we were still in the park as the gates were being closed. We went in a Tally's and had a Macallum each. I paid with a ten shilling note. Her eyes widened over a spoonful of ice-cream.

'In the money, eh? I suppose ye stole it?'

'You could put it like that. I got it for a poster.'

'A what?'

I told her about my 'homework'. Artwork of all kinds on the kitchen table: posters, signs, lay-outs for adverts, sketches for birthdays, all that sort of thing.

'Does your mother no' mind?'

'Only when she has to set the table.'

'Does it no' make a mess?'

'Not at all. And if I get a jammy mark, I just incorporate it into the design. But I don't just do drawings.'

'What else?'

'I write letters.'

'Letters?'

'Aye. Half-a-crown a time. Five bob for fancy script.'

'Who pays ye to write letters?'

'You'd be amazed. Mostly old people though, and people wi' problems. That kinda thing.'

'What kinda problems?'

'I couldn't tell ye that – professional confidence, an' that.'

'Of course.'

I was beginning to feel I was impressing her. 'I do job applications as well.'

'Oh?'

'Aye. I got a fella a trainee job wi' Marks and Spencer.'

'Did ye?'

'Aye. It sounded a great job.'

'Why didn't ye apply yourself?'

'I did.'

'Whit happened?'

'I got turned down!' She laughed. 'Anyway, I didn't really want the job.'

'A manager's job at Marks and Spencers would do me.'

'OK. I'll write a letter for ye.'

'I'll write my own letter, thank ye.'

'Have ye no faith in me?'

'I haven't got half-a-crown!'

We sat in that Wellshot Road café for ages till it, too, was closing, then I walked her home to Pitcairn Street and we stood at the back close, sharing a cigarette, and muttering hoarsely in the darkness.

'I think ye should get a job. A proper job, I mean.'

'I'll think about it,' I said, wondering how we could get together when the cigarette was in one or other of our lips at all times. Then her big sister came down the stairs with the dog. It barked joyfully and bounded up to us. For a minute I was afraid it thought I was a tree!

'Is that you, Mary T'resa? Who's that wi' ye?'

'S'all right, Kath, this is John,' Terry called. 'John whit?' she whispered urgently.

For a minute I was flustered. 'Er . . . Cairn –.' I began.

'Tell "John" it's time ye were up the stair,' replied Kathleen. 'Come on, Prince.'

'Goodnight,' whispered Terry, and she and Prince bounded up the stairs together after the big sister. I hadn't even kissed her! I didn't even get a pat of Prince. I took a long time to walk back to Williamson Street, but by the time I reached our door I had made a momentous decision – I would join the youth club! For Mary Theresa McFarlane's sake.

'There's a divinity that shapes our ends . . .'

In my case it was a tall, young, bespectacled Irish curate at St Michael's called Father Joseph Power. He had come to Glasgow from Cork via Rome with a great love for community drama and especially the one-act play. He decided that the St Michael's Boys' Guild should have a drama group in conjunction with the Children of Mary. Having been one of his altar boys, he decided that I should appear in his entry for the 1946 Catholic Drama Festival in something called *Thread o' Scarlet* along with the other ex-altar servers he had coerced: John Donnelly, Jim Hutton, Charlie Kelly, Bill Hutcheson and Bill Moran. Reluctantly giving ourselves over to rehearsal, we came nowhere in the competition, but I must admit to having enjoyed painting on my villain's moustache and pretending to be English. 'Sure, they'll never know you're not, over in Kinning Park,' said Father Power genially.

If at first you don't succeed, then give up gracefully, was my motto at the time, but I had a funny premonition about this drama business. Terry was amused.

69

They had a quiz one night at youth club, and I won first prize.

'Who is the Old Lady of Threadneedle Street?'

'The Bank of England,' I yelled, and I had won.

The youth leader (John McAllister, ex-RAF aircrew) gave me an envelope with something in it. Great – pound note, I thought. I could do with it.

'What did ye get?' It was Terry, flushed from another badminton win.

I was just waiting for her to ask me. I took the envelope out of my trouser pocket where I had folded it, quoting grandly as I did so, 'There was an elderly lady in the city, of great credit and long standing who had lately fallen into bad company.'

'Here, are you being cheeky?'

'Sheridan to Pitt the Younger in Parliament, 1797.'

'Whit are ye talkin' about?'

'The Bank of England. Oh, blast!'

'Whit's up?'

'Look at this.'

My prize wasn't money. It was two theatre tickets.

She took them and read, '*The Righteous Are Bold* by Frank Carney. The Citizens Theatre. 22nd February at 7.30 p.m. What's wrong wi' that?'

'Mebbe I could sell them,' I said.

'Why sell them?' she asked.

'Who wants to go to the theatre?'

'I do.'

'Oh. When is it?'

She looked at the tickets again. 'Er . . . 22nd. On Monday.'

'D'you really want to go? I mean . . . to a play?'

'Ay.'

I was genuinely surprised. I'd never known anyone before who'd wanted to go to a theatre. *Five Past Eight* at the Theatre Royal perhaps, or Tommy Morgan at the Pavilion, or variety at the Empire, and of course the pantomime at the Alhambra with people like Robert Wilson and Will Fyfe, but a play – never.

'OK,' I said reluctantly. 'If ye fancy it.'

'Ye'll have to wear a suit. Have ye got a suit?'

'Of course I've got a suit.'

I didn't dare tell her it was a bright blue suit, cut spiv square like a bandleader's with wide shoulders and narrow legs. It was not a beautiful thing, but was mine. Anyway, it was the only suit I had, except for an old brown one which was flecked with poster paint and had a cigarette burn on it.

Because Terry had to work late that night, we arranged to meet at the theatre.

'You'll be there?'

'I'll be there,' I replied dolefully.

'Good. Fancy a game of badminton?'

'No, thanks. I've got my name down for billiards.'

On the night of the play I was waiting at the front of the theatre quite early, because I was in town in any case. I had found myself a temporary job at the Ministry of Food in Pitt Street, issuing ration books and working in the mail-room. Orders for letters and posters had fallen off drastically, and caught between the female pincer provided by my mother and Terry, I yielded to commerce and found myself a job. I had been interviewed by a Mrs Henderson that day, and, much to my disgust, I got the job. I was nothing more than glorified office-boy. What would Brother Clare say if he heard? He had succeeded Brother Germanus, and tried his best to keep me at school after fourth year, but I was adamant to do my own thing and wanted to leave.

'You're a fool.'

'Yes, Brother.'

'And you're a coward. Running away from your Highers. That's all you're doing.'

He was right.

Now I was standing in front of the Citizens Theatre at Gorbals Cross. I had to admit I was a little bit excited. It would be a new experience and I was all for new experiences. As I stood, little women in fur coats and what seemed like no legs kept scuttling past me in pairs going into the theatre. They didn't look like the kind of women I knew and they didn't sound like women I knew. Some of them even sounded English.

Then Terry came running up, flushed and lovely. 'I see what you mean about the suit,' she said, when she got her breath. 'Have ye got the tickets?'

'Aye,' I answered. They were still in the envelope.

Our seats were in the stall, at the right-hand side and on the centre aisle. The place was crowded, and I seemed to be surrounded by fur coats. I could smell a funny smell, like damp. A sort of fustiness. Was that how all theatres smelt? I looked around me and took it all in. The plush curtains, the lights, the people in the boxes, the chatter of all the different conversations around us, which hushed at once as the lights started to go down. So this is where they put on plays? I settled back in my seat ready to be bored. The curtain went up with a swish, and the lights nearly blinded me. At the same time, what seemed to me like a gale blew from the stage into the stalls. It was the natural downdraught caused by the quick rise of the heavy curtain but it made me squirm in my seat. Now I saw why they all wore those fur coats. Gradually, I got used to the stage lighting, and I saw a man sitting at a fireplace, appearing to stir the embers with a poker. A young woman came in at the back and spoke to him. 'Da,' she said. The play had begun . . .

It was an Irish play about a young girl being possessed by the devil and the attempts of the parish priest (Sir Lewis Casson, no less) to exorcise her. Lennox Milne was the young girl. I think Sybil Thorndyke was in it as well, but at this distance I can hardly remember the cast – only the effect that play had on me. Of course, it was little more than melodrama, but to the Catholic population of Glasgow it was a compelling piece of theatre. For me, in fact, it was a riveting and life-changing experience. For that's what it did. It changed my life. Not immediately, of course. Everthing takes its own time, but I found myself so caught up in that world the play had presented to me, so involved within it, that I found it difficult to come out at the end of the performance. Not only to come out of the play, but to come out of the theatre and back to the real world. Because this was the dream world that I had been, perhaps subconsciously, looking for, in my drawing, in my attempts at writing, in my reluctance to apply myself to studies, and in my lack of anxiety for a proper job. There was something came to me that night that I couldn't quite understand. I had just the beginnings of a suspicion that perhaps I would like to be up on that stage. In that world. Part of that dream. Although I never said anything to anyone, I had to confess to myself that I might want to be an actor. Of course the idea was ridiculous. I mean, how do you become an actor? Especially if you're Scottish and you come from Glasgow and from Parkhead into the bargain. There are some things one has to face, and one is that being an East Ender is not always an advantage.

I took Terry home, but for once I hardly said anything.

'You're very quiet. That's a change.'

'I'm thinking.'

'What about?'

'I think I might want to be an actor.'

And she laughed.

'What are you laughing at?' I said.

'You, an actor? Don't be daft. Remember Father Power's play?'

I shrugged. 'I suppose you're right.'

Nothing more was said on the subject.

But I could hardly get to sleep that night. I was still in the world of the play we had seen. And to think they were just actors on a stage. It must be great to be an actor.

I asked Father Power about it after confession one night.

'Ah, well,' he said, 'It's a fine thing the drama, as long as ye don't rely on it for your crust. There's a whole lot of hungry actors, don't ye know. But I'll tell ye what, I'll talk to some friends who know a bit more about it than I do, and I'll let you know. Now just say five Hail Marys and make a good act of contrition . . .'

'Thank you, Father. Bless me, Father, for I have sinned . . .'

And that's how I became involved with the Marian Players.

They were a group of Catholic schoolteachers and professional people who were keen amateur actors. They met every week in a house in Byres Road to discuss art and drama and Glasgow Celtic, and occasionally put on mostly Irish plays at the Athenaeum. One of the committee, Mr Kennedy, took me aside on the first night. He was a kindly, big man who was an optician by day and a leading actor by night. He looked very theatrical to me. But then I wasn't very sure what 'theatrical' was.

'I hear you're interested in the theatre, my boy? Well, now, I think we could give you a start.'

My heart jumped. This is great, I thought – I'm in.

'Yes,' he went on, 'we're doing a little thing called *Today and Yesterday*. A comedy, you know.'

I didn't, but I nodded eagerly.

'A little thing by Heppenstal.'

'Oh, aye.'

'Yes. Well, we need somebody on the curtain. Would you oblige?'

And that was my first ever job in the theatre. I turned a wheel at the side of the stage of the Athenaeum Theatre to open the curtain and turned it again to close it.

'Ah, well,' said Father Power, 'sure it's a start.'

Meantime, the second Catholic Drama Festival had come round. This time we were to do *Julius Caesar*! And I was to play Mark Antony. The producer was our former quiz-host, John McAllister, and his casting method was idiosyncratic to say the least. He announced at the club one evening that he was entering us for the festival in an excerpt from *Julius Caesar* (Act Three, Scenes I to III) and that only the boys would be required. There was a groan at this, but John, who had survived bombing raids over Germany wasn't put off by puerile rumblings and said that any boy not taking part would be denied badminton and billiards during the period of production. Since these were the main reasons most of us came to the place, we knew we had no option. The next shock from the mild-mannered John was, 'Right, all the boys on the floor, please.'

Sluggishly, we ambled on to the badminton court.

'Right, tallest on the right, shortest on the left, please.'

Much shoving and pushing and ribaldry, but we finally got it.

'Right, this is what you're all going to play. Now listen carefully and every boy remember the name that I tell him. OK?'

'OK', we chorused, and starting at the 'tall' end John made his way down the line, with a Penguin Shakespeare in his hand, giving a character to each boy as he passed, without even looking up. 'Caesar–Cassius–Mark Antony–Brutus–Casca etc.' He certainly couldn't be accused of directorial bias!

John later explained that since he didn't know who could act, or who couldn't, it was just as fair as anything else to make a random selection on the basis that big parts deserved big boys and small parts, small boys. He would let fate decide who played what, and fate decided that I should play Mark Antony. What really decided it, of course was that I was taller than Robert Wilson, who played Brutus, and not as tall as John Davitt who was Cassius. My pal, Bill Hutcheson, was Caesar. He was the tallest boy in the club. It was also decided that since there were no parts for the girls, they would make the costumes and the props and generally assist on stage management. I understand they entered into an arrangement with Kent Flour Mills of Parkhead, through contacts that Helen Flynn had, for an unlimited supply of hessian for the tunics and we boys were instructed to bring our Scout belts and sandshoes in for adaptation to the Roman. Everyone was further encouraged to steal at least one curtain from the house for use as robes, and little Josie, who was an apprentice hairdresser, was told she had to curl everybody's hair.

'But I've only wan pair o' tongs,' she wailed.

'You've only one pair of hands, Josie,' retorted John coolly.

Rehearsals were conducted against a background of normal club activity and 'Trebonius' (brother Jim) had more than once to retrieve a shuttlecock! Mr McAllister was quite imperturbable, and with his head buried in his Penguin, hardly noticed anyway.

I took to it all, not so much like a penguin, but like the proverbial duck. I loved the whole rehearsal process, the direction, the

With Alison's godfather, John Gregson in Miracle in Soho *1958*

discussion, even learning of the lines. It was in that youth club hall at Parkhead Cross I got my first-ever applause.

One night at rehearsal I was leaning over Big Hutch as he sprawled uncomfortably on the floorboards, imploring me with his eyes to get on with it, but I was in no hurry, I was enjoying the drama, the situation, the words . . .

> Pardon me, thou bleeding piece of earth,
> That I am meek and gentle with these butchers;
> Thou art the ruins of the noblest man
> That ever lived in the tide of times.

And so Mark Antony goes on in his peroration over the body of Caesar, till it ends with the famous lines:

> Cry havoc! And let slip the dogs of war;
> That this foul deed shall smell above the earth
> With carrion men, groaning for burial.

But Hutch only groaned under his breath, 'Oh, for God's sake.'

The script then says, 'Enter a servant' (Jim McLean), but as I was emoting lustily, the Forest of Dunsinane advanced gradually from the other end of the hall and eight of the boys carrying their billiard cues in their hands now semi-circled the rehearsal space, drumming the butts of their cues on the floorboards, grinning hugely and calling out, 'Great stuff, John.'

'Good on ye, son!'

'Whit aboot that, eh?'

'Who's this Shakespeare anyhow?'

It was a heady moment. Naturally, the ring of boys prevented the servant's coming on, so he headed off for an orangeade and the rehearsal was abandoned.

So the weeks went by, and John McAllister managed to keep his cool, and me in check, and at last, it was the night of the competition.

The girls had done a great job. We all looked truly Roman. The purples, the reds, the blues, the belts and the togas, the flags and the shields – it was all very impressive. Except perhaps that the hessian scratched a little and Popilius (wee Bobby McClymont) insisted on wearing his socks with his Roman sandals. I seemed to have no nerves at all and revelled in it. It's not that I was cocksure, but just that I was so enthusiastic. But it wasn't over yet. I had just reached the big moment:

Friends, Romans, countrymen, lend me your ears;
I come to bury Caesar, not to praise him.
The evil that men do . . .

I was aware of a restlessness in the audience. The costumes were indeed splendid, mine particularly so, but it was unlined, and the girls, having no knowledge of stage requirements, had made no allowance for the heat of the hall, of the lights, for the general tension, and for actor's sweat. It was pouring off me, which perhaps assisted the emotional effect, but when I got to the line, 'When that the poor have cried, Caesar hath wept' our audience laughed. I looked down at my own chest, and saw why. There on the hessian, under the magnificent scarlet, a huge roundel had appeared, proclaiming:

KENT'S FLOUR MILLS, PARKHEAD.
MORE BREAD FOR LESS DOUGH!

It was also unfortunate that my next line was, 'Ambition should be made of sterner stuff!' More laughter.

At the end of the evening, the adjudicator was very understanding. Mr George Paterson Whyte was no doubt used to such stage eventualities, and brushed it aside as a small thing, but for me it was a disaster. I wanted to get home right away, but John McAllister wouldn't hear of it.

'You might get something for the commercial,' he grinned.

'Now, we come to St Michael's and their *Julius Caesar*. Well . . .'

I hardly heard what the adjudicator said as I sat with Hutch and Davitt at the back of St Margaret's Hall. It was hard to take the smooth, dulcet tones of his professional voice seriously. Drama adjudicators do not speak as other men. They live in another world of speaking from the diaphragm and carefully received pronunciation. It's hard to imagine an adjudicator going into a shop and asking for a half-pint of milk and five Woodbines, please. Suddenly, both my friends were nudging me on either side.

'Hey, that's you, John.'

'He's talkin' about you.'

'Whit aboot that?'

'Get you.'

Apparently, the adjudicator was asking for the boy who played Mark Antony. Would he please stand up. John McAllister looked round from where he was sitting, but there was no way I was going to stand up and be further embarrassed before everyone.

77

'I'm so sorry he's not here,' went on Mr Paterson Whyte, 'because I'm going to do something that I have rarely, if ever, done after a competition of this kind, and that is to recommend that this young man, er . . .' he consulted his notes 'yes, John Cairney, who played the part of Mark Antony for St Michael's, become an actor on the professional stage.'

There was a reaction all round the hall at this, especially as we hadn't won anything. I noticed that Father Power was beaming, but John McAllister was shaking his head in amazement.

'It is not something I say lightly, believe me, but if John is not already embarked on a career, then I think he should seriously consider becoming an actor. Now, we come next to the Sacred Heart Drama Group from Bridgeton in their . . .'

'You an' Errol Flynn!' whispered Davitt.

'Can I have your autograph?' scoffed Big Hutch.

But it was the way the man said 'actor' – not '*act*ir' as we did, but ac*tor*. He made it sound so grand, grandiloquent, in fact. He made 'professional actor' sound, not like a job at all, but like a learned profession; no, even better, a noble calling.

'There'll be no holding you now,' said Terry later that night as I walked her home to her new house in Riddrie. 'There's only one thing.'

'What's that?'

'How do you get to be a professional actor? It's no' as if ye can sign on at the broo, and say "Any vacancies for actors?"'

I laughed, and she continued, 'I can't imagine there's a great call for actors in Parkhead.'

'Have you been to Celtic Park recently?'

'They're clowns, not actors,' she replied.

'And since when did you become a football authority?' I said.

'I'm not, but you forget I work for the local paper.'

I mused over her question for days. She was right. How did one become an actor?

I talked the matter over with Mrs Kay Henderson, my 'temporary' colleague and mentor at the Ministry of Food, where I was still stretching out my summer appointment as long as I could. I had a cushy number there. Mrs Henderson did most of the work, while I just kept out of the way, but we had lots of good chats at the tea-break, this amiable widow and I. She suggested that I write to John Casson at the Citizens Theatre, and, why not, since I liked writing, try to write a play. If I could get that put on, I could appear in it and get paid for it, and that would make me a professional actor.

It was a simple plan, so we made a start by writing a letter to John Casson on one of the government typewriters. Unfortunately, soon after, my 'cushy' job came to an end with the end of food rationing. What could I do now? So, every afternoon, on the kitchen table, I wrote a play. It was a play about Pontius Pilate and all in blank verse: serious, well-intentioned, innocent and entirely without humour. But it passed a lot of afternoons in front of the kitchen range in Williamson Street.

John Casson was too busy to audition me, but his secretary gave me a cigarette, and John himself joined us for a cup of tea. The thing to be was utterly committed, he insisted, but, personally, he would rather do market-gardening. We talked for so long, this ex-naval commander and the East End tyro, I could have read *Man and Superman* to him. However, he promised to see me again some-time. And he did.

Then, in the way things happen, a chance meeting set up another theatre chance. Mrs Henderson's brother was a pianist at the BBC and he mentioned that he'd heard in the studio that Molly Urquhart was starting up a semi-professional company in an old church in Rutherglen. Kay wrote me a note telling me to get out there right away. I did, and met a man called Bert Ross who engaged me at once as a juvenile simply because they didn't have one. I got thirty shillings a production, which was nearly as much as I got at the Ministry of Food. I got to speak lines in things like *Are You A Mason?* and *Bombshell* but I was ludicrously over-cast and woefully inept, but I was the only one who didn't think so! I have no idea what ground-less hope sustained me, but something did.

Duncan Macrae came one night to the theatre. He was already emerging as one of Scotland's greatest character actors and comedians, but he visited that night as a personal friend of Molly's. Somehow he and I got into a long discussion, and he suggested can-didly I might have the arrogance to make an actor, so why didn't I go right in at the deep end and try for one of the smaller com-panies in the West End. The West End? Wow! I wasn't even ready for Rutherglen Rep.

'The West End of Glasgow, you idiot,' intoned the tall actor.

He had been a schoolteacher amateur with the Curtain Theatre. Now it had been enlarged into the fully professional Park Theatre and dear John, as I soon learned to call him, said they were now auditioning for a production of *Doctor Faustus*. I was at its elegant steps in Woodside Terrace, overlooking Kelvingrove Park, the next morning. John Stuart, a business man and theatre enthusiast, had

79

converted his large townhouse into a pocket theatre and had asked
Kenneth Ireland to form a company to present plays there.
Another young hopeful attending that morning was John Fraser
from the High School. We were both accepted, and I was asked to
hand in my card to Mr Hume in the office. What card? Your
National Insurance card! I didn't know I needed one. I was still
technically an art student. So my first job in the theatre was to
report to the Central Labour Exchange and collect a brand-new
National Insurance card with its brand-new number inked in:
LR642088B. I delivered it next morning to the Park Theatre office
with pride. No one could say now that I wasn't a full-time professional actor. And in only just over a year from George Paterson
Whyte's advice. I wrote to tell him I had taken it, but my letter was
returned. He had died of cancer.

As he had rightly guessed, however, this theatre world was my
world. Everything I had done so far had tended towards it. From
the beginning, rehearsals were fun as well as work, performances
were exciting if not demanding, and I made some good friends:
John, of course, Jimmy Sutherland, Brown Derby, David Gourlay,
and Moira Lamb who married the boss, Kenneth Ireland. It may
have been Glasgow's smallest stage, but it was big enough to give
me a start. I made my professional debut as Robin, the clown, in
the *Faustus*. I was then cast as a Jew in *Salome*, to be followed by
Lachie, the Scots soldier in *The Hasty Heart*, but instead John
Fraser and I received another government intimation. This time,
it was nothing to do with insurance cards, but was, in fact, our call-
up for National Service, effective from Monday, 5 April 1948. So
much for my nascent theatrical career – five months it had lasted.
Never mind, this was only an interruption. By law, the Park
Theatre had to take us back at the end of our service. John and
I shook hands after our last-night party at the Grand Hotel at
Charing Cross.

'See you in 1950!' he said, and went off to the Army.

'Roll on,' I answered, and reported to the Air Force.

Suddenly there was a family bombshell. Old Uncle Eddie had
decided to marry his Jeannie. A date was fixed so that I could be
their best man before I left Glasgow. Uncle Eddie was married at
St Bridget's just like his father and brothers, but the surprise of the
day was the appearance of the estranged Swan family: Aunt Ellen,
Uncle Andrew and my cousins, Jimmy, John, Gary and Margaret.
Margaret was exactly my age, and she was beautiful. The 'drastic
action' had finally been taken by my wily old uncle, and at the same

time a Cairney family chapter had ended and a breach in the family wall closed up.

I joined the RAF in Padgate, Lancashire, but in the entire two years I wore its uniform, the RAF never joined me. I tried my best, but despite being considered for a permanent commission, my only triumph was when I sang 'My Ain Folk' in the NAAFI at the end of recruit training. As a result I was put into the entertainment pool and posted to Germany as an accounts clerk in the Berlin airlift. Not that I did much accounting – or lifting. I was too busy organising concert parties and taking courses. I found that if you went on a course, you could see Europe and learn something at the same time. Anyway, it was all part of my actor's idea of gaining life experience.

I was mistaken once for royalty in Celle, a little town near Hanover. With a friend, I had gone to the local theatre. We took our seats high up in the balcony. It was some kind of musical evening and really rather boring, but from where we were sitting we could see that one of the boxes above the stage was empty, so we decided to change our seats. In the box, we sat back in style, only to notice a flash of braid in the front row. It was the group-captain, our CO and his party. We scuttled back in our chairs into the shadows of the box where we could just see the stage and no more, but were safely out of our officers' eye-line. As other ranks in further training, we weren't even supposed to be off the station. Then we noticed that, as each turn came out on stage, they bowed to our box in their solemn German way before performing. I couldn't resist giving a gracious hand wave back! The white flashes on our caps must have given them the wrong impression and since they couldn't see us clearly they misconstrued our anxiety to remain discreetly in the shadows. We thoroughly enjoyed our unexpected importance, but decided it might be better to leave before the end.

Even after this, I went to theatre as often as I could. For the equivalent of a penny, I sat in the front row this time, and saw Furtwängler conduct *Tristan und Isolde* in the Opera House in Hanover. It was the first building the Germans rebuilt out of the ruins. Not a shop or an office block, but an opera house.

However, the very best thing that happened to me in Germany was not learning to ski, or ride a horse, or even catching up on my skimped education. It was in being gloriously seduced by Ingrid

81

Bergman! Well, she looked like Ingrid Bergman. It happened in Cologne.

Up till that time, my previous sex experiences had been a series of skirmishes in the park, and a few hand-to-hand 'close' encounters in Glasgow, but this was to be a glorious battle, and the victory was mine – I think. The first shots of the battle started in a night-club. On the Hogmanay of 1948 I was celebrating in true Scots fashion with a group of friends as the hour of midnight approached when I realised that it was already midnight back home in Scotland. I began to lead my table in 'Auld Lang Syne' on the xenophobic grounds that if it were New Year in Scotland it was New Year everywhere! Not unnaturally, the Germans and English present resented this assumption and an argument developed, which soon led to blows. But help came in the formidable form of a Private Speakman, who was an Englishman with the Seaforths, a Scottish regiment stationed nearby. Speakman was to win a VC the next year in Korea, but he really earned another one that night in Cologne.

'Who touches wee Jock here'll 'ave to bloody well deal with me,' he growled, a bottle in each hand.

They did, or tried to. During the fracas 'Wee Jock' landed under a table and there beside me was a beautiful girl in a trench-coat and gumboots.

'I am Hilburga,' she whispered.

'And I am delighted!' I said.

Whistles, shouts and the scampering of service boots all around us told us that the military police had arrived. We could hear Speakman take them on as well.

'He is brave, your friend,' said Hilburga.

'He's nuts,' I replied.

Then all the lights went out. Always a good dodge in a police raid. That's what they used to do in Glasgow billiard halls.

More shouts and Hilburga was in my arms under the table. 'I am afraid. What is it they are saying?'

'Happy New Year in Scots,' I chuckled.

A torch was shone in our faces. ''Allo, wot we got 'ere then?' The typically mindless voice of police authority intruded on our below-the-table intimacy.

Hilburga's arm shielded me. '*Hier ist mein Mann,*' and a stream of Hun abuse followed which wasn't 'Happy new Year' in German, I can tell you that.

'Begging pardon, I'm shewer,' said the voice behind the torch and it switched off.

'Thanks,' I whispered.

'It is nothing. I hate *polizei*.'

'So do I. Police aye are up my nose an' a'!'

'*Was ist?*'

'Sorry. Nothing.'

Luckily, I wasn't in uniform that night. With my concert party activities, I could wear 'civies' quite a lot of the time, and I did, mainly because my sports clothes were a lot smarter than my air-craftsman's uniform. We watched the various legs moving around then, as the lights came on again, and tables and chairs were being picked up, we came out from our shelter and slinked out. A German shouted something, but Hilburga shouted something back, and we were up in the street.

'You are soldier, *ja*?'

'*Nein, ich bin* Air Force.'

'*Ach*, RAF, *ja*. I do not like RAF.'

Standing as she was with bits of bombed buildings behind her, I could understand why. Then I remembered Clydebank. 'I don't fancy the Luftwaffe either.'

She smiled.

I noticed the lovely, even, white teeth. That's when I saw the resemblance to a young Ingrid Bergman.

'I like better the Navy,' she said.

I didn't say anything.

'What is your name?' she asked.

'John.' I felt terribly shy all of a sudden, as the drink and excitement were wearing off. I was standing alone in a German street with a beautiful girl and it was in the early hours of the morning. Let's hope they don't have a bed check at the station, I thought. I am already AWOL. 'I think I'm going to be sick,' I mumbled.

I started to sway, and she grabbed me quickly.

'Come,' she said, 'I give you coffee strong for your drink.' She took my arm, and took me home. Her home. It was at the top of an outside stair. She put her finger to her mouth, asking me to be quiet while she unlocked the door. I had to wait till she lit a candle before I could see that we were in a tiny, cluttered room dominated by a circular table and with two large chairs at an empty fireplace. There were books all over the place, and a rickety old typewriter. Among the things on the sideboard was a framed photo of a smiling German naval officer.

'*Mein* father,' she said simply as she took off her coat.

I could see why she preferred the navy.

She was wearing a red woollen cardigan buttoned up to the top, and a plain, black skirt. 'You like my dress?' she asked wryly.

'I think you're lovely.' And she knew I meant it.

'I will get you coffee,' and she moved through a bead curtain.

I sat on one of the big chairs. I was cold, so I lit a cigarette, leaving out one for Hilburga. She sat in the other chair and we smoked, and drank the very strong coffee and talked in a funny, yet utterly agreeable, lop-sided way. Saying one thing, meaning another. At times she would get impatient with her own lack of English vocabulary, but we would laugh about it. I learned that she was studying to become a translator, English and French, that her father was now in the Argentine, that her brother was taken prisoner by the Russians, and that her mother and sister had been killed in an air-raid. She had been away from home at the time with her school. She went to the Cockatoo Club to try to catch an English officer, who would give her chocolate and butter and cigarettes, and she wore her coat because she didn't have a dress.

I reached over for her hand. 'Sorry, I'm not an officer,' I said.

She smiled again. 'Never mind, Johann, you have nice singing with your songs.'

I attempted to retrieve my hand, but she held it firmly.

'Ach, your hand it is kalt. Come,' she said, 'we will go to bed. It is warm there.'

I gulped, but let myself be led through the bead curtain and through a make-do kitchen area and into a room beyond which had a brass bed, of all things.

'It was from our old house. I bring here myself in a cart. The bathroom, you call it, is outside.'

'It's all right.'

I was trembling all over as I started to undress, and my fingers were numb. I tried not to look as she unbuttoned the cardigan on the other side of the bed. I tried to look nonchalant, and unimpressed, but failed miserably. She was about twenty or so, blonde, full breasted and with the kind of waist only steady hunger gives you. Her skin was the whitest I had ever seen, and when she had only her light blue underpants on, she skipped past me, saying, 'I will get other candle. You like candles?'

I could only nod. I didn't trust myself to speak. I wasn't sure whether to keep my air force games shorts on or not. They were the type that had no flies or aperture and were tied at the front. I had both hands on the bow when I heard her return, and almost involuntarily, I jumped between the sheets with them on.

As soon as she joined me, I tried to clamber all over her: '*Nein, nein, nein.*'

It may have sounded like a call for help – 999! – but instead it was an appeal for me to take it easy – we had plenty of time. This was how Hilburga introduced me to foreplay and real love-making. A gradual, and ever-ascending process of kiss, touch and embrace which as surely fires the imagination as much as it does the body and allows the girl to be a partner in the enterprise, and certainly not a sleeping partner. I'd never met a girl like this before. She wasn't a girl but a woman. And not any woman, but Eve, Cleopatra and Ingrid Bergman.

I felt her reach down and slip off her panties. This was my signal to do the same, before my young and eager manhood burst through the cotton material and made its own way to where it was meant to go. We were at that moment in a deep kiss, but I reached down and pulled hard with one hand – and pulled the tie into a knot! I tugged again even harder and only succeeded in making the knot tighter! All this under-cover effort did not do much for romantic passion, and when we broke off to see, Hilburga couldn't help but laugh. I had pulled the cord so tightly that I couldn't move the damned pants in any way. I tried to unpick the knot, but it was firm – which was more than I was by now. I felt so stupid. And very frustrated. She was out of bed again and out of the room and in a moment she was framed in the doorway with a large kitchen knife.

'I will cut it,' she said.

That's what I was afraid of. 'No, it's all right.'

She put the point of the knife in the knot and in minutes I was as nude as she was but 'with all passion spent'.

'I'd better get back,' I muttered bleakly, reaching for the pants again.

'*Ach, kleine Johann, nein –*'

'But aye,' I said, getting dressed. 'I'll be shot as a deserter if I'm not there by first parade.'

She was sitting up in bed, her head on her knees, watching me. 'Goodnight, Johnny,' she said softly.

By this time, I had my trousers on again and was buttoning my shirt. I picked up my sports jacket and tie and leaned over the bed to her. She didn't move. I reached up and turned her face to me. Her eyes were moist. She pulled her head away. Saw the knife was still lying there. I rose up with it in my hand and made for the door.

I was about to open it when she said, 'I told you I not like Air Force.'

I turned, and she looked so lost, sitting up in her own bed that I went to her at a rush and took her up in my arms. This time she gave to me. We kissed hard and long.

'Johnny,' she said eventually.

'Yes?' I found I was breathing hard.

'Please to put away knife.'

I found I still had it in my hand. I threw it down on to the thin carpet, and threw myself on Hilburga. This time she did not protest . . .

It was bright daylight when we awoke. I started up in a panic, yet with absolute exhilaration in my heart. Such love, or was it love-making, I had known with this fair daughter of the Herrenvolk. The Dennistoun Palais was never like this! As I came out into the morning sun, I came face to face with her neighbour peering out from behind her half-open door. I raised my right arm in salute. '*Heil Hitler!*' I roared, and went down the stairway on air.

I came down to earth with a considerable bump, however, as soon as I got back to my room in the German barracks that was our station at the time.

I skipped in the back way to find that my room-mate had reported me missing, and that the RAF Regiment Police had been out all night looking for me. Ah, what the hell. I didn't mind, it had been well worth it. I'd better report to the guardroom. The sooner I got it over with the better. I was supposed to be rehearsing a play in the sergeants' mess. But first I had to get to the NAAFI. Sugar, chocolates and cigarettes, she had said. I would surprise her tonight with cartons of each. We had arranged to meet at the entrance to the Malcolm Club in Hanover at 7.00 p.m., after I'd been to rehearsal and got out of my uniform again. I must remember to wear normal underpants this time. I was carrying the boxes into my room when I saw the two RAF policemen sitting there. One on my bunk and one in my chair. They never even got up as I staggered in.

'Bit late for Christmas, ain't it?' said one.

'Bit late all round, if you arsk me,' said the other.

Hilburga didn't get her sugar or her chocolate or her cigarettes. I was walking on air when I left her that morning, but my feet didn't touch the ground once the police got their hands on me. I was on a Dakota before I knew where I was and on the train back to RAF Cardington before I realised what had hit me. I was demobbed a week later. This is what saved me from a fate worse than death at the hands of the RAF police, but it's what also prevented my seeing that wonderful girl again. I couldn't write to her. I didn't know her address. I didn't even know her second name. I wonder if she ever met her officer?

It was April 1950 and I was home again in Glasgow. Johnny Fraser and I met in Ferrari's Café next to the Empire Theatre and swopped notes. He had decided to join up with the old Park Theatre in its new guise as Pitlochry's Theatre in the Hills. I wasn't sure I wanted to go into theatre straight away. A lot had happened to me in the two years and I wanted to digest it for a bit. I was accepted provisionally as an undergraduate of Glasgow University in the Faculty of Arts for the Session 1950–51 to commence in October. I was even given a generous grant by Glasgow Corporation which covered fees, books and basic living expenses. I would, of course, continue with my theatre interests at the same time, or rather part-time, until I had graduated, after which I could always apply again to my first boss, Kenneth Ireland, and take to the hills.

This was the plan during the summer of 1950. But then it was announced in the press that a College of Drama was being set up in conjunction with the Royal Academy of Music at the Athenaeum and would open in the coming September. Young people wishing a full-time career in the theatre were invited to apply for the three-year course. I decided to apply and was given an audition date. I did Hamlet's 'Advice to the Players', and something from Shaw, and was accepted to begin as a first-year student on Monday, 11 September.

I reported with nineteen other pioneer drama students at ten o'clock that morning to find a well-dressed little man in a wing-collar and bowler hat standing on the steps of the Athenaeum at St George's Place. He was waving tracts in one hand and raising the other in exhortation.

'In God's name, and that of his Kirk in Scotland, I call on you to denounce the stage and all its works. As ye are the true children of Calvin, I urge you to step back from the abyss surely facing you if you embark on this course of Satan and take up his promise of sin and damnation. Save yourselves now while there is still time. Turn back. Turn back even at the very door.'

I paid little attention to the little man's rantings and walked past him. Some laughed at him but I felt sorry for him. He was standing at the wrong door!

The drama college entrance was in the old Liberal Club building and there we gathered in the ground-floor hall to hear Colin

Chandler, the director, welcome us and introduce Mairi Pirie, our movement teacher, Geoffrey Nethercott, our voice teacher, James Arnott from the university, Sheila, the secretary, Tommy, the stage electrician and Willie the janitor. Seven of them and twenty of us, that was the full team assembled on that first day at the brand-new college: 'We few, we happy few, we band of brothers . . .'

There were, of course, other students in the evening course, and children on a Saturday, but we were the kernel, the élite corps, the pick of the bunch. I felt elated, excited, impatient, but above all, relieved. I had found my path, my vade-mecum, my only way and I couldn't wait to get started. Dame Sybil Thorndyke and her husband, Sir Lewis Casson, came on the Thursday and declared the place opened officially. Dame Sybil gushed magnificently and told us in high West End tones to keep our lovely Scottish accents, and Sir Lewis mumbled in his false teeth about the importance of being heard at the back of the gallery. I think that's what he said, I couldn't hear him properly! I saw their son John Casson in the audience. I asked him how his garden was growing. He looked right through me. Everybody was there, James Bridie, whose idea it was to start a drama school, and Duncan Macrae, who didn't know me either, and some of the parents. But not mine. I hadn't told them yet. I don't know why. Somehow, I'd never got round to mentioning it. They thought I was at the University!

'Do you sell fruit?'

'What?'

'I said do you sell fruit from a barrow?'

'No, I was an art student. Worked in an office, was in the RAF –'

'There's something wrong with your voice. It's very odd. Thought perhaps you might have strained it.'

'No – at least I don't remember.'

This was the first conversation I had in the voice class with Geoffrey Nethercott, our voice teacher. He was intrigued by the natural, and inevitable, urban huskiness of my voice, and in fact sent me for examination to the ear, nose and throat hospital, where it was found I had a nodule on my epiglottis.

'Just like Caruso,' Geoffrey beamed, when he got the report. But there the similarity ends. It is a fact, nonetheless, that I have a singer's speaking voice. That is, the chords don't seem to close properly until they're in full action, and good tone can really only be achieved by pumping hard with the ribs and belting it from the diaphragm. All this, of course, I didn't know at that time and had to learn.

'From now on,' said Mr Nethercott, 'and at all times, you'll all have to speak English.'

I thought I spoke English, but mine was the drawling patois of the streets, peppered with 'A'right?' 'OK?' 'you know' and 'know whit I mean?'. These all had to be ironed out, and it was a difficult process. But a start had to be made. Mine was made that very night at Parkhead Cross. Supporting the Linen Bank as we had done for years by leaning against it, a group of us were standing wondering what we would do with ourselves. One of the boys asked the time. These were the days before what we called 'wristlet watches', so I glanced across at the clock at the opposite corner on the Bank of Scotland building and enunciated after a very deep breath, 'Tw-en-ty meen-utes to-oo ni-ine.'

'What the hell's up wi' you?'

'I am spee-eking Eenglish!' I replied haughtily.

'Disnae sound very English to me!' said somebody else.

'Eet ees the way I have to spe-eek from now on,' I said, persisting in my Dalek tones.

'Not wi' us, you don't,' they said, dispersing generally, and I was left mouthing to the railings of the gentleman's convenience. It was a hard struggle learning to speak again, but I persevered.

'Whit's wrang wi' our John?' said my mother.

'What do you mean?' said Dad.

'Do you no' think he's talkin' funny?'

'John's always talked funny,' said Dad, and went back to his crossword.

It was a different matter with my dancing career. It never even got started. We assembled in the movement room, five boys and fifteen girls, the boys in black tights and white shirts, the girls in long practice skirts, when Miss Robertson, the dancing teacher, entered briskly, without even a 'good morning'.

'We'll begin with simple taps,' she said.

'I though that was a bugle call!' I muttered to Stan Giolouras.

'You there!' She was glaring at me. 'Yes, you. Outside!'

'But, Miss . . .'

'Outside, I said.'

'But . . .'

'Please leave the class. I know trouble when I see it.'

So I did, and stood out in the corridor wondering what to do and where to go.

Colin Chandler passed. 'What are you doing here?'

'Miss Robertson threw me out the class. Said she knew trouble when she saw it.'

'Well, she should know,' said Colin, and carried on his way.

So I never got to be Fred Astaire, and went to the changing-room and, with a secret relief, got out of my tights. I didn't have tap shoes anyway.

One of the most significant jobs in the first session had nothing to do with either voice or movement, but possibly came under the heading of pest control. All five boys, Stan, Bob Baird, Jimmy Copeland, Campbell Lennie and I, were ordered one morning to go down to the basement of the nearby Athenaeum Theatre and get rid of the rats. Some of the girls had been mucking about in one of the two theatre dressing-rooms and had been rather put out when a rat appeared and ran along the dressing-table in front of the mirrors. The girls ran out screaming and refused to go back into that dressing-room. They insisted on sharing with us next door. We didn't mind. Not having a theatre cat, Colin armed we boys with hammers and half bricks, organised us into a rat-pack next morning and deployed us into the Athenaeum catacombs. The idea was to hit the pipes with the hammers and drive the rats out into the open, then belt them with the bricks. Stan had the better idea of hitting the pipes with the bricks, then belting the rats with the hammer. I didn't contribute much. Given my rat phobia, I kept finding excuses to become less involved, but Jimmy Copeland more than made up for my reluctance, being an ex-water bailiff. He was picking them up in one hand as they scuttled past him. If they had all sold by their tails, we would have made enough between us to have had a very good lunch in the Ivanhoe that day. But I didn't feel very much like lunch.

Gradually, both staff and pupils settled down and a good working routine was established. I knew I was enjoying the happiest time of my life. I couldn't wait to get in each day, and was almost reluctant to leave at the end of classes; whether it was fencing, make-up, movement, or voice, I gave myself to everything wholeheartedly. I was even allowed back into the dancing class on condition that I made a vow of silence to Miss Robertson. Twice a week we went to lectures at the university on poetics and the history of drama, once a week to the art school for the history of costume and design in the theatre, once a week to the academy of music for singing and musical appreciation. I was having a first-rate grounding in the fine arts and I knew it. But the question still had to be faced: how would my father react to my becoming an actor?

The question was settled for me by the end of the first term. We were due to give a public demonstration of our class work in movement and speech. I had to be Lysander in *A Midsummer Night's Dream* in my new careful 'English' voice, and take part in a mime demonstration with Jean Martin, Sheila Prentice and Hilary Gillies. I felt more than a little self-conscious following Mairi Pirie's graceful mime instructions, and made sure that none of my mates from Parkhead would see it or hear about it. I wasn't so sure about my parents, until one morning a card came through the letter-box, addressed to Mr and Mrs Thomas Cairney at 20 Williamson Street, Parkhead, Glasgow E1, inviting them to attend a lecture demonstration by Mr Colin Chandler and students of the College of Drama at the Athenaeum Theatre, Buchanan Street, on Tuesday, 12 December at 7.30 p.m.

'Whit's this?' said Dad, peering over his new specs at the embossed card. 'Mair o' your fancy friends?' he asked, looking up at me.

This was it. This was the moment. I took a breath, and said, 'No, Dad. That's me.'

'Whit?'

'I mean – I mean – I'm in that. *Early Stages*, it's called.'

'Whit?'

'The demonstration.'

'Whit are you doin' in a theatre demonstration?' he said.

'I'm at the college,' I said simply.

'Wait a minute,' said Dad. 'I thought you were at the university.'

'But I am – in a way.'

'What do you mean – in a way?'

'Well, it's all part of it.'

'The soup's gettin' cold,' my mother interjected.

'Look, I better explain,' I said. 'I'm a full-time student at the College of Drama, and I have been since last September.'

'I wondered what was goin' on,' my mother said quietly.

'And what does that mean?' said Dad.

'I'm going to be an actor.'

'A whit?'

'An actor.' I couldn't bring myself to pronounce it as Paterson Whyte had done, but it had the same bombshell effect around that table.

Jim just laughed. Naturally he had known all about it, but

91

presumed that our parents did too. 'Hi, diddle-dee-dee . . .' he began. 'Shut up,' I snapped at him.

'Just a minute,' said Dad. 'Let's get this straight. So you're not goin' to be a teacher?'

'No.'

'And you're not goin' to do that commercial art thing?'

'No.'

'You're goin' to be an actor.'

'Yes.'

'Paint your face and talk like a lassie? Is that it?'

'No, Dad –' I tried to say.

'No, John,' he went on. I could see he was angry, and Dad never got angry. At least never with Jim and me, only my mother. 'No, no, you listen to me. No son of mine is –'

'Och, leave him, Tom.' My mother seemed quite unconcerned, as she put out the second course. 'Let him be. It's just the daft sort o' job that'll suit him. Eat up, for God's sake, or yous'll a' be late for the match.'

It was Celtic v. Third Lanark, so nobody was in a great hurry. During the game, I glanced round to Dad at one time, and he was looking at me very strangely.

'Hell of a game,' I said.

'Aye,' he said, and looked back to the pitch.

My mother's premonition outweighed my father's suspicion, so I was free to carry on. The demonstration went very well. My mother and father did attend – after some persuasion.

'What did you think?' I asked them when I got home.

'Some very nice lassies,' said my dad.

'I thought you sounded awfy affected,' said my mother.

This didn't spoil my chances not long afterwards of getting my first radio job. A couple of lines in *The Birds*, a Scots version of Aristophanes, which very properly got the bird next morning.

That Christmas, I worked in the Post Office along with hundreds of other students of all types, and very cold it was in the back of that lorry delivering cart-loads of Christmas cards up closes. I soon got a transfer indoors to the sorting and very boring that was. Then, remembering the lesson of the St Mark's woodwork class, I worked out a diversion. Not having *Music While You Work* any longer, nor any access to radio as we sat there in our dreary ranks sifting the cards into their various pigeon-holes, I started to sing Christmas carols with Gerald McGrath, a handsome big devil who was doing opthalmics. An ex-St Mungo boy too, Gerry was quite a character and

With Sammy San in the recording Studios for HMV Abbey Road, London – 1958

had a very good baritone voice to which I added harmony in my reedy tenor. One of the postmen came along and told us to be quiet as we were disturbing the workers, but the 'workers' protested loudly, saying they were enjoying it, so Gerry and I got up from the sorting and for the rest of the shift we entertained them with every song we knew from 'The Bold Gendarmes' to 'Ye Banks and Braes'. By the end we were down to Benediction hymns, but since our voices were giving out by then I don't suppose anyone noticed. I was sorry when the Christmas rush was over and we had to break up the act.

Being still required by my mother to work every day of the holiday, my next job found me in a woodyard in Old Shettleston Road. A bundle of students suddenly found themselves standing outside the 'office' of this very scruffy little establishment, and the little man behind the desk had no idea what to do with so many of us, so I suggested that he should take our names at least.

'Good idea,' he said, 'let's hiv a' yer names. Here, you dae it.' And he gave me a notebook from a drawer. It had three names written on the first page.

'What's this?' I said. 'Horses?'

'Naw, dugs,' he answered. 'S'a'right, they never come up.'

So I took the names, then asked him, 'What now?'

'Well, I've got two loads tae come in an' two tae go oot.'

'Right,' I said, spotting a chance. 'How many of your own men do you have?'

'Four.'

'Well, it's simple. We've got nine students here, so we divide them up and assign them to each of your boys – that's a couple of lads each they'll have.'

'Aye, that's right.' He nodded. 'Ah, bit, four intae nine – that's wan ower.'

'That's right,' I said, 'that's me.'

'An' whit dae you dae then?'

'I take the names,' I said, 'an' I can be the reserve, just in case.'

'Just in case o' whit?'

'Sickness, absenteeism, a death in the family.'

'Oh, aye,' he agreed.

So I became clerk of works in an East End woodyard for a couple of weeks. I noted the times each day, and helped make up the wages and answered the phone by the stove in the office, while outside better men than I were sawing, cutting, chopping, loading and generally breaking sweat. The best times, however, were the break-times. I used to organise debates, picking a motion from a story in that morning's paper and selecting two teams of three, who each had to speak for two minutes on fanciful motions like: 'That this yard deplores the lack of courtesy shown to men by the average Glasgow woman, and recommends that she refer to him in future as "Mister".'

It was great fun and passed half an hour easily. Often it was difficult to get them back to work.

'Bloody talkin' shop,' the wee foreman would growl.

'Better jaw-jaw than war-war,' I said in a Churchill voice.

'Whit the hell are ye talkin' aboot?'

The ones who enjoyed it most, however, were the permanent labourers, who not only welcomed the diversion, but showed themselves, like many working men, to be unexpectedly well-read, and first-rate debaters.

One of the older men, and one of the smartest, came from Baillieston. He was sorry when we all had to leave again after the holidays and gave me a shake of the hand. 'You're your Uncle James ower the back,' he said.

I couldn't have been more warmly thanked.

In the New Year, I took part in my first ever rag day and the student revue which followed at the old Lyric Theatre. One of the highlights was the Burns supper in which I was reluctantly involved as Rabbie. Little did I know! I was more concerned about my singing spot, where I had to render 'Take Thou this Rose' accompanied by Arthur Blake on the piano. My singing was accompanied by calls from the gallery like 'Take Thou This Coin!', 'Take Thou This Sausage Roll!', 'Take Thou This Toilet Roll!'. The stage was littered at the end of my first song, and I didn't bother about a second. However, I made a couple of pounds in coppers.

My singing had been more appreciated that morning outside Lewis's department store in Argyle Street. It was about eleven o'clock in the morning and I was on the back of a lorry with students from the music academy, one of whom had an accordian. He was playing 'Mother Machree' so I started to sing it, while the other students went among the shoppers rattling the collection cans under their noses. An old wino leaned over me, smelling heavily of a few minutes before, and hoarsely invited me to 'Shingit'gain, son, jus'furmee, eh?'

'Sure, Dad, just put your shilling in my can.'

'Nae borrer,' he mumbled, and pulled out a roll of fivers!

I sang 'Mother Machree' at least three times and I got a fiver a time as he had promised. I might have got more, but an earnest fellow-student reported me for putting a fiver in my pocket, and I only got away with it by saying that my can was full up. But it was a near thing. I vowed to go straight after that!

I was glad to get back to the routine of college and to the regular rehearsals of our first production. All the time, the end of the first session was rapidly approaching, and with it, our first real public performance, which was to be Oscar Wilde's *The Importance of Being Earnest*. I was to be Algernon Moncrieff and Ellen McIntosh, a deep-throated young actress from Dunfermline, was the Lady Bracknell, and magnificent she was. So much so, she was known as Dame Nellie thereafter. My big moment was off-stage, after the first scene. I was coming down the narrow wooden stair at the side of the stage and was met by the wide-eyed figure of little Mildred Linton from Falkirk.

'Here, John,' she said, 'you were good.'

'Naturally, Mildred,' I replied, still in my Algernon voice, 'what did you expect.'

'I thought you were a right chancer,' she said.

Millie and I became really good friends after that. She used to pick the poems for me to read in the diction class. We were really supposed to prepare them, but I never did. I just winged it, and hoped for the best with whatever sweet wee Millie put in front of me. I think Geoffrey was suspicious, and Millie was beginning to feel a little taken for granted, because one morning I got up and advanced to the front of the class with Millie's *Oxford Book of English Verse* open at the place, as she had given it to me and read:

Wake me early Mother dear, for I'm to be Queen of the May!

After that, I chose my own pieces.

It was also in the diction class that I got nil out of twenty for a test piece. It was Mercutio's 'Queen Mab' speech from *Romeo and Juliet* and I gave it all I had which, in Mr Nethercott's opinion, was precisely nothing. But it is a rare feeling to be so gloriously and utterly wrong. Or maybe I was right, who is to know? I never even got a mark for attendance. Never mind, I shall never be other than eternally grateful to Geoffrey Nethercott. Against all the odds, he gave me a voice. Odd perhaps, but it is mine, and I've been glad of it. Whether it is attractive or irritating matters little. What really counts is that it is instantly recognisable as mine. Not, you might suppose, the ideal vocal instrument for the protean actor, but then I am not a mimic or an impressionist, I am an actor, of whom the voice is only a part and not the whole. This was a lesson learned early.

I was a very happy student. I had found a congenial vocation in pleasant surroundings with attractive and stimulating companions. I was enjoying myself and if there were a catch in it I hadn't found it yet. I had energy and enthusiasm, but more importantly, purpose. I knew where I was going and I didn't care how long it would take me but I had a sneaking suspicion I'd get there – wherever it was! Meantime, mine was but to enjoy. Relax and soak it all up, for these were truly the happiest days of my life. So far.

But once a Catholic . . .

Wally Butler, a music student who had been the producer of the *College Pudding Revue,* came to me with the idea of forming a Catholic Arts Guild to act as a focus for Catholic talent emerging in the west of Scotland. He knew of my first experience with the Drama Festival, and thought we could get together and encourage Archbishop Campbell to provide premises and such-like practical support. This was duly forthcoming, and auditions were announced in the Catholic press. We were overwhelmed by the response, and the irony was not lost on me. Here was I, a first-year drama student, with five months' professional experience, and a couple of productions at Rutherglen Rep, suddenly taking auditions and arranging to produce and direct a new company before the session was over. We put on three one-acters by Thornton Wilder at the Athenaeum and sold out. I also discovered a genuine talent in a young girl called Collette O'Neil.

'I am going to do something I've never done before,' I said. 'I'm going to advise you to become a professional actress.'

I had not forgotten George Paterson Whyte! Collette did become a professional actress. A very successful one, I am happy to say. Gerard Slevin was another product of this time. I suggested another production of *The Righteous Are Bold* with all the best performers from the current year's Drama Festival, but the project didn't take off. Wally was offered a television job in Manchester and I was asked to play William in *As You Like It* at the Citizens Theatre. Nobody seemed keen to take our places, so a good idea for young Glaswegians foundered.

I learned then that any new movement is always one person's indestructible enthusiasm in the face of all odds, and my enthusiasm was beginning to self-destruct. Anyway, I had gone off the whole idea somewhat. It was getting a bit too 'Catholic' for me anyway. I was starting to feel like a pass-keeper! Besides, Father Power, whom I thought would make an ideal chairman, suddenly died one morning, standing in his braces, shaving in front of the bathroom mirror. It seemed an augury, so I let the Catholic Arts Guild die as well.

John Casson had come to the college to give a talk on production and asked for me specifically to play a small, but good, little part in his production of *As You Like It*. I suddenly found myself among the 'big boys': Jimmy Gibson, Paul Curran, Roddy Macmillan, Andy Keir, Fulton Mackay, and a very unusual English actor with a famous name, Michael Martin-Harvey, son of the great actor. For six weeks, I was backstage at the Citizens among the smells and the sounds of a successful theatre company at work, and I was totally at ease. I knew this was my world and I revelled in it. In the play, I had to work closely with Michael, and he and I got on very well. I have always got on well with old actors. The further they go back, the better. They have stories of other actors, other times, that I never fail to find fascinating. And anyway, they have survived in a hard, if magical trade, and their hardihood, if nothing else, does them credit. Of course, to have lasted at all, they must have had something, and there was no doubt that Michael Martin-Harvey had something.

His famous father's belt, for one thing.

This was the belt worn by Sir John when he played Hamlet, and now Michael wore it as Touchstone. On the final Saturday night, he came along to the big crowd dressing-room and gave it to me.

'Might bring you luck,' he said.

I stammered out my thanks as he placed the relic in my hands.

'These things should be used, I say, not left around in drawers or hanging up in museums. My father'd be delighted to think some young fellar's wearing it, you know. Have it. Wear it yourself if you ever play the prince. Have to take it in, of course.'

By one of those coincidences again, my next small part was with the Wilson Barrett company which was about to rehearse *The Only Way*, an adaptation of Dickens' *Tale of Two Cities*, and the part of the hero, Sydney Carton, now played by matinee idol Richard Mathews, was in fact created, and made famous by no less than Sir John Martin-Harvey! Just for luck I wore the Martin-Harvey belt under my costume. Michael was right. I had to take it in!

Wilson Barrett was the last of the old, gentlemen actor-managers. He himself was the son of a famous actor-manager, and throughout

the 1950s he had no less than three full-time companies touring in
Scotland doing comedies, classics and thrillers. As I mentioned, the
classical company were doing *The Only Way* and we students were
hired as extras and small parts. This time I was Gabelle, servant to
Carton, with a nice little moment just before Carton's: 'It's a far, far
better thing I do . . . etc.' The best thing I did was to get up on the
guillotine beside him!

During all this time, class work continued, of course, with lessons,
lectures, play rehearsals and demonstrations. I had the feeling that
the staff were learning just as much as we were and the curriculum
was being evolved gradually around our needs. Where we were
lucky as students was that since nobody in Scotland then was quite
sure how the actor should be trained, they took no chances and
taught us everything! Dalcroze eurythmics, poetics, how to 'cleek'
a flat, the proper method of setting out a prompt book, the whole
history of dramatic representation, everything it seemed, except
cookery and how to deal with tax problems. This last would have
been very useful! College always made it very clear we were not
being trained for a job. There was no guarantee whatsoever of
employment once we had graduated. We were being prepared for
a life in the theatre, and whether we lived that life as actors or directors or teachers of drama was up to us and the community, but I
had a funny, sneaking suspicion that I wouldn't become a teacher,
even though I knew I would qualify. I wanted unashamedly to be
a professional actor.

1951 was the year of the Festival of Britain. This was a national
celebration of culture and entertainment held throughout the year
to mark the centenary of the great Victorian census of 1851 and also
as a cheeky defiance of the grim austerity that had marked Britain's
post-war years. Every city, town, village and hamlet in the country
had to do something in the year and the West Highland community
around Duror, north Argyll, decided to put on a play. It was called
Murder in Lettermore and was written by local writer Angus MacVicar
who, being a Kintyre man, knew how to write for the local actors,
but there weren't enough of them to cast his courtroom drama
which dealt with the Inveraray trial of James Stewart for murder in
1752. So, Captain Rio Ritchie, a John Buchan type recently demobbed from the regular army, had the 'super wheeze' to engage
professional actors to supplement the amateur nucleus, since it was
the Festival of Britain and all that. However, when they found out

what it was going to cost, they quickly decided to involve us at the College of Drama. Since we were training to be professionals, we qualified on the first count and since we did not require to be paid anything more than expenses, we were acceptable on the second. This was all the more pressing since Kentallen, the adjacent village, had also decided to do a play, Compton Mackenzie's *The Lost Cause*, a Jacobite romance about Bonnie Prince Charlie and Flora MacDonald; but since *Murder In Lettermore* had already drained most of the local dramatic pool it was decided to merge forces and present the two plays under a single banner and call it a West Highland Festival for 1951. A neutral producer was appointed, Mr R. Christie Park of Dunoon, the County Youth Organiser.

Ten of us, under Mr Chandler himself, reported by bus to Cuil Bay and were distributed around the various houses. I landed up with Captain and Mrs Ritchie – which was 'absolutely super' but, unfortunately, I was paired with Harry Walker and not Jean Martin as I had hoped.

We were cast variously between the two plays. I was Lord Lovat in the Compton Mackenzie and it was only when we got there I learned that Bonnie Prince Charlie was to be played by the twenty-three-year-old president of the Glasgow University Dramatic Club – one Jimmy MacTaggart, of later BBC fame. Jimmy and I had already met. He had sacked me from the cast of Shaw's *You Never Can Tell* to be done by the university when he learned I was training to be a professional actor. 'Unfair advantage!' he claimed, but the truth was we both fancied the same girl in the cast. I can't remember her name. Now I was to be Lord Lovat with Jimmy and our Hilary Gillies was to be Flora MacDonald, complete with the very plaid worn by the real Flora; that is, if one is to believe Compton Mackenzie who loaned it specially for the production.

Someone said with awe, 'To think that this was actually worn two hundred years ago.'

'By Compton Mackenzie, no doubt,' muttered someone else.

I was only cast for this play, and wasn't in the MacVicar opus at all, until Hamish MacGregor, the local star thespian, got suddenly 'nervous' and took a little too much of the 'wine of the country', as it were, on the night of the dress rehearsal, no doubt for strictly medicinal purposes. To no avail apparently because Hamish was very much 'indisposed' for the opening performance.

'Bloody fool,' said Colonel Ashworth.

'Damned shame,' said Captain Ritchie.

'Oh, dear,' whimpered Canon Collins.

'He'll have to be replaced,' insisted Mr Fraser, the stationmaster and secretary.

'We haven't got anybody left,' said Mr Reynolds, the bank manager and treasurer.

'We'll need somebody,' exclaimed R. Christie Park of Dunoon.

'Get Cairney,' ordered Colin Chandler.

I was in the local bar chatting up Jeanne Menzies, a local girl, who, like everyone I met in Argyll, seemed to have an English accent. That morning I had a press photo taken with young Miss MacAlpine-Downie and the even younger Lady Fitzgerald. Both were on horses, and very 'horsey' though pretty with it, and both were in the plays: 'Jolly good fun,' said Miss MacAlpine-Downie. I was surprised Jeanne hadn't been cast to appear in either of the plays. She was certainly attractive enough, in a dark, striking, dramatic sort of way.

'No fear,' she drawled in her mannish voice, 'wouldn't be seen dead on a stage.' And that was that.

She was at art school in London and, being home on holiday, had been roped in to help with costumes. Now she was sitting with a gang of us round a roaring fire after dinner one night, while the rain bucketed down outside. It was a typical West Highland night in high summer!

Young Robert Russell suddenly appeared at the door looking for me. 'The colonel says you have to come to the tent.'

'What, at this time of night? He must be joking.'

'The English man in the raincoat says you have to come.'

That was Colin. That was different.

'What have I done now?' I wondered as I sloshed through the rain to the marquee, where the lights were still on. What was going on, I wondered.

We rehearsed from the moment I put my nose through the tent flap until five o'clock the next morning. Fed by soup, mince and drams at regular intervals till I felt nearly as bad as old Hamish. After a bath, a nap, lunch and another rehearsal in the afternoon, I was word perfect and opened that night as the Duke of Argyll, and romped away with the notices. I think it was just 'nerves' but a different variety from Hamish's. Where he was low, I was high, and in that mood, you can do no wrong. The only trouble was that every paper had me down as 'John Kearney' and it was he who got all the plaudits.

John Cairney didn't do too badly either as Lord Lovat, so

between them, Kearney and Cairney had a great West Highland Festival! But the best was still to come.

As the rains came down, the county just put on their macs and raised their umbrellas. To them, I'm sure it was no worse than a point-to-point, except that in this case, the points concerned were between the edge of Cuil Bay and the foreshore of Loch Linnhe, where Peter McIntyre had to land Bonnie Prince Jimmy. Now Peter, from Eriskay, had sailed all over the world as a merchant seaman but he never had a harder journey than coming round the head of the bay trying to land 'the actor folk'. A gale was blowing, but it was less meteorological than biological. A veritable gale of laughter. As the spectators huddled on the hillside caught their first glimpse of a very bedraggled Flora MacDonald, the historical plaid now about her ears, its redness matching her nose, and saw her handsome prince, now a decided green, lurching at the side, Peter, the oarsman, swearing mightily in the Gaelic, sought to beat wind and tide and derision and bring the cob round the corner for the third time. The cast, huddled in a bunch against the wind, hid their hysteria behind their plaids and it was a laughing 'Lord Lovat' who strode across the shingle to greet a nauseous Chevalier and a very dispirited Flora. Eventually, and with much cursing, the prow was pointed in the right direction. At long last they got the boat in after the choir of schoolchildren had sung the song of welcome over and over again like a litany, and when dear old Jimmy stood up like a trooper to make his royal landfall he stepped over the side and disappeared! For a moment we got a glimpse of his startled face, now ash-white, over the circle of kilt spread like a ballet tutu around him, then he sank like a stone, leaving only a forlorn white wig bobbing on the surface of the water and our Hilary (and his Flora) sobbing on the gunwales of the cob. Or was she laughing too? Peter, meantime, was striding through the play in progress on his way to the pub, muttering imprecations against all theatricals and throwing off his bits of costume as he went.

Some days, though, in that beautiful setting were magical. The sun going down behind the hills of Morvern and Ardgour, with the silver of the loch shimmering into the pink and gold of the bay, and Jeanne and I lighting her Gauloise cigarettes to keep off the midges, and trying to remember that I was really here to work. But it's hard to be serious in the Highlands. I couldn't be serious about Jeanne, but what was alarming was that she seemed to be getting serious about me, and I didn't mean that to happen at all. I was certainly fascinated by this Chelsea Highlander, but I didn't love her. I couldn't love her – I mean, she wasn't real. Nothing was real about Duror of Appin, the little place with the big ideas, Brigadoon with a Home Counties accent, my little play home in the west! Then one Saturday night, it was all over and we were home again, and no doubt Duror got back to abnormal!

I thought I'd said goodbye to Harry Walker when we dispersed in Glasgow, but he turned up again at Barry Camp where I was next sent to be a waiter at a territorial army camp. The Open Golf Championship was to be held at nearby Carnoustie and I was determined to see it. The only way I could do so was to work at nights at the camp and see the golf by day. Since I had gone to Duror I had no money for holidays so this was one way of getting a change of scenery before I had to report for rehearsals for *The Thrie Estaites* at the Edinburgh Festival. Anyway, I liked watching golf. I reckoned without the responsibilities of 'waiting', however. My attitude must have been wrong or something, but I couldn't take these clerks and newsagents as men born to command or lead others – especially the two I had in my section. They seemed determined to make my life difficult, and kept delaying their meal orders, then when I had them in, changing their minds, or when I did bring them something, they asked for it to be taken back. At length, I came up to them one night and told them it was a set meal and plonked down whatever I had on the tray. Naturally, they were annoyed, and being genuine snobs, complained noisily.

As a result, I was confined to kitchen duties and I didn't really mind, even when I was put on to dishwashing. I could think my own thoughts while I cleaned, but, unfortunately, I was given to singing while I worked, and the cook didn't like my singing. I told him that was too bad, but I couldn't repress my natural *élan* and he would have to put up with it. He was unused to having his kitchen authority questioned, but I pointed out that I wasn't in his army, not even part-time, and continued to strangle 'La Donna e Mobile' in my best John McCormick manner. Next minute, a bowl whistled by my head and thudded into the wainscoting near the window. I wheeled round, and there was the cook, his completely bald head a sea of mottled veins, raising a floured fist to me and swearing like a trooper and not at all like the sergeant-cook he was. I told him to restrain himself – well, not quite in those terms, but to that effect. This caused him to come round the table, apron flying, so I hurled the pot I had in my hands. Unfortunately, it was half-full of greasy water and most of it went over his corrugated dome. He picked up a huge carving knife and came after me. I dashed to the other side of the table. He followed me round. He came on again. I got to the other side, and so on, round and round the rectangular kitchen table. Harry Walker came in from the dining-room and, surveying the chase, could only mutter dolefully, 'Aw come oan, keep the heid!'

Our table-chase was only halted by the arrival of the CO. The cook immediately skidded to a halt, coming to attention at the same time, like a Disney cartoon cat after a mouse. I was the mouse, and impelled by the centrifugal force of the pursuit I hurtled past the gaping officer (who was an estate agent in real life) and straight out of the kitchen. Out of the camp in fact. Harry Walker brought his sad, bear's face to tell me I was to 'Chuck it in'. I had lasted a week. I never got to see Gary Player, Tony Lima or the young Lee Trevino.

Being an extra in the 1951 production of *The Thrie Estaites* at the Edinburgh Festival meant sleeping three in a bed. There were nine of us in one big room in Mrs McPherson's lodgings in Danube Street and there were three big beds, and all I know is that last to come in at night had to sleep with his head at the foot of the bed. At least the other two could turn their backs, but latecomers had to contend with two pairs of feet, which wasn't a happy prospect, even if you'd had a few beers. Our digs were exactly opposite Edinburgh's only brothel. Being Edinburgh, it was very discreet, but being a brothel, it was known to everyone. We used to see the girls in the mornings taking the air. I bet they didn't sleep three in a bed! Or maybe they did!

In order to escape our overcrowding, I was happy to get away first thing in the morning, and it was generally the next morning when I got in again in any case. No matter how early I got up, I was never earlier than Duncan Macrae, who had his own room, of course, as befitted our star. And anyone less like a star I could not imagine. An eccentric, yes; a character, without a doubt; a leading man, in every sense; an actor with comic genius, certainly; but never the 'big star' in the accepted sense. He made a practice of walking each morning to rehearsal, which meant a good hike through Stockbridge, over the Dean Bridge, through Princes Street Gardens and up the Mound. I tried as often as possible to walk with him, or rather, I ran alongside. He had this loping, gangling stride, which seemed to cover leagues with every step,

104

and all the time he would be gesticulating with a long left arm to emphasise some point or other, while with his right, he would be indicating points of interest on the way. Like all great artists he had extraordinary energy and enthusiasm, and I couldn't believe my luck that I was involved professionally with such a man so early in my career. In fact in my pre-career, as it were, since I was technically still in training. Duncan Macrae was the first of the greats I met and he was to remain for a long time as the yardstick by which I measured the others.

One of those 'greats' was the director of *The Thrie Estaites*, Dr Tyrone Guthrie. He would have needed a milestick for measurement, rather than a yardstick. We all looked up to him in every sense, since he was six feet five in his shoes, and six feet four in his slippers – which he often wore at rehearsals. My first impression of these festival rehearsals was of Mrs Guthrie coming down the aisle behind the great man carrying his slippers in one hand and a flask of tea in the other. Tony, as everybody called him, was a big man in every respect. He made a point of being rude to his principals, but never to his extras. He gave to us all the benefit of his vast experience and theatrical wisdom, assuming, quite rightly, that the leading actors could take care of themselves – which they did. Every point of direction was accompanied by an anecdote or aphorism, and the rehearsal days went blissfully by.

It was my first Edinburgh Festival, and I think my most memorable. I walked and talked with Duncan Macrae, Tony Guthrie put his arm round my shoulder, I heard Kathleen Ferrier and Dietrich Fischer-Dieskau sing, and every night, sitting on the steps of that Assembly Hall stage, I willed Fulton Mackay to drop dead or at least break a leg, as I was understudy to his king. Fulton, however, was made of stern stuff and survived the whole run without as much as a cough! We took the production to the St Andrews Halls in Glasgow afterwards, and it meant I got a decent night's sleep at least, as I was back in my own bed again – alone . . .

A second year joined us now at the college, among whom was one who immediately became a good friend, Andy Stewart. We got on so well that before the end of the year we had decided to take out a student tour in the summer holidays. At least it would be better than working in a woodyard. As putative professionals we did everything in a very professional way. We got all the right permissions and approvals, we worked out a sharing scheme with the cast and the college secretary made a stencil letter for us, a copy of which we sent to virtually every town clerk in Scotland.

THE YOUNG STAGERS

60 St George's Place
Glasgow, G2

Tel: Douglas 4101

15th May, 1952

Sir,

The Young Stagers is an entirely non-profit-making society of young people in Glasgow and the west of Scotland, professionally interested in the theatre and particularly – Scottish theatre. Its aims are to promote the presentation of Scottish plays in Scotland, and to arouse enthusiasm generally for our waning national drama. It does this by undertaking annual summer tours of performances by its own company of players.

We begin this year by contemplating a tour embracing your district among others, commencing Monday, 30th June, and finishing Saturday, 2nd August, 1952, at points yet to be determined. The play being presented on this occasion will be Torwatletie by Robert McLellan, an uproarious Scottish costume comedy in three acts.

If you are interested in seeing this entertaining work performed by our company at any time during the aforementioned period in your locality, please complete the attached questionnaire and return it as soon as possible to us. We can then arrange our itinerary accordingly. Thank you.

Provisional date of arrival in your area is _____

Further details will be forwarded as required.

Until we hear from you,
I beg to remain, for
'The Young Stagers'
Yours very sincerely,
John Cairney

Andy and I were quite pleased with our professional approach. While we awaited replies we rehearsed our play after hours in the common-room, and we made sure that all our particular friends were in it. Jean Martin, Sheila Prentice, Aileen O'Gorman, and, of course, my particular favourite, Mildred Linton. The whole cast, in fact, went through to Falkirk for a rehearsal at Millie's house, which turned into an all-night party. Even though the term work was becoming more strenuous and the university lectures more demanding, we still had plenty of time for parties, and there were many.

106

Gradually, over the weeks, *Torwatletie* emerged as a production and, to our amazement, most of the town clerks replied agreeing to take us. As a result we now had a tour which seemed to last most of the summer and would cover most of the east and north of Scotland. We were thrilled, and that was an excuse to have another party. Any excuse was good enough.

Then one day, while I was rehearsing Sophocles' *King Oedipus* at the college, I, as Oedipus, was with Andy in a scene where he was a shepherd, and Colin Chandler as the director was trying to stop us making a gag out of the stage direction, 'Oedipus lifts the shepherd' when the secretary suddenly appeared and told Colin he was wanted in the office. He broke the rehearsal while he went down, and Andy and I clowned about for the benefit of the rest of the cast. By now we were an accepted double act in the college. Suddenly Colin appeared at the door looking very grim. There was an immediate hush in the rehearsal-room. Colin then said just the one word, 'Cairney,' and beckoned me to follow him. I looked at Andy, shrugged and followed.

In his office were two men in plain clothes who could not be anything but policemen, and, believe it or not, I was asked by one of them, 'Where were you last night?'

I said, 'Why?'

'Never mind why,' snapped the other. 'Give us your whereabouts if you please.'

I suddenly realised it was almost the clichéd situation: 'Where were you on the night of . . .?' I was being grilled. It was almost like a scene from a play. I looked to Colin, but he looked even more solemn that usual.

A voice went on, 'Well, where were you?'

'Eh? Er . . . I was at a party in Clarence Drive.'

'Glasgow?' snapped one of the policemen.

'Why, is there another Clarence Drive?' I said with a weak smile.

'Don't be silly, Cairney,' growled Colin.

'Well, what's up?' I asked.

'Do you know a Mildred Linton?' said the first detective.

I glanced at Colin again. 'Of course,' I said.

'Is she a friend of yours?'

'Yes. Mildred's a friend –'

'A special friend?'

'What do you mean –'

The other policeman broke in abruptly. 'Mildred Linton was found murdered in a Falkirk park this morning.'

107

There was absolute silence. I looked at Colin. He was looking down. I looked at the two policemen. They were staring fixedly at me. At me? They thought I . . .? Mildred? It was impossible.

'It's impossible,' I muttered.

'What's impossible?' growled one of them.

'She was at a rehearsal on Friday. We're doing a tour –'

'There'll be no tour, I'm afraid,' put in Colin.

'Have you proof that you were where you say last night?'

'Well, yes – half the class upstairs.' I was hardly taking them in now. Mildred?

'When did you get home?'

'What? Oh, I stayed the night.'

'Can you prove that?'

'Ask any of them.' I nodded upstairs. 'So did they.'

I wasn't bothering about their questions now. I was thinking of poor wee Millie. I thought you were a chancer, she had said. I really felt like one in that room between these two anonymous men. What terrible chance had she taken? Poor little darling.

After a time Colin told me I could return to my class, but he added, 'Say nothing to the others. I'll be up in a moment.'

'Yes, sir,' I said, and closed the door behind me. I didn't go back up to the class. I walked straight out into St George's Place. I wanted some fresh air. Of course there was no tour that summer. There was to be no Young Stagers Company because there was now no Millie. I never learned what actually happened. It was in the papers, but apparently her mother had remembered her speaking about me and we had all been to that party in her house. The police were just checking up, I suppose. Doing their job. It gave me a terrible fright just the same. But the fright was nothing compared to the shock of hearing about Millie that way in that office.

It was the first time that the outside world had intruded on the ideal small world we had built up for ourselves within that year-old college of drama. Ours was a positive arcadia of little delights, based largely on the daily exercise of our bodies, our imaginations and our total sensibilities. It was my first realisation of how real to the actor his unreal world is. It takes the shock of a cruel, harsh incident like Millie's murder to suddenly make one aware that the outside world goes on. And what a rotten, dirty, filthy world it can be at times.

However, the fact remains, it does go on, and so did we. I found that my relationship with Terry McFarlane was deepening to what families call an 'understanding'. Nothing was actually said, but it was accepted by everyone around Parkhead that we were 'going together' and I was happy enough to go along with things. She was attractive, and a good girl, and seemed right for me in every way, so I didn't mind the relationship at all. It was relaxed and comfortable, and just what I needed. I think Terry would have liked things to have been formalised, even if only to please her girlfriends. But I suggested that since I had only a year to go before graduating, we should wait till then and see what happened. I wasn't in any way using it as an excuse. I took it as almost inevitable that Terry and I would become engaged, then marry, find a good flat up some East End close and start on our many children. What I wasn't sure of, though, was where my acting ambitions would take me. Certainly not up an East End close.

I spent the summer with the Fraser Neal players in my first and last experience of weekly rep. We played places like Paisley and Greenock in second-rate theatres with third-rate plays, like *White Cargo* and *Smilin' Through*. The actors were jaded professionals of an older school and green hopefuls like myself. But just occasionally in a production we pulled it off. The hit of that summer was Tennessee Williams' *A Streetcar Named Desire*, which was such a success around the smaller dates that Fraser Neal brought it to the Empress at St George's Cross in Glasgow. This was very much a working-class area, and they made no bones about their likes and dislikes. I was cast as Stanley Kuwolski and was doing my best to impersonate Brando, even to the extent of lifting the girl (Irene Corcoran, Tommy Lorne's daughter), and throwing her roughly on to the bed. The only difference was, at the Empress I lifted her up all right, but, unlike Brando, I dropped her. In order to cover this, I pretended to kick her, at which the house went into an uproar – the stalls being outraged and the balcony yelling its approval. I ended up by pulling Irene by the arm towards the bed as the lights went down. *Streetcar* was not one of my early triumphs.

I was glad to return to the Edinburgh Festival, this time in a musical production called *The Highland Fair*. Robert Kemp had adapted the Romeo and Juliet story in terms of two Highland clans. Once again I was hired as an extra. Once again I was with Mrs McPherson, but the overcrowding was less on this occasion. I believe the authorities had stepped in and regularised her sleeping arrangements! Tony Guthrie, the great beaked demi-god, was once again the director, and on the first day of rehearsal called me aside and drawled in his nasal way, 'Want you to make yourself useful.'

I said, 'As what?'

109

'Don't know. Find something to do,' and pushed me back into the crowd.

Since the play was called *The Highland Fair* and was concerned at several points with the normal activities of a fair, I decided to make myself a fairground seller, and had props make me up a tray with shoulder straps, so that I could walk among the people on stage, generally among the principals, during the action, selling my 'wares'. I decked myself out with a tricorne hat and a tartan waist-coat and generally enjoyed myself. Roddy McMillan, who himself had a small singing part, commended my idea of using a tray. This was a mistake, as I immediately had the tray enlarged and filled it with more gaudy trappings. By the end of the week I had such a large tray and it impeded the action to such an extent, that Roderick Jones and Ian Wallace and other principals were making large detours around me on the stage, till Guthrie stopped the rehearsal and asked if I would like to set up shop with a stall centre-stage. Amid general derision I said that would be a great idea. I was told to halve the tray immediately. It was a lovely, happy and most successful production, and on its high note I was happy to report to the college for my final year.

Before doing so, seven of us were directed to the Citizens to be shouting students in the production of Bridie's *Anatomist* which was to star Alistair Sim, as part of the Bridie memorial season. We had very little to do other than make noises, but it was fascinating to watch Mr Sim work. Here was my next Scottish 'great'. The problem was in filling in time between the student entrances, and since so many of us were cooped up in the crowd dressing-room at the top of the building, it led to games being developed – one of which meant scribbling with greasepaint on the long mirror. This developed to such an extent that we could hardly see our reflections in the mirror after a time, and one night there was a pencilled note saying, 'Please clean mirror, as I don't know how to get the stuff off.' And it was signed, The Cleaner. This led to conjecture about who The Cleaner was, and what her name was, and to a general discussion on women's names and the importance of the right name for the right girl, incongruous names and beautiful names and so on. Then, for some reason, I took up the stick of make-up and wrote 'Sheila Cowan' on the mirror.

'Who's that?' asked Alex McAvoy.

'Haven't a clue,' I replied, and started to try and rub it off.

With Carole Lesley Operation Bullshine *ABPC 1959*

The start of that year's session at the college was unique, in that it was the first time that the full complement of students – from first year to third year – had now been attained. So Colin made a speech of welcome. By this time our original twenty-five had been reduced to twelve, and the second year original twenty-five were now twenty, but there was a pristine complement of twenty-five called the new first year, among whom to my astonishment was Miss Jeanne Menzies who had forsaken both Chelsea and Duror of Appin to become a first-year drama student. Just for company, she had brought Sappho, her Irish wolfhound, who stood nearly three feet in her bare paws and was now tethered to the door of the janitor's cubby-hole downstairs. I made a note to keep well out of both their ways: Sappho and Jeanne's.

As we were all assembled in the lecture room, Colin read out all the names, starting with us. We felt very much the old hands as final-year students, and listened with interest to the names of the new first year. You can imagine then my astonishment when I heard Colin read out the name, 'Sheila Cowan'. I jumped. That was the name I had written on the mirror only the night before. I looked round to see who had answered, but by this time he was on to other names, and I couldn't tell who had spoken among all those new faces. As soon as we were dismissed to the common-room, I began to make enquiries, and found that the owner of the name was sitting at the end of the table, looking at her class instructions. I immediately went to her and caught my breath. I was looking down at the most devastatingly beautiful girl I had ever seen in my life.

'Excuse me,' I said, 'are you Sheila Cowan?'

She looked up at me and I had never seen such eyes. 'Yes,' she said.

In exactly that moment, in the time it took her to reply, I had completely and utterly fallen in love with her.

'I wrote your name in a mirror.'

'Get lost!' And with that, she brushed past me and made her way through the crowded, chattering common-room to the door.

I followed at once, but was stopped by Alec McAvoy. 'Here, John, funny you should write that lassie's name on the –'

But I was already pushing past him on my way out into the corridor. No sign. I looked over the banister, and caught sight of her fair hair bobbing up and down on the lower staircase. She was going into the ladies.

I was waiting on the lower landing when she came out. 'Look –' I began, but she moved quickly past me again and hurried down-

112

stairs. I ran after her, even when she continued outside and turned up into West Nile Street.

'I know it seems daft –' I kept trying to explain, but she wouldn't listen and kept on walking up towards Sauchiehall Street. I then put myself right in front of her and refused to let her pass. I could see she was angry. I suddenly stopped bantering in mid-sentence. We looked at each other in absolute silence as we stood on the pavement. Only then did I realise it was raining and that umbrellas were stepping off the pavement to go round us. Luckily, we were almost at the door of the Lido Café, and I hurried her in before she had a chance to protest.

'No singin', no noise,' said Domenico, the proprietor, as soon as he saw me. The Lido was one of our student resorts.

'Don't worry, Domenico, I'm not Gene Kelly, I never sing in the rain!'

We found seats up near the back of the café and, removing our wet things, settled in. I just sat there and feasted myself on this girl, Sheila Cowan.

'Whit d'ye want?' a voice mumbled.

'I just want to look at you.' I replied, still staring.

'Eh?'

The tone brought me back to earth. I then saw it was Carla at my side, Domenico's young sister, and his waitress. 'Two espresso, please.'

'*Due espresso, si,*' muttered Carla, leaving me to continue staring.

'This is very embarrassing,' said Sheila, looking around her.

'I'm not at all embarrassed,' I answered.

But I certainly was when the coffees came, for I found that I had no money! There were many days when I was a student I had no money, and this happened to be one of them. I tried to explain to Carla that I hadn't been to the bank, that I was a regular customer, and all that, but she just sighed and turned away.

'I get Domenico,' she said.

He was hovering over me within seconds. 'Wassa trouble?'

'No trouble, Domenico, it's just that I –'

'There's no trouble at all,' a cool voice interjected. It was Sheila, very cool, quiet and composed. 'My friend here and I were arguing about whose turn it was for the bill. I insisted it was mine. How much did you say it was again?'

She was looking up at the stocky little Italian, her purse open in her hands, a dimpled smile on her face. What class, I thought. What style. What a girl!

113

'*Due espresso?* One and a sixpence.'

She gave him a florin. He fumbled a long time for the sixpence change, but she waited, and took it. Then lifting her cup she turned that gaze on me. 'Cheers,' she said, and took a sip, but her eyes were smiling.

And that was how I first met Sheila Cowan – my name on the mirror. Of course, I told her the full story, and at the end of the day's classes, I took her down to the Citizens Theatre to see for herself, but the mirror had been cleaned. A typewritten label was stuck on the glass warning that the management would take strict action against anyone defacing the dressing-room mirrors in such a way again. However, if you looked closely enough, you could just see, very faintly, the name 'Sheila Cowan' still on the glass.

'Believe me, now?' I asked.

'Thousands wouldn't,' she retorted quizzically.

This girl was like no other I had ever met. I was fatuously infatuated with her from the start. A whole new happiness had come in to my life. I woke each day to the sunny knowledge that in a few hours I would see her. I almost ran to college every morning, and couldn't wait for class breaks so that I might meet with her, and steal her away to some quiet corner for as long as I could detain her. I walked her back to the girls' hostel in Bothwell Street every evening. I resented every occasion that took her away from me. In short, I was overwhelmingly in love with this seventeen-year-old, and I didn't care who knew it. Everybody at college did. Especially Jeanne, who had us both up at her flat in Hill Street for coffee and Drambuie.

'Cradle-snatching I would call it,' she drawled through the cigarette smoke. 'On the other hand, given your own age – '

'Twenty-two.'

'Yes,' said Jeanne, 'she could hardly be said to be grave-robbing, could she?'

'Hardly,' I replied, sipping my Drambuie, but savouring the sight Sheila made on the couch opposite beside Sappho the wolfhound.

'Thank God, I have Sappho!' said Jeanne.

'You must remember she's very young, and new to Glasgow.' Colin Chandler was his grave self, and was eyeing me very closely from the other side of his desk.

'Yes, sir,' I said meekly.

114

'By comparison you're a man of the world.'

I felt quite flattered, until he added, 'A small world, admittedly.'

'Yes, sir.'

'But the world of theatre is a small world, a small closed order, if you like. It wouldn't do to have the monks fraternising with the nuns, now would it? We'd none of us ever get any work done!'

'No, sir.'

'She's just beginning, and you're about to finish. It's an important time for both of you, so for God's sake go easy. I'm not asking you to repress your normal instincts, but just to keep them under control, at least till after the final performances. You've come on a long way in three years, don't mess it up with just one fence to go. Try a cold bath every morning.'

'We haven't got a bath in our house, Mr Chandler.'

'What? Oh no, of course not. You'd better get back to – what are you rehearsing?'

'*Hedda Gabler* with Miss Gordon.'

'Of course. Off you go.'

'Yes, sir.'

I met Andy in the main hall, beaming. 'What did you get – a hundred lines, "I must not snog with Sheila Cowan in the common-room", or words to that effect?'

'No,' I said. 'I think Colin meant I must not be caught snogging with Sheila Cowan in the common-room.'

'Never mind, see you and Johnny Grieve in the Ivanhoe.'

'Why, your birthday or something?'

'No,' replied Andy, 'I've just heard from Johnny Groves that I'm to be in a film.'

'No?'

'But aye – *Rob Roy* for Walt Disney.'

'Great, Andy. What are you playing?'

'Mickey Mouse, I think. See you.'

Good for wee Andy. Or young Andrew, as Colin called him.

Sheila Cowan had exploded like a starshell in my life to such effect that for a time I was blinded to almost everything else. My part as Eilert Loveborg in the *Hedda Gabler* meant that I had to grow my first beard, or at least try to. A pretty, or rather un-pretty, miserable affair it turned out to be too. Wispy and apologetic could best describe it. It mattered little in the college rehearsal-rooms, but it caused all kinds of comment around Parkhead. My mother looked especially annoyed. 'It's neether wan thing or another,' she complained. 'It just looks as if ye hid a bad shave, that's a'.'

115

My metamorphosis to drama student, while it didn't entirely surprise my mother, didn't always please her either. My sartorial fancies were sometimes so extreme in her eyes that she would often cross the road to avoid me if she saw me coming, either trailing my coat like a cloak, or with my shirt outside my trousers, or my tie unknotted at my neck. I was much given to such affectations, I'm afraid. I thought them very daring and Bohemian. My mother had other ideas. 'Like a bloomin' rag-man, oor John!'

It was hard to be artistic in Parkhead.

It was also becoming slightly uncomfortable with Mary Theresa. Not that anything directly was ever said. That was the trouble, very little was said when we were out these days. At least by me. Terry would prattle away happily about her doings at the office, with her girlfriends at the club, family happenings. She very rarely asked me about specific events at college. It was an alien world to her. What was worrying was that I could feel that her world, which was also my world, was becoming increasingly alien to me. Not better or worse, but more and more different. I might not be a monk as Colin had said, but if Terry were a nun, she was in a very different order. We had seemed to have everything in common, but now we had less and less. On a superficial level at least. There were increasing strains, more quarrels about nothing, dates were postponed, delayed, broken off. Not being a fool, she was becoming suspicious, but being a wise girl she said nothing. We went more often to the pictures. That way, we didn't have to talk so much. If we didn't talk, we couldn't argue. If we didn't argue, we couldn't fight, and if we didn't fight there would be no danger of my saying too much, or saying something I didn't mean, or worse, saying nothing at all. I might hurt her, and I didn't want to hurt this little Glasgow East Ender for the sake of an East Coaster. I liked them both too much. I loved them. Could I love them – both of them?

One night Terry and I went to the Three Ps (Parkhead Picture Palace!). It was showing *Ivanhoe* starring Robert Taylor, Joan Fontaine and Elizabeth Taylor and, as I watched, in the way of all young romantics, I became Robert Taylor, Terry was Joan Fontaine and Sheila was the young Elizabeth Taylor. Come to think of it, not bad casting! I sat through the film that night, matching my growing real-life dilemma with the film's, or rather, Sir Walter Scott's, fictional situation and matching its development and outcome with my own. Walking home, Terry asked which of the two women I preferred. I hummed and hawed and said something about their being

116

very different types, which was why they were cast that way in the film.

'I would've imagined you'd prefer Elizabeth Taylor, somehow,' said Terry.

I said nothing.

As Christmas approached, things got worse instead of better. I had to make up my mind and do something about the situation. Sheila and I had both become involved in an opera co-production of Sheridan's *The Duenna*, with the music academy people next door. I was cast as the tenor lead and Sheila was a dancer. It allowed us extra time together, but when Terry came with some St Michael's friends to the Athenaeum to see the production, I was left with a straightforward choice. Who was I to go home with: Sheila or Terry? Terry naturally expected I should go with her, so I did. We became engaged not long afterwards. It was an impulsive and abrupt decision, taken in a back close in Salamanca Street, Parkhead, when Terry was staying with friends of hers, the Flynns. In so many ways, it seemed the right and inevitable thing to do. I had almost finished my training, my mother liked her, my dad liked her, Jim liked her, and I liked her. She gave me a silver cigarette-case and I gave her a ring, which she chose in the Argyle Arcade one Saturday morning. The Sheila Cowan episode was over. I thought I could then get back to work.

Our main college production at the time was *The Family Reunion* by T. S. Eliot, a kind of Greek tragedy in modern dress. It was to be 'rehearsed' for us, which was the training phrase then, by Peter Potter, a handsome, English ex-army officer who had lost his leg in the war, and had come north to direct the Citizens Theatre Company. I was to play the lead, which had both happy and unhappy consequences. The happy result was that, thanks to Peter's subtle direction, I got fabulous notices, especially in the *Scottish Daily Express* by Robin Millar, who was also a well-known playwright.

However, what caused some unexpected bother was the photograph in the paper that day which accompanied the interview and the notice. I had come home from the performance, or rather the party which followed it, to find a strange man sitting at our table having tea with my mother and father. It was the *Express* photographer. He needed a photograph for the morning edition, and didn't know I wouldn't get in till two o'clock. From their general bonhomie when greeting me, I'm sure the two men had more than tea while they were waiting. I was made to get back into the suit I had been wearing. I had to sit facing the back of a dining-room chair, then turn back to face the camera. I don't know why he wanted it like this but it was to suggest something of the 'neurotic character, perplexed by guilt, on the verge of insanity, ecstatic and ironic by turns, credible, whether subtle or explosive'. I don't know whether I managed it on one of our kitchen chairs, but that was the photo which appeared the next morning, as a result of which I had another visitor the next night. This time my father was out and my mother looked very uneasy, for the new visitor was a plainclothes policeman.

Not again, I thought. What is it this time? 'Och, it's nothing at all, Mr Cairney,' he soothed in his Highland tones. 'Just a few enquiries, but we'd like you to come to your station – at your convenience, of course. But would tomorrow morning be convenient?'

'What time?'

'Before you go to the college or at the dinner-time if you prefer.'

'I'll come at nine. Can my father come – ?'

My mother broke in. 'We'll no' bother your father. I'll come wi' ye.'

'Just as you like, Mrs Cairney,' said the oily Highlander. 'I'll just let myself out.' He was so smooth, I'm sure he got out through the letter-box.

At nine the next morning, my mother and I were in the Southern Police Station. At ten we were still there, and at eleven we were still there. I wasn't even given a chance to ring the college. There was something very funny going on. The general attitude towards me was pugnacious to say the least, and my mother was growing visibly upset. I was moving gradually from irritation and anger to very definite apprehension.

Then a sergeant suddenly said, 'Right, you, this way.'

I presumed he meant me and followed. I was taken into another room where a row of men were standing against a blank wall with a harsh light shining on them.

'Have you any objection to these men?' said the bad-tempered sergeant.

'Why should I? I've never met them before.'

'Bloody comedian, is it. Right, just stand against the wall.'

'What?'

'Just take a place against the wall with the others.'

'What's all this about?' I cried.

'You'll find out soon enough.'

Two women then came in accompanied by another policeman. They walked slowly along the line, and then one woman looked at me and turned away, whispered something to the other woman who

118

whispered something to the policeman who nodded to the sergeant, who said something like 'Humph' and the women were led out again. A little girl came next with a woman who was obviously her mother, and when the little one saw me, she burst out crying and turned to her mother, who looked as if she were going to say something to me, but pulled her girl away and ran out. 'Humph,' said the sergeant again.

The constable brought two older girls in, who stood in front of me and seemed to argue in whispers. The terrible truth then dawned on me. I was in an identity parade. The perspiration broke out on my face. I looked along the line. I was the tallest person there. I was the youngest. I was the only one with black hair. I was the only one in a suit. In fact, I stood out like a very sore thumb. I got very sore indeed, and made to walk to the sergeant to point this out, when I was grabbed by two other policemen and forcibly restrained in the line, at which I started yelling. The two girls in the room ran out. The other men in the line, whom I now saw to be plainclothes policemen, and a couple of prisoners obviously let out of the cells, were removed and I was left struggling between two policemen as a senior officer came in. I really let go at this man, and insisted I had not been given any notice whatsoever of this intention or told anything about why I was here, and what was much more important, I was missing a rehearsal at the college.

This final incongruity seemed to get through to him and I was taken into his office. He explained that a prowler had been active around the South Side, bothering little girls after school. One of the mothers had seen him for a moment as he ran off through a back close. As he looked back at her, his face and expression were exactly like mine as I appeared in the *Express* newspaper the morning after *The Family Reunion* – 'neurotic, guilty, insane'; no wonder she thought I was the prowler! Luckily for me they had exact dates of the incidents around Pollokshields, and when I checked with my diary, I found that on each occasion, even more fortunately, I was in rehearsal at the college. A quick call to Colin Chandler confirmed this, and the superintendent said I could leave at once. Would I like a police car?

'No thanks,' I muttered, 'but I wouldn't mind an apology, or a word with that sergeant.'

But he never answered.

I went in search of my mother. She was crying in the waiting-room. Just then the children and their mothers came out of another room. I drew their attention to my mother, and asked them to be

119

a little more careful before they level accusations at anyone from newspaper photographs. I've never been able to take a press notice seriously ever since!

I didn't do any Christmas holiday work that year. Instead I swotted T. S. Eliot in the Mitchell Library. My thesis for university was to be on 'The Poetic Drama, with special reference to Eliot's *Murder in the Cathedral*'. I was also building up a harmony singing act with Liz Grieve, and Norman Quinney on guitar for *College Pudding 1953* and Andy and I were gradually adding to our comedy routines for occasional cabarets. It was this college revue, incidentally, which introduced 'Ye Cannae Throw Yer Grannie Aff A Bus' to the tune of 'She'll be Comin' Round the Mountain When She Comes'. One way or another, I tried to keep busy and out of Sheila Cowan's way. Anyway, she didn't lack for boyfriends. On the contrary. One of her most persistent admirers was a very likable Earl of Doune who was quite keen she should become his Countess.

The big event in every Charities Week at Glasgow University is the Charities Ball when the students meet to elect the Charities Queen for that year from the finalists submitted from every college and further training establishment. Sheila represented our college, and the music academy, not surprisingly. I remembered I had put her entry in at the beginning of the session. Inevitably, she won and was crowned by Lord Inverclyde on the night of the Charities Ball. This resulted in the whole glare of the west of Scotland publicity machine being focused on her, and I was left with some very mixed feelings. On the actual night of her crowning in the technical college, I remember I stood outside for ages before deciding not to go in. I was supposed to be there with Liz Grieve and Sheila was there with her boyfriend, a nice, Protestant mining engineer from Fife. A boy from her own background. A good match, as they say. Ah well, good luck to them. I should be just as happy with Terry McFarlane, a good Catholic secretary from Riddrie. A girl from my own background. A good match as they say! I walked home along Duke Street wondering if I'd get a refund on my hired white tie and tails. At least, for once my mother thought I looked very smart, so I suppose it was two pounds well spent! Time to get on with things now. I had plenty to occupy me, not the least of which were the preparations for the diploma performances.

But I couldn't damned well get Sheila Cowan out of my mind. At last I had to face Terry with the truth. It was the least she deserved.

She was remarkably calm as we stood outside her front door in Riddrie. I didn't want to go in.

'I suppose you'll want your ring back.'

'No, it's yours, you keep it.'

'I don't want it. What use is it now?'

It was then she started to howl. It was such a heartbreaking cry, incongruously at odds with the difficulty she had in taking the ring off. I stood there feeling helpless, hopeless, immature, but honest. She took my hand, put the ring in it, ran in, and the door shut behind her. I stood for ages waiting for her mother or father or sister or brother to come out, but after a moment or two, I walked away. It was only then I noticed that the ring had bitten right into the palm of my right hand. I didn't go home. I went to Sheila's flat at Lansdowne Road. I wanted to tell her at once. But she wasn't there. Where was she? Doune Castle? I walked up to the coffee stall at Charing Cross and had a coffee among the prostitutes, hoping and praying that I had done the right thing by a wonderful girl. By two wonderful girls. But for the moment one had to be more wonderful than the other. I went home really miserable. I should have been elated.

Next day, it was break-time before I saw Sheila. In the voice lecture room I showed her the ring. She was appalled that I had broken off the engagement. She knew the whole Terry McFarlane story. I tried to offer her the ring, since it was really no use for anything else other than an engagement! Her answer was to take it and chuck it into the corner. I spent most the next hour, when I should have been at a *Shrew* rehearsal, scrabbling on my hands and knees trying to find my twenty pounds' worth. Thanks to Willie, the janitor, I eventually found it again, and wondered what I could do with it. Sheila simply would have nothing to do with me in the next few days, so I did the only manly thing possible. I crawled back to Mary Theresa! But she didn't want anything to do with me either! I remember leaving the ring in her mother's bathroom, stuck in a bar of soap. She could sell it at the Barras, or get her brother, Robert, to do it. I didn't want to see it again. I was genuinely fond of Terry, I had sincerely loved her, but it was almost a brotherly love now and that was of no interest to the healthy young girl she was. I felt I was throwing away something fine, but I couldn't do otherwise. I was bewitched by Sheila. Bewitched, bothered and bewildered. I wondered what could bring us together again. It was her bust that did.

We were both in a production of *The Marvellous History of St*

Bernard, being performed in the college library. She was playing an angel and was standing in such a position that every boy in the cast had a wonderful view of her cleavage.

Somebody said, 'They can't be real.'

Charlie Johnstone, who was in Sheila's year, said knowingly, with a leer, 'You can take it from me boys, they are.'

At which St Bernard's father – me – suddenly belted him right in the teeth, which meant he made his next entrance holding his nose, and St Bernard's father entered wringing his hand. Sheila had noticed and later, during the play, I caught her eye, and she winked. A great surge of elation went through me. I could have kissed Charlie Johnstone.

After the rehearsal, Sheila and I couldn't wait to change and escape the building. We ran most of the way to the Station Café opposite the bus station, where we thought no one could ever come, and by both talking at once, we more or less caught up with every-thing. During these fervent exchanges, who should then enter but 'Rupert Brooke' Doune, his sister and his brother, who joined us at the table for egg and chips all round, and to propose that both Sheila and I come to Perthshire on the next weekend for a visit. Everyone knew it was for a leisured appraisal of Sheila in ducal surroundings. But she didn't seem keen to go. I tried to persuade her, realising what a catch she was making in this young man. I must confess that my persuasions were half-hearted to say the least, and a very nice trio of aristocrats left later knowing that they had lost a future countess to a future actor.

With Sheila off my mind, as it were, I was then free to properly concentrate on the Final Diploma Show. With her help and encouragement, I felt I could do no wrong, especially now that it seemed I was being offered the gold medal on a plate. I was scheduled for three parts in three pieces. To play Petruchio opposite 'Dame Nellie', which was good casting for both of us, to play a lovely romantic juvenile in Somerset Maugham's *Home and Beauty*, and to repeat an excerpt from *The Family Reunion*. I hoped there would be no photographers this time! I had never been as nervous or tense as I was for that afternoon of performances, nor as relaxed and easy for the evening repeat which followed it. The reaction from the audience on the matinee suggested that I had indeed carried off the main prize, and Harold Ballantyne from the Citizens approached me before the results to get my reactions.

'Hold on, Harold, no announcement's been made.'

'I've been watching drama long enough to spot a winner,' Harold said. 'Now tell me . . .'

But before he could carry on, Colin came out of the office to announce, 'The winner of the first James Bridie medal is Mary Ellen Donald for the part of Mademoiselle in *The Provok'd Wife.*'

There was a gasp. Mary Ellen was indeed clever and pertly attractive, but the opportunities she had been given compared to those offered Ellen McIntosh and myself were minimal. She had come in on the rails and pipped us both at the post. I was as surprised as Harold Ballantyne who hurriedly excused himself, 'Excuse me, Miss Donald, can I have a word . . .'

It was almost a relief to be performing without the strain of trying for a prize, but I hadn't been left empty-handed. Ellen and I shared the silver and, what was much more important, the main prize, professionally speaking, which was a year's contract at the Citizens Theatre to start in the autumn, and Andy Stewart and I had a hundred pounds each in our pocket from Alec Guinness, so I had plenty to be pleased about.

It was years later that I learned what had happened about the gold medal. The panel of judges had included Wilson Barrett, who had employed me in *The Only Way.* He blackballed a decision to give me the medal with the comment, 'He's insufferable enough now. If we give him a gold medal, he'll be impossible. Tell you what. Let's forget him for the medal and I'll give him a job.'

A telegram arrived at Williamson Street soon after – we still had no telephone – asking me to report to Fred Ferne, the manager of the Alhambra Theatre in Hope Street. Fred was a Cockney and quite a character.

He wasted no time in coming to the point. 'I got a telegram 'ere from Mr Barrett, who'll be known to you.'

I nodded.

'An' 'e tells me 'ere, in this 'ere telegram, that I gotta sign you for 'is company for the comin' year.'

I beamed at Fred, but he went on.

'Now, before we start layin' eggs, we gotta count chickens.'

'I beg your pardon?'

'We gotta talk money.'

I had never been in this situation before and wasn't sure about it. But I managed to mumble, 'Of course.'

'What do you want?' Fred was direct.

'How much have you got?'

'Don't be bloody silly. You give me a figure.'

'For the week?'

'That'll do.'

I thought quickly. I had no idea what to ask, so I said, 'I'll have to ask my father.'

'I might have known. You bloody Scotch. Always cagey about the pennies. Right. I'll give you till the mornin'.'

'Thank you.'

I couldn't wait for Dad to get back that night. He was home again from the Ministry of Works and was now employed as a vague kind of foreman somewhere. I managed to corner him in the room and whisper urgently out of my mother's hearing, 'How much do you earn, Dad?'

'Mind your own bloody business.'

'No, I need to know . . .'

'Why?'

I told him about the Fred Ferne discussion.

'What's my wages got to do with it?' he asked, mystified.

'Oh, come on, Dad. I need to know.'

He bit his lip, glanced round in the direction of the kitchen, then whispered furtively, 'Nine pounds without overtime, but – don't tell your mother.'

Next morning I was sitting opposite Fred at exactly the time I was due.

'Well,' he said, 'what's it to be?'

'Eight pounds a week,' I said.

'What?' he exclaimed.

'I've talked it over with my father,' I said quickly.

Fred leaned forward. 'Listen, son, I got orders to start at ten, coulda gone more.'

'Eight'll do fine, Mr Ferne.'

'Why's that?'

'I don't want to earn more than my father in my first job.'

There was a pause as the genial Fred leant back in his chair. 'You bleedin' Scotch are funny.' He leaned forward again. 'Tell you what. You can have this.' And reaching into his wallet, he produced one of the old large white five pound notes with Please Pay the Bearer, scripted prominently, and handed it to me.

'What's this?' I asked.

'Let's just call it a good luck token,' he said. ''Ere, sign 'ere.'

And I signed for the Wilson Barrett company summer season of

1953 to 'play as cast', eight performances a week, at eight pounds a week.

'A pound a performance, you might say,' said Fred, grinning.

My mother insisted on accompanying me to the theatre train. The Guinness hundred pounds had been spent entirely on a new wardrobe, most of which I wore self-consciously up the platform. Every single thing I had on was new, and I'm sure it showed. When I got to the carriages marked 'Wilson Barrett company (Glasgow to Aberdeen)', I felt wonderfully proud to be in a band of professional actors as one of them. My mother went off giving me a shy little wave. I found space in one of the carriages beside one of the old English actors in the company, Eric Maxon, who was playing Crabtree in this production of *The School for Scandal* in which I was Snake. It's a lovely part for a young actor. He's on at the beginning and on at the end and in the middle you have time to sit at the side and enjoy all the performances.

Eric and I became good friends, and decided to find digs together when we got to Aberdeen. We consulted our digs list and selected one which suited our small part salaries and got settled in. Eric taught me to look under the mattress right away as soon as I got into my room. 'First of all, you might find some money, and second of all, if the place is damp, that's where it shows, and it don't do to lie in a damp bed, especially if you're lying alone.'

Eric didn't have much to do in the play either, but I noticed that his dressing-room was so far away from the stage at His Majesty's that he might have been making up in Dundee. I remember suggesting to the stage director that it would be surely more polite and convenient if older actors were given dressing-rooms nearer the stage, thus saving on preparation times and their old legs. I was abruptly told to mind my own business.

The first night and the date of my debut proper in the theatre was Monday, 1 June 1953. This was terrible timing on my part for it was also the day before the Coronation of Queen Elizabeth, first or second, depending on whether you're Scottish or English. It was also the day the news broke that New Zealander Edmund Hilary had climbed Mount Everest with Sherpa Tenzing on 29 May, so very little press attention was given a young Glasgow actor's professional debut.

This didn't stop me, however, from trying to make my presence felt in the company. Using the very legitimate hint given by my character's name, Snake, I employed everything I knew to suggest his reptilian characteristics. I stressed every sibilant in the text, especially at the ends of words and I must have been a real pain to my colleagues, except to the young girl with whom I played my first scene, also making her debut, Edith McArthur. She was very nervous before the curtain went up on that first June night. I felt very gallant in being able to reassure her. The scene went well and the only trouble was my reluctance to get off when my exit lines came. Applying the same *raison dramatique* to my movement as I did to my voice, I positively oozed from centre-stage to down right, taking all the time in the world, and being encouraged by most of the actors en route, with a jab in my ribs, a knee in my thigh, a foot on my toe, with varying whispered imprecations like, 'For God's sake, get on with it!' 'Get a move on, will you!' 'Get off!' and in one instance, from one actor who shall be nameless, 'Fuck off!' Undeterred, I maintained my pace and got my hard-won round of applause, and reluctantly departed the scene.

Just as long as I took to get off, poor old Eric seemed to take to get on. He took such ages getting made up, dressed and prepared, that by the time he made his way down the five hundred and fifty or so stone steps to the wings, his little scene was often over. The irony was that due to the deft fill-in playing by the other actors on stage, his absence was hardly noticed. The poor old fellow was then left with nothing to do but about turn and then walk all the way up again. I used to go up with him and keep him company and listen to his stories of old actors. He had a framed picture beside his little tobacco box of make-up, and this picture showed an older actor kneeling down centre-stage, and behind him a most dashing, handsome and virile young juvenile, poised with sword in hand at a window up-stage.

'Who's that?' I asked, pointing to the figure in front.

'Sir Henry,' he muttered, almost reverently.

'Henry?'

'Irving, my boy. Irving.'

'And who's that at the back?'

'That is I, my dear boy, 'tis I, as they say,' helping himself to a little whisky from the hip flask he always carried. 'Strictly medicinal, old chap, and always post-performance.'

He never ever offered me any, but then again, it was a kind of medicine that I didn't need at that time. He was off-stage so often that the company hardly noticed and the stage director didn't take any action. Everybody liked old Eric. But one evening he didn't come in at all. I was asked where he was, and I told them that he always went to the cinema in the afternoon, like many of the old actors did. For them it was comfortable and warm and cheap. He was found in an Aberdeen cinema slumped over his stalls seat, quite dead. I was more upset than I expected, and when I went to his room that night, I could almost feel his presence there, or at least the presence of all the actors there have been. Here was I in the first week of my job, and I was being given hints of a tradition that went all the way back to Burbage. This old man was only the latest exemplar.

I looked at the photo again as little Kathleen Hill, the stage manager, came in to clear up his effects.

'Who's that?' she said pointing at the photo.

'Sir Henry Irving,' I answered grandly.

'Who was he?'

'My dear girl,' I expostulated.

'Who's that at the back?'

We both looked at the curly-haired young actor, so full of energy and purpose and ambition.

' 'Tis I,' I whispered, ' 'tis I.'

As it happens, Snake was my only part with the Wilson Barrett. I was cast as Romeo, but the Citizens Theatre took up their contract option earlier than expected in order that I might appear in the 1953 Edinburgh Festival repeat of *The Highland Fair*. This depended on how I fared at the singing audition. I reported to the Citizens Theatre as requested, and found, by one of those silly coincidences, that the young man who was allocated the time just before me was dressed in identical gear. We both had black polo necks and green corduroy trousers. Neither of us wished to make any closer wardrobe scrutiny. We had both been in the previous year's production, and already knew each other, and he was surprised to say the least that I was there for a singing audition. He was very much the singer, as was obvious from his required rendition of 'My Love Is Like A Red Red Rose'. He really had a most beautiful voice and an engaging manner to go with it. His acting voice was that of a singer, however, and when my turn came, I asked if I might do the acting section first, as I knew that my singing voice was that of an actor.

I was only into the second verse of my song when, clapping his hands loudly, Tony came loping down the central aisle, intoning nasally, 'Enough, enough, enough.' I thought, goodness, was I as bad as that? But he meant he had heard enough, and offered me the part of Alastair, the tenor lead, there and then. So instead of playing Shakespeare's Romeo, I played Kemp's Highland Romeo, and sang him rather than speaking him. The other young polo neck declined to understudy and took another singing engagement. Although I knew him then as a forestry student, he later became better known as Kenneth McKellar!

My own career as a singer was somewhat chequered. My vocal condition was a mystery, known only to God, for only He knew what was going to come out when called for. At times it was positively thrilling and at other times chilling! This was of course due to my lack of professional training. I had a good natural lyrical tenor voice. I had been given the rudiments of singing practice while at college, but I lacked the intensive application required for the best kind of vocal production. Besides, the acting demands militated against the singing demands in most cases. The former was pulling the voice down into the diaphragm, and the latter pushing it up towards the forehead. Poor thing, it never knew whether it was coming or going. But occasionally I got it right.

This encouraged Tony Guthrie in his kindness and foresight to offer me, via the Scottish Academy of Music, a Caird scholarship to Rome to study singing for two years. His argument was that I was sufficient an actor to produce the voice in performance, but I needed further training to develop the singing aspect. If I did, asserted Guthrie, a surefire career in opera presented itself, especially the operas of Mozart, Donizetti, Bellini and the like. Tony was so enthused about this idea that he took the trouble to come to our room and kitchen in Parkhead, positively filling it as he leaned over the kitchen table to impress upon my mother the need for my studentship to continue for at least a further two years so that I could go on with my singing.

'Another two years?' said my mother. 'He's been in the hoose since he left school, and never a penny I've had from him, other than what goes in his mooth. And the little I have hid I've put on his back. So, his faither and I think it's time he got a joab. And this Citizens Theatre seems to be a regular enough joab for a while at least.'

Guthrie could only shake his head, especially when my mother continued, 'Besides, oor John cannae sing.'

'But when have you heard him sing?' asked the learned doctor.

'Every New Year and sometimes at weddings.'

'Hardly the best circumstances for a proper judgment of vocal potential,' muttered Tony dryly.

'And when would he begin to earn some money if he took up this opera singing, or whatever ye call it?'

John Cairney . . . the Fan Club photo!
The television troubadour – 1960

'I don't suppose he would be earning real money until his forties.'

'In his forties!' exclaimed my mother incredulously. 'Away, for God's sakes, that's worse than his dad.'

So I didn't get to be an operatic tenor!

If I occasionally got my voice right there were many occasions, of course, when I got it very wrong. One such was at the Assembly Hall in the middle week of the run when I was delayed by a Canadian ballet dancer in the corridor and was subsequently 'off', meaning I'd missed my cue to enter. Lea Ashton, the stage manager, came running forward and threw me on by the ear. I burst into song and was relieved to know that it came out like McCormick, effortlessly and easily with a wonderful relaxed power. It was a duet with the soprano. I had two duets with the soprano, and unfortunately, on this occasion, I was singing the other one. I saw the conductor's curtain close with a gesture as the orchestra sank dismally with him, and I carried on, desperately converting my line into a harmony of hers, till I found out where we were. She approached me, eyes popping, mouth moving like a fish, signalling the correct song to me, and somehow we got it and got off – quickly. The rest of the cast were killing themselves, but Tony Guthrie was not amused and my singing career effectively ended there. I was relieved to get back to my own world of the theatre and reported to the Citizens for the first day of the winter season.

I met up with John Fraser again, now a rising film star with Associated-British, and he and I shared juveniles in that first Citizens' season under Michael Langham, although we were both together in *The Laird of Torwatletie* which I got to be in after all. I was a very ineffectual juvenile lead, however, and squirmed particularly under my tennis racket in one play: *Witch Errant* by Leslie Storm. But I was seen in it by Mrs Olive Dodds, casting scout for the Rank Organisation who suggested I contact her should I ever decide to come to London.

Michael Langham didn't waste time in teaching me some real theatre manners. I had come to the Citizens with quite a fanfare, and imagined I would be Hamlet within the fortnight. Instead, one of the first parts I had was as the tramp in Ostrovsky's *Diary of a Scoundrel* who had no lines at all but had to appear at the window in the second act. I was insulted at this casting but vowed to be the best tramp he'd ever seen. I began by appearing at the window a little earlier than my cue, then I opened the window and looked in. I then came round by the door and listened. During all this time the scene was going on. I even ventured in at one point, giving

130

myself a maniacal giggle which stopped Ronnie Fraser and Jimmy Cairncross in their tracks, but Michael never ever said anything. By the first run-through, I had a positive ballet going on up-stage, and with my huge red beard, and long cloak which I gave myself, I felt I couldn't be missed. I wasn't, at least by Michael. In his quiet, charming way, he complimented me on my hard work, but suggested I might do it a bit further up-stage, then a bit further, and further. By the dress rehearsal I was up by the window again, and by the opening night I was behind it again, just as the author intended, and there I remained for the run. 'Oh, and by the way, John,' smiled Michael, 'cut the laugh!'

The highlight of the season, however, was a Scots play: *Right Royal* by Alexander Scott in which Ronnie Fraser and I were cast as the bastard sons of King Dod of Fife, inimitably played by Duncan Macrae. It was a musical and again it gave me a chance to sing. The young Alexander Gibson, no less, was our conductor-pianist. Ronnie and I had a duet, but somehow or other, we were always at the end of the singing rehearsal call, and we could never get together with Alex and the piano.

'Look,' he said, 'you don't need me to teach you the notes. You've got the key, just mug it up for yourselves and we can get together later on.' We did just that. We mugged it up to such effect that it might have been the duet from *The Pearlfishers* we were performing instead of a mock-comic duet between two clowns. Ronnie had a good baritone voice, and I subscribed my tenor, and we sang the silly song just as well as we could. On the first night, we had to encore it three times! We lay flat on our backs, with our heads in the floats, kicking our legs in the air, while Duncan Macrae fretted in the wings waiting to come on. It was a sweet moment, and, the later Sir, Alexander was grinning with delight in the pit. I can't meet Ronnie Fraser yet, without he bursts into:

> We're princes rare, although we're pair,
> Wi' kings an' queens we're rankit,
> Frae each affair, a royal heir
> On the wrang side, o' the blanket!

It was the annual Citizens' Christmas pantomime which gave me my best chance to date. Michael Langham was baffled by the Glasgow pantomime and wasn't sure how he should go about it. At a meeting of the whole company at his flat, he suggested we should write our own and he would co-ordinate our efforts. This was right up my

131

street and I got down to working out what kind of demon king I
was to be. I decided to make him a student who worked on the trams
during the holidays, giving him comic doggerel, which I wrote with
actress Effie Morrison, to sing and speak in the action. I had to sing
'Brother, can you spare a dime?' and was able to adapt it to 'Once
I built a tramway, made it run . . .' etc. I enjoyed myself hugely. So
did everyone. Our panto was an enormous success. I had my doggerel verse at the tip of my tongue, delivered at top speed to the
tune of 'The Irish Washerwoman':

> Students on summer vacation from varsity
> Frequently find a spondulical sparsity
> They can hardly frequent the old bars
> Wherein once that they
> Used to frequent wi' the cheque for their fees.
> Go on the cars and the dibs are immediate
> Why waste your time on the body collegiate
> I'm doing fine by remaining an eedgie-it
> Sigh no more ladies, and Gil-no-more Hill!
> . . .

I couldn't help thinking, standing there in a tram conductor's
uniform with a university scarf around my neck, that I hadn't
travelled far from the five-year-old boy who stood at the end of a
tram, nearly twenty years before, asking the passengers to make the
sign of the cross! In the transformation scene, I got to wear white
tie, top hat and tails and sang 'That Old Black Magic' with the
orchestra, and being able to put in lines like, 'Round and round you
go, like a bus that's lost in a fog . . .' I was having a ball.

Little Abie Barker, an old variety artiste, now playing small parts,
came to the dressing-room before the opening night, and stood
behind my chair looking into the mirror: 'You're gonna be a big
thstar, thun,' he lisped to his own reflection. 'You've got it. I should
know. I havenae.'

One of my first visitors was another variety name – Tommy York.
He was a singer/comedian and feed to Tommy Morgan, a Glasgow
comic, and huge name at the time in his pavilion summer shows.

'Tommy'd like to see you,' said Mr York.

'Delighted,' I replied.

Tommy Morgan lived at Kelvin Court, off the Great Western Road,
which is Millionaires' Row to most Glaswegians. I went up there one
morning to meet Mr Morgan. He was smaller and slighter than he

looked on stage, and he wore a dressing-gown over a casual shirt and slacks, but the voice was unmistakable, a Glasgow fog-horn sifted through sludge and fifty cigarettes a day. 'I hear ye're a bit o' a comic?'

'I'm an actor, Mr Morgan.'

'I'll no' haud that against ye. Tommy here –' he nodded to Tommy York who was sitting at the window '– says you can sing a bit, an' you've got timin'.'

'Oh?' I couldn't think what to say.

'We were put on to ye be wee Abie Barker. He thinks ye'd make a comic. Whit d'you think?'

I didn't know what to think. I spluttered something about being an actor again, and if the part had laughs in it –

'Listen, son,' he interrupted roughly, 'actors are ten-a-penny, an' that's dear fur some o' them, I can tell ye. But a good comic, who can put over a song, and his a bit o' personality, ye can build a show roon 'm. Me an' Tommy here, think we might be able tae dae that wi' you if you fancy it?'

I spluttered vaguely again.

'I havnae seen ye mysel' mind, but I hear good reports o' yer caur conductor sketch. Wrote it yersel, I hear?'

'Well –'

'Write yer ain material. That's a bonus, I can tell ye. Must've peyed a fortune tae writers in my time, right Tommy?'

'Right.'

'The auld caurs, eh? Ye know – John in't it?'

'Yes . . . er, aye.'

'Aye. Ye know that Ah wance toured for two years withoot gettin aff a caur. Know whit I mean? Nae trains or motors or buses or anythin' – just a plain auld caur. Airdrie tae Paisley, Milngavie tae Rouken Glen. They could take ye onywhere, that right, Tommy?'

'Right.'

He and his namesake then discussed Glasgow trams and their numbers and their various destinations, before he got back to me.

'So whit we're sayin' is this. We're willin' to give ye a bob or two, I mean were no' skint, right, Tommy?'

'Right.'

'We'll see ye all right if ye'd like tae join up for the summer season, an' gie me a haun in some o' the sketches, try yer ain haun at this an' that, see if we can build ye up like, gie ye yer ain spot, that sorta thing. Whit d'ye say?'

'Well –'

'If it's money, ye could hiv a ton up tae start wi' tae see how we go.'

My East End quickly translated that into a hundred pounds a week! I was getting ten at the Citizens.

'Ye could rise tae a half-grand if we gie ye shares later on.'

Five hundred pounds? This was mad.

'It's not the money, Mr Morgan.'

'Christ, whit else is there?' He laughed. 'Right, Tommy?'

'Right.'

'It's just that I've only started as an actor –'

'Listen, son, I'll tell ye. I'm gettin' oan, I'm no' as young as I look ye know, an' I want tae start takin' things a bit easier. We think if we could get a smart boy, he'd take some o' the work aff me. Right, Tommy?'

'That's it. Ye see, John, there's a lot Tommy here can show a young fella. Tricks o' the trade, like. For instance –'

Tommy interrupted gruffly. 'When we want your opinion we'll ask for it. Right?'

'Right.'

He then turned to me with a kindly look on his craggy face. 'The thing is, son, what wid ye really like tae dae yersel'?'

There was a pause as I tried to gather my wits. This was all too bewildering for me. 'I'd like to play Hamlet one day.'

'Who?' said Tommy Morgan.

'Hamlet,' I said. 'Shakespeare.'

'Shakespeare? Jesus Christ! I'm offering you real stardom and you want to ponce about in Shakespeare. For coppers.'

'Yes,' I said.

He leaned right into me. He smelled of cigarettes. 'Yer'e a mug,' he whispered. 'Right, Tommy?'

'Right.'

One talks of 'dying' on the stage, that is of failing in all one's effects and finding the audience entirely unresponsive, and I must confess I nearly died on the last night of this pantomime. And I mean literally died. There was the usual last-night party and this drifted on, as these things do, to the digs of some chorus girls in the theatreland district of Glasgow between Hill Street and Renfrew Street. Johnny Fraser and I found ourselves sitting facing each other across a gigantic fruit bowl. It was filled to the brim with a special punch the girls had made, which, to me, seemed like a few slices of orange peel and some apple core laid in a bath of gin. The trouble was that as the guests came in, they proffered their drinks contribution to the hostesses, who promptly emptied it into the fruit bowl. As a result, it was a lethal mixture which was brewed. Being quite innocent of drink combinations, and wholly unsophisticated in party practices, I just sat helping myself to tumblers of this stuff, until I passed out.

I came to lying in a corridor, gazing up at a very strange ceiling, with people occasionally stepping across me on their way here and there. I staggered up, desperate to find air, and somehow got to the street again. I had no idea where Glasgow was, never mind Parkhead. I remember lying in a gutter in the Saltmarket, which was a reasonable halfway point between where I had been and where I was going. I must have needed the rest. I got home eventually, but it was my mother who told me later what happened after that. She and my father had been wakened by an almighty crash. She came in to my bedroom to find me slumped over the piano stool, which was on its side on the floor. Apparently I was fully dressed and quite green. She called my father, who took one look, recognised the symptoms, wrenched off my clothes, and dragged me to the sink, where he put his fingers down my throat and made me sick. He then laid me in front of the kitchen range on my stomach, and kneaded the small of my back until I was sick again on the towels he had put around my head. Gradually, my mother said, I went from green to lime to yellow to white to pink and back to normal. At which he lifted me again, put my head under the cold tap and let it run until I was spluttering for breath. He then dragged me back to the bedroom and laid me on the bed, while my mother dried me again, put on my pyjamas, pulled up the bedclothes, and left me alone to sleep for two days. I missed the first day of rehearsals, and I didn't feel I could go back on the next. I needed a doctor's line, so I reported to his surgery. Dr Bernard Cutler took the cigarette from his lips long enough to tell me that my semi-coma had been caused by self-induced alcoholic poisoning. But he wrote down 'flu' on my medical certificate and in a cloud of cigarette smoke, waved me away.

Sheila returned from her Christmas holidays for the new term, and I met her at Queen Street Station. It was a lovely, bright sunny January day, and an old man stopped us on the pavement, raised his bowler to us, and smiling pinkly, said, 'You look so happy, you two, that if I were a minister, I would marry you.' And nodding politely to Sheila, he replaced his bowler and walked away. Right there and then, in the street, I kissed her.

The little pink-faced, bowler-hatted, city gentleman had put an idea into my head, and once there, it refused to go away. Marry Sheila? Why not? Would she have me? Why not? I don't remember ever asking her, and she certainly didn't ask me, but somehow the idea took hold between us, and we decided to do something about it as soon as we could. At the soonest this could only be at the end of the theatre season, and Sheila's second year in the last week of May. She had by this time made a hit herself as Regina in *The Little Foxes*, and show business pundits were already prophesying a big career for her in films. The prognosis was also friendly to me, so we thought that together we had a reasonable chance of surviving matrimony. Sheila met my parents, who were polite but reserved. My mother made no bones about the fact that she much preferred Mary Theresa. My father on the other hand never could resist a pretty girl. The only problem was Sheila's parents. She had told them during the spring break and I gather she very nearly didn't get out of the house again. There was no option for it, but to go through myself and see them.

I took the blue bus on its long journey from coast to coast, and met Willie Cowan, by appointment, on the Kirkcaldy promenade. After an hour walking up and down the Prom in the snow he took me to his pub, where we spent most of the time watching boxing on TV. 'I suppose you might as weel come tae the hoose' he said eventually. I was glad to. I had missed the last bus. 'My, you're just a rickle o' banes,' was how Sheila's mother greeted me. 'Your hair's awfy black,' said her young sister, Heather. Sheila was never mentioned by anybody. I slept in her room and nearly froze to death. I was glad to get on the bus the next morning. At least it was warm and the conductor was friendly.

Sheila met me off the bus in Glasgow, thankful to see me still in one piece. We went to the Lido Café for a celebratory coffee. Domenico was the first to know the big news. We didn't tell anybody else. Next day it was in all the papers.

The final production of the Michael Langham season was a touring repeat of Roddy McMillan's tenement play set in the then contemporary Glasgow. Alex McAvoy and I played brothers, to such effect that my mother said when she saw it, 'That's no actin'. That's just John and Jim.'

At the very end of the season, we toured the play at the Paisley Theatre where I had played in *Streetcar* as a student, and at the Empire Theatre, Greenock. The last day of the last week was our wedding day. The theatre gave us a canteen of cutlery and a bread board, and the cast of the play clubbed together to buy me a lighter.

We were married during a Catholic Nuptial Mass. During the previous two terms Sheila had been taking instruction in the Catholic Faith at St Aloysius from Father William Dempsey, so we were married by him on the last Saturday morning of the run of a play appropriately entitled, *All in Good Faith.* I hoped it was an omen.

I must admit I had more than a twinge of doubt as I stood with Jim at the altar rails. Arthur Blake was playing the organ and most of the Citizens Theatre and nearly all of the college had turned up. Since the Cowans wouldn't attend, we didn't invite the Cairneys or Coyles, but that didn't stop them all turning up, including dear old Uncle Eddie, and some nearly-forgotten schoolmates. It made me very nervous all of a sudden. Besides, I still felt guilty about Mary Theresa.

'Jim,' I whispered.

'Don't worry,' he said, 'I've got it.'

'Got what?'

'The ring.'

'It's not the ring.'

I glanced back at the huge church. It was rapidly filling up. The company were playing the parts of the respective families. Paul Curran and Madeleine Christie were in Sheila's parents' place, along with Fulton Mackay and Alex McAvoy. Duncan Macrae was presiding over my side, with Andy Stewart and Roddy Macmillan among others. I could see my own parents at the back. Lots of cousins. Domenico and Carla. I panicked.

'Jim.' (Another whisper.)

'Whit's it this time?'

'I can't go through with it.'

'Whit? Are ye sick?'

'No. I'm scared.'

'That's a'right. That's normal.'

'But, Jim – '

Just then the organ blared out again. There was a rumble of feet as people stood up, and I could feel the sweat stand out on my brow as I stared fixedly ahead. Suddenly, in a rustle of taffeta, she was there beside me. I turned to look, and there was Sheila smiling at me. She winked.

'Do you take this woman . . .?' Father Dempsey's voice seemed miles away.

'You bet!' I shrieked inside myself, but a grave outside voice murmured circumspectly, 'I do.'

The *Daily Express* provided the wedding car in return for an exclusive on the photos. They also chipped in for the wedding reception, a white wine affair at the Royal Hotel in West Nile Street, which Jim had organised. He and Meta Reilly, Sheila's college pal and bridesmaid, hit it off very well. They were finishing off the white wine with Peter Thompson, Meta's boyfriend, when it was time for me to leave for Greenock for the Saturday matinee. I asked Sheila if she was ready to go.

'Leave her with us,' said Jim.

'Yes,' said Peter. 'What a way to spend a wedding day – sitting in the wings of the Greenock Empire.'

'What do you suggest?'

'She should stay here and help us finish the wine.'

'What happens when the wine runs out?' I asked.

'Remember Cana?' quipped Sheila. 'And I'm with J.C.,' she added glancing at Jim.

So I deserted my wife after only a couple of hours and left her for a matinee at the Greenock Empire. It's funny to think that both the Greenock Empire and the Royal Hotel have now been demolished, but they both looked very good in 1954.

Jim delivered Sheila to the evening performance and went home to sleep off the wine. After a party in somebody's Glasgow flat, Sheila and I left for our secret hide-out – a flat in Oakfield Avenue. It was actually the basement of a big house. The rent was modest as we had the responsibility of making sure that the furnace/hot water boiler that shared the basement with us was kept lit at all times. The landlady took a risk in hiring a newly married couple to keep her furnace going. Luckily, 29 May was a warm night, because the furnace went out!

In the meanwhile, the BBC had been looking for me, as had the Rank Organisation. Since I had not told anyone where we were going for our honeymoon, not even Jim, nobody could find us. Some imagined we were in Spain or the south of France, but all the time we were in Hillhead. Our secret came out one night when we went to the Odeon in Renfield Street to see a Guy Mitchell film and met Jim in the queue.

'What have you two been up to?' he said, ingenuously.

He told us about the telegrams to the house, so we went there next morning. I learned I'd been offered the part of a village lad in a television play called *Knock*, adapted from the French by

Robert Kemp. Andy Stewart was to be the other lad, and Moultrie R. Kelsall was the star. It was to start on Monday.

The BBC gave the company a first-class return on the train to London, plus accommodation for a couple of weeks while we rehearsed and transmitted the play live from the Lime Grove Studio. I persuaded the railway to give me two second-class singles for mine. When Jimmy Crampsey, the director of the play, heard about this, he arranged to pay the difference himself, and so Mr and Mrs John Cairney travelled in style to London on a one-way ticket, with two tea-chests, two cases and twenty pounds in cash. Our entire wordly possessions. Sheila certainly didn't marry me for my money!

We had our first fight almost as soon as we arrived. We got to the hotel in Russell Square and I insisted on unpacking everything, except the tea-chests, even though we were only going to be there for a few nights before we found a flat somewhere. Andy had to come down and act as placator.

However, all was forgotten in the heady foreignness of London, the new excitement of television and the strangeness of being married. The job itself was the last thing to worry about. The parts were no problem. Avoiding the BBC male dressers was, for both Andy and myself. Moultrie Kelsall, our leading man, was misleadingly abrupt and dour, and our main scene was with him. We, as patients, were to have our chests examined by Dr Knock, and in order to liven things up a bit, I had make-up put a little cow's head on my chest, so that when I opened up my shirt, the sight of it would give Moultrie a bit of a laugh in rehearsal. I also added a 'Moo' sound for better effect.

Moultrie didn't laugh, he was absolutely furious. 'Don't you dare resort to such undergraduate nonsense in a professional rehearsal,' I was told.

I tried to suggest that it was just a bit of fun, and anyway it had been Andy's idea, but he wouldn't hear of it. I was in disgrace from then on.

Television was live then. A show or a play was given a date and a time, and it would have to be an enormous act of God to prevent the programme going out on that date and at that time. So, on 2 July 1954, at 8.25 p.m., *Knock* or *The Triumph of Medicine* went out to the few viewers that were then around the country. When the moment came for me to open my shirt for the examination, I did so on cue, to reveal not a little cow's head, but a huge cow's head. It covered most of the small chest I had then. Moultrie's eyes came up to mine, at which point I emitted a soft, 'Mooo-ltrie!' He jabbed me viciously with his stethoscope and turned away. But I could see

139

that he was 'corpsed'. The good man had a sense of humour after all. As for Andy, he was making all kinds of agricultural sounds just off camera, and I kept going while it was on me. I couldn't do much else because the operator was killing himself. Of course it was unprofessional, but it was delightful too. It was real, and it was live. It was some time before the script could be resumed as written, and I'm sure we added a few minutes to the running time. Moultrie himself laughed longest about it later.

We had to stay on in London for an extra few days to give a further performance on the Thursday for Mrs Pandit Nehru. This was the fashion then, that if someone requested a repeat, the actors were merely reassembled and it was done again. It was expensive but it was the only way in pre-pre-recording days. Not that we actors complained. It meant another full fee.

During the waiting time, Jimmy Crampsey called Sheila and me in to see him, as he was very worried about my remaining in London. I assured him I wasn't worried at all. I had a screen test and now Sheila had a screen test. Between the two of us we would get by, but Jimmy was worried about my throwing up the further Citizens year which would have given me leading parts, and a chance to put a bit by before trying for London. For instance he said, 'How much have you got left?'

Sheila looked in her purse. We had about four pounds left.

'For God's sake,' Jimmy said, 'what are you going to do now?'

'Well, we'll get your cheque and a repeat to follow.'

'God almighty,' he said, 'that's only about another four pounds. What are you going to do then?'

'Well, by that time one of us should have a job.'

'Doing what?'

'Acting, of course.'

And I was right. We all attended the party following the final transmission of *Knock*, and found ourselves in the back room of the White Horse pub at Lime Grove. A singsong began and for some reason, I found myself with a solo. Maybe I was the only one who knew the words, but as I finished, a tall, balding man came over to me and said, 'Do you sing, professionally I mean?'

'Not really,' I replied.

'Would you?'

'That depends.'

At which the tall man produced his card and said, 'Come and see me at the Centre in the morning.'

It was Campbell Logan, the BBC producer, and he wanted a

singer-actor to play one of the leads in a children's serial, to start rehearsals in the following week. Someone had dropped out of the cast at the last minute; could I take over as Jean Baptiste Lully, the French composer? I would have to sing and play the violin, or, at least, mime to Eugene Pini. 'No problem,' I assured him. 'I've been on the fiddle for years!'

Unfortunately that weekend was a holiday, and I found that my second BBC cheque for three guineas was worthless as all the banks were closed. I rang Jim – who else – who was now a professional footballer in Portsmouth. He promised a five pound postal order for the Monday morning. Meantime we had to live through Saturday, Sunday and Monday. We did – on milk, egg and buttered potatoes. By this time, we had a garden flat out in Roehampton, and on the Saturday evening, Sheila and I walked to Richmond Park, aware that this was our honeymoon proper. We would try to make it last as long as possible. At least till the Post Office opened on the Tuesday morning.

We were at the counter at one minute past nine, and by quarter past we were tucking into bacon, egg and sausage in a nearby café. I felt then I could go to rehearsal in a Scout hall in St John's Wood. Sheila went home to write to her mother. She wanted to tell her about the screen test at Elstree. It was for a film called *Geordie* about the Scottish Highland Games, and Sheila was asked to test for the part of Bill Travers' girlfriend. She must have made a good impression for she was offered the role a few days later. She also had an agent, Mary Harris, who rang to arrange a return to Elstree for make-up tests and wardrobe fittings, as the action called for her to be ducked in water at one point. She came home that night to our new flat in Lansdowne Road, Holland Park, just a few doors away from Anne and Jimmy McTaggart, feeling quite chilled and complained of tummy pains. These got so bad in the next few days that she went to the local doctor, a young Indian, who gave the usual medical blanket reaction, 'A virus, you know. There's a lot of it about.'

There certainly was. She was pregnant.

In the meantime, the children's serial had been seen by the director of the Bristol Old Vic, John Moody, and also the Christopher Mann Agency, and, as a result, within twenty-eight days of arriving in London, I was on the books of one of the best theatrical agencies in Britain and had a two-year contract at the Bristol Old Vic. I couldn't wait to tell Jimmy Crampsey.

The only problem now was that Sheila had to make a decision, either to stay in London and make that film, while she still had her superb figure, then follow me to Bristol, or come with me now and forget the film. Without a second's hesitation, she turned down the film offer. She said she didn't fancy being ducked in water. I think the truth was that now she was pregnant, she didn't want to do anything other than think of that baby. Sheila had found her real vocation – motherhood.

The Theatre Royal, Bristol, is one of the oldest stages in Britain. It was now the home of the Bristol Old Vic company. Even in 1954, it was highly prestigious, and I was very pleased indeed to have been offered a place there, even though it meant I had, for all intents and purposes, to become an Englishman overnight. Thanks to my train-ing, this wasn't totally impossible, though there were certain linguistic hazards to face. One was the very first line I had to offer on the English stage in the very first play of the season. It was a period piece called *The Road to Ruin* by Thomas Holcroft, and my opening line was, 'I think Harry must be half mad.'

Ordinarily this would pose no problem to any actor, not even a Glaswegian, but given the tensions of being a new boy in a new company in a new place, coping with a new style in a very old play called *The Road to Ruin*, it came out with me on that August night in Bristol as, 'I think Horry must be haff maud.'

Michael Allinson, playing the scene with me, couldn't believe his ears. 'I beg your pardon,' he drawled languidly.

I pushed my cane into my mouth, gritted my teeth, and said, 'I think Herry must be hoff mud.'

By this time, the audience must have wondered what sort of play this was going to be as I hadn't even succeeded in getting out the first line.

So I took a deep breath, and changed my whole intonation. 'I think . . . Harry . . . must be . . . half mud. Damn.'

'Ah, I see what you mean – I think,' said Michael quickly, and we got on with the rest of the scene.

But what a way to begin one's career in the English-speaking theatre. I suppose it was only natural nervousness, but that's when vowels slip and training gives way to breeding. I had few problems after that, at least on stage, and soon settled in to the company.

I had to miss some performances as Claudio in *Much Ado About Nothing* because I was called to Glasgow suddenly. My father was seriously ill after an ulcer operation. This was the first of his illnesses, and he was never really the same man again. Ted Hardwicke took over from me as Claudio, and was a great improvement I think. His father, Sir Cedric, flew from Hollywood to see him in the part. I flew to Glasgow to see mine in a hospital ward. I couldn't help think that while Ted was with his father in our theatre, I was with my father five hundred miles away after he'd emerged from another kind of theatre. I'm glad to say, both fathers recovered from the experience. So did both sons – thank goodness. It was around this time I made another life-changing decision, and like all such decisions it was made impulsively. I bought my first car!

When Sheila came to the Christmas production of *The Two Bouquets* the management jokingly gave her two seats. Cracks were made now about her being a 'two seater'. This must have been in my mind when I accompanied one of the actresses in the company, Yvonne Furneaux, who had joined us for *Ondine*, to the Bridge Motor Company in Redlands, to help her choose a car. I don't know why she asked me to go with her; I knew nothing about cars. It must have been because I was the only actor available that day, and I suppose she thought she might get a better deal with a man by her side. Some women are funny that way! Anyway, Yvonne found her car and while she was attending to all the necessary details I looked around the other cars on the lot. I saw a little Morris Tourer, Series E – a two-seater – with only nine miles on the speedometer. I looked again, yes, that's all it was, nine. Dodgy, I thought.

The salesman approached and I asked, why the low mileage?

'Oh,' he grinned, 'the manager'll tell you all about that.'

Just then, the manager came out with Yvonne and he told us a most unusual story about that car. It had been bought by a couple for their twenty-one-year-old son, who had newly graduated from one of the universities just at the outbreak of war. It was kept at their home for his return, but he was shot down during the Battle of Britain, and the car never moved from the garage. The nine miles on the clock was the distance it had taken from the first garage to their house. Every six months or so, someone from the Bridge Motor Company had gone to their garage to tune the little car and turn over the engine, so that it was always 'in good nick' as they say in the trade. It had sat there all through the war, surviving the Bristol air-raids and nearly ten years of post-war corrosion and the passing of all those days and nights since the Battle of Britain and now, with the death of the surviving parent, was in absolutely mint condition and available for sale on the orders of the estate. The manager said that nobody believed the mileage or the state of the chrome or the perfect bodywork, or the pilot story, but he assured us it was all true and the lawyers could confirm it. I must say the state of the vehicle bore him out.

'How long have you had it?' I asked.

'Coupla days.'

I turned to my companion who was now anxious to go. 'Wouldn't you like this one, Yvonne?'

'No, thanks. Don't like open cars. Blows my hair about. Which reminds me, we'd better get back. Come on, I'll drive you to your digs.' And she strode with a new proprietorial air towards a Hillman Minx.

The manager looked back to me. 'Well, sir, what d'you think? Or do all you theatricals hate open cars?'

I looked at the little beauty standing there, shining in the winter afternoon sun, and I knew I was in love again.

I bought it there and then for two hundred pounds.

There were two snags though. I didn't have two hundred pounds and I didn't have a driving licence, but I so loved the car's history that there was no way I wasn't going to have it. I made the usual call to Jim now playing football for York City FC. I got the promise of a hundred pounds. The manager and I shook hands on it.

I made immediate application for a test. From time to time over the years I had tried to drive Jim's Fiat, and my father's old Singer Sports, so I had a rough idea about gear changes and so on. I had no compunction at all about taking delivery of the car myself one free afternoon and driving it, in a series of kangaroo jumps, to our flat in Clifton. In every spare minute, I rehearsed being a driver in the alleyway beside the theatre under Ted Hardwicke's tutelage, and, occasionally, Yvonne's, when she had the courage. I took at least a decade off the instructor's life on the morning of my test. It was not that I drove badly. I was just dangerous. We were missing parked cars by millimetres, and making emergency stops at every traffic junction, so it was no surprise when he told me that he was 'failing me on this occasion', although it took him some time to complete the form once we were safely parked, due to his shaking hands! Never mind, I got it without any trouble a few weeks later, and Cleopatra never travelled in greater triumph on her barge than Sheila did down Park Street in our little brand-new 1939 Morris Tourer, Series E, with only twenty miles on the clock. The only difference was Sheila was going backwards as I couldn't get out of reverse!

Jennifer Mary Elizabeth Cairney was born on 19 February 1955 during a performance of *The Merchant of Venice*. Stage management had been rung and they had the wit to put a note in one of the caskets, which normally enclosed scurrilous and ribald messages from them to the actors on-stage, but on this occasion all it said was: *'It's a girl!'* Paul Lee, playing the Prince of Aragon, read it out to the audience who applauded, as everyone in Bristol knew that Gratiano's wife was expecting a baby. But a girl? I couldn't believe it. Not a son?

At the end of the show, Ronnie Hines, whose wife was also expectant, accompanied me and the flowers and a bottle of whisky in Ted Hardwicke's car (I think mine was in the garage having a bump knocked out – as was Sheila, in a manner of speaking!). Off we flew to the Bristol maternity hospital. The boys and I finished the whisky before we got out of the car I think, and the flowers were forgotten in the rush. When I finally got to Sheila she was kneeling up on the hospital bed with only a short nightie on, her face mottled with perspiration and effort. It had been a long labour. I gave her a long, long hug, then plucked up courage to look in the cot on the other side of the bed.

I had never seen anything so ugly as that little, wizened, screwed-up infant face only a few hours old. I don't know what I had been expecting, but somehow I was taken by surprise. It was the first newborn babe I had seen, so I didn't know what to expect.

But I must have made my reaction pretty clear because Sheila was saying. 'Are you disappointed?'

'Of course not, but she looks – '

'She looks just as a baby should look, so just let her sleep and she'll be fine.'

When I came up the next night after the show, I was shown to another room. There was no sign of Sheila or the baby. I sat there for a while twiddling my thumbs, as out of place as any man felt in a maternity hospital. While I was sitting there, staring at the wall, I became aware of how hungry I was. Looking around Sheila's locker, I thought I might find a biscuit or a piece of cake or some fruit or something, but all I could see was a covered glass with milk in it. That'll do, I thought, and gulped it down gratefully. It was much sweeter than usual. They must have put sugar in it.

When the nurse brought Sheila back with Jennifer, I heard the nurse say, 'And did you manage to express some, Mrs Cairney?'

Sheila replied as she was settling Jennifer in the cot. 'Yes, I left it on the – '

'Oh!' I said, and felt my face reddening. The empty glass on the locker beside me now seemed about eight feet tall.

'John!' cried Sheila.

The nurse burst out laughing, and left the room. And I rose quickly to go and have another peep at Jennifer. She looked much better than she did the night before. Then she started to cry.

'What's wrong with her?' I asked anxiously.

Sheila said, 'She's hungry.'

'Oh!' I said.

And that was Jennifer. Of course, within a month, a little month, I was wheeling about the streets of Clifton the most beautiful baby girl in the world. And she was. And I have the family album photos to prove it!

We moved to a bigger flat in Alma Road soon after, in order to gain an extra room for the baby, and to my eternal shame, I swopped my beautiful Morris Tourer for, of all things, a Ford Popular. The Tourer was only a two-seater, and we needed space for the carry-cot. Such are the problems of young parents. It was one of the worst decisions I ever made in my life, and I've regretted it ever since. I loved that car.

The Crucible by Arthur Miller was the main offering of the first half of the first season, and it was a tremendous experience being involved in the British première of such an important American play, which Warren Jenkins had directed brilliantly. The cast, led by Edgar Wreford and Rosemary Harris, was very strong. First-rate actresses like Annette Crosbie, Pat Sands, Phyllida Law, Perdita Nielson, and Mary Savage were the women of Salem and the girl playing Tituba was Barbara Assoon, a black actress. I remember when I pushed open the trapdoor in that very old theatre to make my entrance and found that ring of female faces staring down at me, for a moment, I actually believed I was in that eighteenth-century American farmhouse situation. I had an extraordinary sense of dislocation which I had never known in theatre before, and hardly known since. The feeling passed of course as soon as I ascended the steps and said my first line, but it was an unforgettable moment.

At the first end-of-season party the theatre club host the artists, and in return, the artists entertain the club members. Sheila and I decided to sing 'Foggy Foggy Dew' as a duet, and as a direct result, she was offered a contract for the following season. This time our leading man was Eric Porter, and our leading lady, Moira Shearer, another Fifer, so Sheila felt a little more at home. Another

Between Dirk Bogarde and John Barrie in Victim *1961*

newcomer to the company was the young Peter O'Toole. For the first time, Sheila and I were in a professional company together.

She did little, however, to protect me from Peter O'Toole, whose impudence and impetuosity on stage struck a responsive chord in me. This resulted in our both being sacked during the Christmas pantomime. I was Marmaduke, the simpleton, to his Alderman Bung. Cicely Suett, the dame, was Eric Porter. He had left Peter and me both on stage at one time, and we got a laugh out of some unexpected business. Then, in the same way that comedians work, we built on that, till neither of us could remember where we were in the script. Sonia Fraser, another of the Old Vic Scottish imports, was on the book, and was trying to yell out to us the next cue, but we couldn't work out whose line it was, so Peter and I went into the prompt corner and lifted Sonia out, still in her chair, then, going either side of her, argued playfully about whose line it was. When we finally agreed, we lifted her back to her place again, and carried on, as per script. The audience, we thought, had enjoyed it all hugely, but Anne Stutfield, our stage director, was not amused, and reported us to Nat Brenner, our production manager, for 'halting the progress of the play in performance'. We were hauled up before John Moody, our director, the next morning, and formally fired, but thanks to Nat's intervention, reinstated that afternoon in time for the evening performance.

I was also retained for a second season soon after which meant a rise in my weekly wage to eighteen pounds which justified another flat move in order to give Jennifer more playroom. We moved in with the Jameses in Chesterfield Road. This was a little further away from the theatre in King Street, and so gave me a bit of a rush at lunch-time. I had to jump off the bus as it turned the corner, hare along to the house, run up several flights of steps, then upstairs to our flat. I generally arrived panting. One lunch-time, I think Jennifer had been giving Sheila a hard time, for it was a very flustered young wife who let me in. My lunch was on the table, and it was something I didn't immediately recognise.

'What's this?' I asked conversationally.

'Never mind what it is,' snapped Sheila, very untypically. 'Just eat the damn thing, and get out of my hair.'

I stared at the strange dish. Sheila was in her experimental phase of cooking, and was not yet the great cook she was to become. She continued to scold, so without a word on my part, I raised the window beside me which looked down on the garden, and taking the plate, threw it out. Then I rose from the table and, grabbing an apple from the sideboard, let myself out, and running again, caught the bus back to rehearsal.

When I came home late that night, I rather dreaded my reception, but there wasn't a sight or sound as I let myself in, and there on my place on the table by the window was that plate again! However, the only thing on it was a recipe, cut from a cookery magazine, which was pasted on to cover the crack on the dinner plate, and on it was the picture of my lunch-time dish! Nothing else. Game, set and match to Sheila!

Being at the Bristol Old Vic meant that one had constant visits from London critics and theatre people, and just as frequently, film casting directors. In my second year at Bristol, I got to know quite a few. One of these was Irene Howard, and she invited me to take a test at Elstree. I was also asked by Bob Leonard to test at Johnny Fraser's studio, ABPC, and Dodo Watts offered me, through Christopher Mann, another film test at Ealing. This film interest was growing all the time in that last year, and I'm afraid it unsettled me rather. Sheila warned me about losing the bird in hand for the possible two in the Shepherd's Bush! On the theatre front, I had been, in the course of the season, featured prominently in the première of a new play, *The Mulbery Tree* by Angus Wilson. This was taken up by George Devine at the Royal Court as part of his season with the New English Theatre Company and he asked John Moody about my availability in the following year.

John and I had a chat and he told me that the new company at the Court was to perform another new play, called *Look Back in Anger* and that Devine had me in mind for that as well.

'It would seem to me,' said John, 'that all roads for the Cairneys now lead to London.'

'Should I go?'

'What does Sheila think?'

'She'll go where I go.'

John grinned. 'And little Jennifer?'

'She'll go where Sheila goes!'

An appointment was fixed with George Devine. We met at the Court and talked about the Angus Wilson play, and then I read a scene from the new play with the young actor who had written it, John Osborne, and the young assistant stage manager who was in attendance, Joan Plowright. George seemed happy enough and we repaired to the pub next door for lunch. I don't know what I said, but suddenly something seemed to annoy him.

He rose. 'I want to withdraw my offer of a company engagement.'

'Why?' I asked, looking up in amazement.

'Because I don't like you,' he replied bluntly.

I wish I could have said, 'And I don't fancy you much either,' but I could only mutter, 'That's reason enough, I suppose. May I finish my beer?'

'As you please.' And he was gone.

I wonder what I said that so annoyed him? Well, how to lose jobs and irritate people. I'll have to watch it, I thought. Especially on my next mission. This was to take Jennifer back to Scotland to meet the Cowans for the first time.

Seventeen hours it took us in that dreadful Ford Popular (including losing the exhaust in Kidderminster). It was seven in the morning when we finally reached Kirkcaldy.

When I put the carry-cot on the pavement, old Willie Cowan came out at once with his pyjama top over his trousers, glanced at the baby, saying, 'My, she's braw, it's Sheila ower the back.' He then reached for my hand, shook it strongly and said, 'Aye, fine. Ye'll hae a dram?'

'It's seven o'clock in the morning!'

'Whit's the differ? It's no' every day I hae a gran'wean.'

A lot of fences were mended in those few weeks in Fife, as we proudly showed off our beautiful first offspring among my in-laws. A baby is good mortar in cementing any breaches in the family wall. I moved my little Bethlehem unit to the west in the final week to make the family circuit around Glasgow. Dad thought Jennifer 'a wee smasher' but wasn't too impressed with the Ford Popular. Then it was time to come south again, but not south-west to Bristol again, but directly south as the A1 flies, to 'The Big Smoke' – London.

It wasn't Bow Bells which drew me, but the rather more tangible prospect of a job at the BBC to play Branwell Brontë in a televised version of the Brontë family story, to be directed by Chloe Gibson under the title *Wild Decembers*. All three of us lived with Chloe in her elegant studio in Kensington while we rehearsed the two-hour piece which went out one Thursday night in the spring of 1956. We were looking for new London digs next day, as Chloe was off to Dublin on the Friday morning, but Peter Potter took us in to his flat in Maida Vale until we found a place of our own, which turned out to be the top of a house in Buckhurst Hill owned by a retired colonel of the Indian army and his mad wife, whom he cared for, poor thing. Actually, I found her quite sweet; it was he who was mad, I'm sure.

At any rate, he got very angry indeed one night, when Sheila tried to make me a curry, and he came storming upstairs in the middle of our meal complaining of the smell. One would have thought that having been in India for so long, he would have been used to it, but perhaps it brought back unhappy memories for him, like the Indian Mutiny perhaps? Anyway, one thing led to another, and before we knew it, he had wakened Jennifer, frightened Sheila and spoiled my dinner. When he then complained about my young wife in other respects which I thought insulting, and even though he was an older man, I'm not ashamed to admit that I hit him. Not too hard, but right on the chin, and he went toppling back down his own staircase in a fall that any film stunt man would have been proud of, and landed at the feet of his wisp of a wife who was laughing her head off. When he came to, he ordered us out of the house there and then.

'But it's ten o'clock at night!'

'Don't care,' he shouted, keeping his distance. 'Out you go, all of you! And at once, d'you hear?'

They could have heard him in Calcutta.

'But we have a three-month-old baby – ' Sheila began.

'Don't care. Out! Out!'

So we were out. I would have gladly hit him again and risked a manslaughter charge, but Sheila restrained me just in time.

'Will you go?' He was screaming by this time.

'When I finish my chicken curry,' I yelled back.

His wife laughed even louder and he dragged her across the hall and the downstairs door slammed behind them.

I turned to Sheila, but she was already packing.

Midnight found us at a garage at Woodford Green. We must have looked a sorry trio. The car packed with all our gear, the pots and pans still smelling of curry, and a baby crying among it all. I asked the man at the garage the best route back to Ealing. I was going to take my brood to Ealing where an actor pal, now turned writer, Tony Marriott, might give us a couch for the night. Give us time to sort things out.

'You don't wanna do that,' opined the garage man, as he filled the petrol tank, 'I got an empty flat up the High Road. You can take the missus an' the little fella up there tonight' (I imagined Jennifer yelled all the louder at being thought a boy) 'an' in the mornin',' the man went on, 'we can talk about fings.'

In a few sentences, that kindly Londoner, Mr Norman, who, as it turned out, was the garage owner, not the all-night pump attendant, eradicated the trauma of the evening for a shaken little family and gave us shelter for the night, which turned out to be our first real London home: Flat 3, 197 High Road, Buckhurst Hill, Essex.

We even had a telephone – BUCkhurst 8964. And all on account of a curry! Lucky for us.

The telephone never stopped all that summer. One television part followed another through May, June and July – each one starting within days of the previous one's finishing. It was a hectic and happy time. Sheila even landed a part; as my sister in *Barnbarrow* and stole the show, but she fretted about Jennifer who had been left with the doctor's family next door. She wasn't keen to work that much, which was a pity, as she got more offers than I did. Not that I was complaining. I was now in another children's serial with Wilfred Brambell, and followed it playing Edgar Allan Poe for Michael Eliot, *Macadam and Eve* with John Laurie, but the sunniest offer of that golden summer was when my Rank option was taken up and I was cast in my first film, *Ill Met By Moonlight*, for which I needed a passport. The locations were to be in the south of France.

Nice was nice. But Draguignon was better. It was a tiny village on the side of a mountain in the Basses Alpes, a few hours' car journey from Nice, and director Michael Powell, standing in the passenger seat of his Bentley, led his Rank film unit up there, much in the manner of Monty leading his troops into battle. That's exactly what film location is like. A military operation, complete with camp followers and hangers-on. The ammunition is celluloid, the commanding officer is the director, the producer is his chief of staff, the stars are his dashing officers and nearly everyone else is a foot soldier, I was a foot soldier, and really very happy about it. I was playing Elias, a Cretan guerrilla working with British officers in a resistance unit, in this Powell/Pressburger film. I had a tentative toe on the first rung of the film ladder, and I was clinging on with a prehensile grip that fully justified Darwin! I couldn't believe that this was all real and that I was here in the south of France, with a film unit.

We were dressing in a laundry in Draguignon when a very Glasgow voice enquired. 'How's it gau'n, Jimmy?'

I looked up, thinking to see a fellow Glaswegian, but there, leaning over the partition of the cubicle was the film's star, Dirk Bogarde.

He grinned down at me. Then, in his usual, charming voice, he offered me his hand. 'Welcome to the asylum.'

I reached up and shook it. 'May I congratulate you on your Glasgow accent,' I said.

'My mother comes from the place,' he answered.

'Nice to find a fellow Glaswegian,' I ventured.

'For God's sake don't call me that, I hated the place. I'm more of a Dutchman really. Cheers for now.'

'Cheers.'

And that's how I started in films, chatting with Dirk Bogarde in a laundry in the south of France. It was still all incredible to me: film stars who acted just like real people, sun every day, luxury at every hand, the exotic and the erotic, and 'cowboys and Indians' up and down those French mountains. And being paid by the day, expenses that were greater than my Bristol weekly wage. I had no complaints at all.

Except perhaps about the dining-table seating arrangements at L'Hôtel Napoléon in Nice. Film units observe a pecking order much like that of any officers' mess, and by virtue of my billing and fee I was among the junior subalterns, as it were, one of whom I found particularly annoying. Or was it perhaps that he found me so? At any rate, at one dinner, after a long day, the waiter made a joke about my being 'M Le Potage' because I was always asking for soup, and put the big soup tureen in front of me. This actor, being very English, very supercilious, remarked to the rest of the table. 'For God's sake, don't let him put his spoon in it. We don't want his Glasgow slum manners here!'

There was an embarassed giggle around the table, and I just looked at the fellow. Then I rose up, the tureen in my hands, and quietly emptied it over his head. Laurence Payne, a fellow Bristol Old Vic actor, had me out of that dining-room in a clatter of cutlery and plates and next night I found I was moved to another table.

Oddly enough, not a word was said about the incident, and the actor, Roland Bartrop, showed considerable English aplomb in greeting me the next morning at the Piera Cava location as if nothing had happened. 'Do you like my hair, John? I just had a special shampoo!'

Much more painful was the film visit made to the French dentist. As part of the action, I had to help Dirk break into a dentist's surgery, at which the script called for us to be caught by Christopher Lee as the German officer. I had to pretend to be the patient and Dirk the dentist. The only trouble was Dirk took his dentist's impersonation quite seriously, and as big Chris Lee watched, inserted the drill into my mouth, and pressed the switch. While Chris was a pretend German and I was a pretend patient, and Dirk was a pretend dentist, the drill was very real, and it didn't know it was only acting. As I felt it go into my mouth, I could see the twinkle in Dirk's eyes, but fortunately, Michael called 'Cut' just before it did just that on my gums!

When it was time to go home again, I was burned black from my days on the mountains, and lean and fit, carrying my wireless equipment up and down, over rocks, across streams and through forests. I had heard from Sheila that she had another job, playing a small part in a tour of *Mr Bolfry*, starring Alistair Sim and Duncan Macrae. So while I was in the south of France, she was in the south of England touring Eastbourne, Brighton and the rest. By the time I came back to London, she was in Manchester. I drove up there to meet her, and was in her hotel room when she returned from that evening's performance. I gave her the fright of her life. She thought I was a Jamaican, and not even the sexy black lingerie I had brought back as a gift was able to soothe the sense of strangeness she felt at being in bed with a black man. When we got back to London she had to report to the Aldwych Theatre each night, and for the Wednesday matinee.

It was one of these Wednesdays that I was babysitting Jennifer, now eighteen months old. By this time we had the first of our German au pair girls, Gisela, and I had given her the day free to go up to London because I was only on standby for the film and didn't expect to be called that day. However, such are the ways of film making that I was!

'But I'm babysitting,' I wailed to the production office.

'I don't care if you're pole squatting,' said an unimpressed official voice at the other end. 'Get here in an hour. Scenes 23 to 30. Your point of view over the road.'

I knew exactly the scenes he was talking about, and it meant a long list of motor car names. Blast it. What could I do? I could mug up the script all right, but what was I to do with Jennifer? I thought of ringing Sheila at the Aldwych, or trying to catch Gisela at the Goethe Institute, but there was no time to do anything. Even the landlady at our Haringey flat, where we now were, was away for the day, so when the film car called for me, I had no option but to grab Jennifer, some nappies and the push-chair, and head for Pinewood.

At the studio I was wrestling with Jennifer in one hand and the push-chair in the other at the foot of the dressing-room block, when a little fellow asked if he could give me a hand.

'Please,' I answered, and let him sort out the push-chair. We strapped Jennifer in, and he then helped me lift both upstairs to the dressing-room. I thanked him at the dressing-room door and he wandered off. At that moment, Chic Murray, the Scots comedian, came out of the dressing-room next to mine, and I heard him call out to my helper. 'Hello there, Norman. You're so small, I almost missed you.'

It was Norman Wisdom. Chic then joined me in the dressing-room to amuse Jennifer while I waited for my call. He also amused me with his non-stop patter.

'Don't worry,' he said, 'I'll keep an eye on the wean here while you're on the set. I'll try out some of my new material on her. If I can get a laugh out of her, I'll get a laugh out of anybody.' He turned to Jennifer. 'Now listen, you stupid one-year-old, did you hear the one about the man who . . .'

In keeping with the tenor of that particular day, it was he who was called to his set before I was called to mine. When I pushed Jennifer on to the set, Michael Powell nearly exploded. But Dirk, who was only there to give a voice off-camera, saved the day. He took hold of the push-chair and walked it up and down in the background while I went in front of the camera. My script action was to listen for various vehicles coming and identify them by their engine noise. I had already done this in long shot on location. Now they were going close. This is normally very stressful for the actor, but on that afternoon I was only aware of Jennifer's being pushed up and down by Dirk behind the camera. When the usual calls for 'Silence' came, my heart was in my mouth. The quiet just before 'Action' in any studio is monastic to say the least, and I dreaded that Jennifer would cry out when she saw her daddy up on this spotlit mound dressed as a Cretan peasant. However, I could see Dirk bending over her and saying something, and, hoping for the best, I went into my spiel. Being preoccupied with Jennifer, I had no time to 'act', and therefore the lines came out naturally and spontaneously.

'Cut!' said Michael Powell, beaming. 'Print. Next set up.'

With relief and gratitude I retrieved the push-chair from Dirk's hand and almost ran with Jennifer out of the studio.

With *Ill Met* in the can, I started the next week in *Miracle in Soho*, and this time the star was John Gregson. He was a genial Liverpudlian with an easier manner than Dirk but with the same charm that that school of Rank Organisation actors had then – the Rank 'charm school'. Most people think that phrase applies to the girls, but, in my opinion, it was the men who had it; Bogarde, Gregson, Kenneth More, Jack Hawkins and the others. John was easy to get to know and his Liverpool-Irish-Catholic background related very much to my Glasgow equivalent. Besides, I was his young 'pal' in Emeric Pressburger's script, and I had to work closely with him on the set. It helps when you actually like and admire what the script calls for you to like and admire.

I was enjoying my new life as an up-and-coming film actor, and did my best to live up to my new status, off the camera as well as on. For instance, I bought a new car. It was a Renault Gordini in silver and chrome, and I was immensely proud of it, though it and I got off to a bad start. The first day I drove in it to the studio, I met two lorries coming round a corner near Slough. I had to take to the banking under a bridge in order to avoid them. It was about seven o'clock in the morning and I think they were just having some fun and games. It was quite stupid and very dangerous, but I never really thought of that as I stopped to check that my lovely new car was still in one piece, and wait for my heart to stop racing. I realised what a narrow escape I had had. I should have been more concerned about being late for my studio call, which, of course, I was. In the studio car park, I was locking the car door, still shaking, when the third assistant on the picture yelled from one of the office windows.

'John, you're late.'

'I know,' I yelled back, and ran to the make-up room.

The scene I had to do that morning was my death scene of all things. Having been badly burned in a previous scene, due to the overturning of a tar boiler, I was to die sympathetically, between John Gregson and Belinda Lee, seated either side of my hospital bed. I must explain that John Gregson and I were part of a Soho road gang, and much of the action showed us laying asphalt in a supposed Soho street. I don't remember much about the plot, except that Ian Bannen from Coatbridge was Belinda Lee's Italian brother, and Billie Whitelaw was my girlfriend. At any rate, that morning at 8.30 a.m. I was supposed to be in that hospital bed, head, hands and arms swathed in bandages ready to die on cue. But, thanks to my highway scrape with the lorries, it was now nearer 9.30 a.m. and I was still in make-up. It was a case of all hands to the pump, or rather all technicians to the rescue. I seemed to be seized on by half a dozen pairs of hands, while bandages were applied all over and a pyjama top hurriedly put on over my ordinary clothes. I was then whirled on to the studio floor, where dear old Emeric Pressburger was waiting, stop-watch in hand.

'In films,' he said quietly, 'time is money, and we have lost a lot of money, while we are waiting for you.'

156

In his Hungarian way, he made it clear to me that he was very angry. I was in bed in no time, still with my shoes on under the blankets, and the red eye of the camera staring unwinkingly. My heart still hadn't adjusted to all the flurried events of that morning, and I realised, too, as I lay there, that perhaps I should have gone to the lavatory . . .

Julian Amyes whispered, 'Action', and Tom, the roadmender (me) proceeded to die appropriately. The only mistake I made was in asking the first assistant before the action if I had time to go . . .

'Hell, no,' he said. 'We're in trouble enough.'

You must remember that not only my head was swathed in bandages, but so were my hands – both hands. When 'Cut' was announced, I almost jumped from the bed, relieved that it had been managed in one take. I now sought another kind of relief, urgently, but the 'First' said, 'Hold it, John, for a still,' and groaning, I went back into place.

Norman Gryspeerdt seemed to take an hour for his still, but eventually he nodded and I leapt from the bed again, holding my hands eagerly out to the first assistant to be released from the bandages. But he was already on his way to the next set-up.

I then went to the wardrobe master on the floor, who said, 'Not my department, dearie. See make-up.'

I made my way to make-up with a great deal of difficulty to be told there that since plaster was used on the bandages, their removal was a matter for special effects.

'Where are they?' I grimaced between my teeth.

'Plasterer's shop, mate,' said the make-up man and went back to making up Billie Whitelaw.

'Where the blazes is that?'

'I don't know,' said the make-up man, laughing. 'Ask at the front gate.'

I about-turned and almost ran from the room.

The plasterer's shop was situated in the workshop area at the end of a long, very long corridor at Pinewood, and is sensibly at a good remove from the sound stages. I must have made a sorry figure as I hobbled slowly along that corridor, my pyjama top over my trousers and my plastered, bandaged hands hanging limply by my side. I realised soon that I was never going to make it to the Plasterers. Then I saw just ahead a very welcome sign, 'Gentlemen'. I looked at my hands again. What was the point? Somebody would have to help me. I stood at the door of the toilet as various gentlemen went in. I hadn't the courage to say to any of them what my particular predicament was. Then I saw Vic, a stunt man. Big Vic, who had once been a Chelsea footballer. Ah, I thought, here's my man.

'Vic, excuse me . . .'

'Allo there, Johnny boy.'

He laughed his head off when I told him.

'They've been having you on, mate. That bloody First', he's a right one. It's been all round the studio, you an' your bothers.' He laughed again. 'Come on, let's 'ave you in 'ere, then.'

I followed Vic to the urinal, where with much giggling and ribald comment, he started to undo my flies. But it was too late. My natural and spontaneous response to release soon wiped the smile off Vic's face!

In the meantime, the scene that I had done weeks before, on the day of Jennifer's push-chair, had been seen by other Rank producers, and one of them, John Bryan, offered me my best part to date, that of Jan, a Malayan student in *Windom's Way*, starring Peter Finch, which was to be shot on location in Corsica. For this part I had to have the widow's peak in my hair removed, with most of my eyebrows, as well as the hair on my chest. I also had plastic discs inserted in my nostrils, but it was worth it. It was a good part. Sheila and I celebrated by buying a £3,000 house in Berkshire, and naturally we called it Windom's Way.

This house was one of a row of steel-framed houses being built at Cookham Rise near Maidenhead, a few doors away from Stanley Spencer, the artist. Sheila, Jennifer, Gisela and I moved there one very hot summer afternoon in a taxi. Our sole possessions by this time, in addition to the canteen of cutlery and the bread board, amounted to a baby's cot and a Roberts radio. Having lived solely in furnished flats till then, we realised in a panic that we didn't even have a bed or a chair. It was then I entered into my arrangement with Heal's. Sheila and I were attracted to this store's good design, but appalled by its prices. However, now that I had three films under my belt, or at least into my Barclay's account, I felt I could make a case for some new furniture as opposed to the packing-cases. The gentleman at Heal's was sufficiently impressed, I think by Sheila, to allow us to open an account, and we ordered our first bed there and then, plus a Parker Knoll armchair and a circular kitchen table in beech with six chairs. On our removal day there were very anxious faces at the windows of Windom's Way as we waited for our first furniture to arrive. While we were doing so, an old, white-haired lady, in velvet high collar and cameo brooch, teetered from the large house across the way, and tripped daintily through the builder's rubble and up to our new front door.

'Won't you come in?' said Sheila.

The old lady darted in like a little bird, her eyes glancing around like a sparrow's. The Roberts radio was sitting on top of one of the tea-chests.

'I see your furniture hasn't arrived,' she said pleasantly.

'Yes, it has,' I said, pointing to the tea-chests.

'Oh,' she said, a little nonplussed. 'You must come over and have tea as soon as you're – er – er – settled in.'

And with that she was gone. We never saw her again.

It was almost dark when the big Heal's furniture van came up Cookham Rise, brushing the trees which ran down the centre of the road. The US cavalry was never greeted with greater excitement than was that furniture van by us.

'Blimey,' said the driver when he saw the house, 'I fought it was the bleedin' AA!'

It was boldly painted black and yellow.

That night, in our spanking, new king-size Heal's bed, we slept the sleep of the just-moved-in! Next day, I flew to Corsica.

The location filming was to represent Malaya, so once again I was staring into a camera up the side of a mountain by day and into another plate of soup in another luxury hotel by night. My table companions had improved considerably, particularly a gossamer-delicate blonde with dark eyes and a neat, slim figure, who asked me, almost as soon as I sat down, 'Excuse me, were you the Demon King in the Citizens Theatre pantomime a few years ago?' It was Mary Ure, our young leading lady.

'Yes,' I managed to gulp.

'You were very funny.'

'Er . . . yes, thank you, I – '

'My mother, and Uncle Allan and I saw it one night when I was home.'

Of course, Mary was a Glaswegian. I'd forgotten that. Although it had to be admitted, she came from a very different Glasgow.

'I was looking forward to meeting you.'

'Thank you.'

The rest of the table were all ears, and I couldn't believe mine.

'May I come and sit beside you?'

I was taken aback. 'Er . . . of course.'

159

She chatted all through the meal to me, of Glasgow, her West End and my East End, of the Citizens, of York, where my brother Jim lived and she had played in rep, of Bristol and Tony Guthrie who had directed her in a medieval morality play – of everything under the sun, in fact, except the film that had brought us all here.

Mary and I continued to get on well all that night and through that night and as the weeks progressed. Almost unnoticed, the working days flew by.

Peter Finch, our star, was the true professional, doing as little as possible for as long as possible but then doing it superbly and simply when he had to. He couldn't drive, which amazed me, but I could, which still amazed me, and often, on free days, Peter, his then girlfriend, Yolande Turner (a lovely girl), Mary and I would drive into Ajaccio or Calvi to see the sights and have a meal.

On one occasion, coming round a corner, thousands of feet up a mountainside, I forced another car to swerve dangerously. As the other car flashed past, I just caught a glimpse of John Bryan, our producer, in the other passenger seat. Unfortunately, he got the same glimpse of Mary beside me. I was up before him in his room next morning.

'It's not that we give a monkey's for you, but were you aware of the cargo you were carrying?'

'Mary's – '

'I know you're just good friends. Well, let me tell you, Cairney boy, she represents nearly £250,000 of investment as far as this picture's concerned, and we don't want to see that lost by idiotic, undergraduate driving up and down Corsican mountains.'

'No, Mr Bryan.'

'Call me John.'

'Yes, Mr Bryan.'

'And another thing, do you know who was driving the other car? I'll tell you. Our director.'

When the plane bringing us all home again was circling London airport, Peter came forward to where I was sitting and asked me to take Yo, as we all called her, off the plane.

'What now?' I asked.

His reply was suitably Australian, but what he wanted me to do was to escort Yo into the public lounge, see her through the luggage bit, and put her into a taxi.

'Please?'

'OK.'

So I came off the plane, and through Customs, between the

160

shapely Miss Turner and the delectable Miss Ure, and there was Sheila waiting to meet me! She didn't turn a hair.

We saw both ladies to a taxi, and Sheila drove along the A4 in the opposite direction, home towards Maidenhead and the other Windom's Way.

'How's the overdraft?' I asked.

'Cleared.'

I leaned over and gave her a peck on the cheek. 'Good girl.'

'Don't let it go to your head.'

Yes, I was a happily married man all right.

Things take time to return to normal after any film location but I was helped in the transition from holiday working to commuter employment by the sudden discovery that I could write song lyrics. The extras used in filming were Orientals of every kind who could be coaxed out of every restaurant and laundry in London. Some of them were actually Malayan, and one of these was Samseer Wahab, a slightly-built, good-looking young Malay married to a London girl. Samseer, or Sammy, played the guitar and sang pleasantly. Most of the Malays sang, and the breaks in filming were delightful as the extras would immediately produce guitars and mandolins and harmonicas. Extras, as a breed, are funny people, and are almost professionally lazy and complaining, but the Malayans and Philippinos were anything but. They were always smiling, easy-going and tuneful. I was drawn to them immediately, for while the Indians gambled, and the Chinese ate, the Malayans sang. They sang traditional melodies unknown to me, but one day in Black Park, in the studio lot behind Pinewood, I started to scribble some words to one of the tunes and showed it to Sammy. He liked the general idea and when I sang the song over, he added an immediate vocal harmony. Just by chance, the sound man had his microphone opened and he picked us up on the boom. We all listened and laughed as it was played back, but then we were called back to the set and I had to start acting again.

Throughout those weeks at Pinewood, Sammy and I continued to play about with lyrics and tunes and before the film was finished, we had quite a song-book. We promised to keep in touch and see if we could do something with our songs, but, like most of these kind of promises, it was given with half a heart. I was due to go on and make a TV film for America with Jeannie Carson at Elstree and Sammy was supposed to go back to being a student of economics.

Neither of us knew what had happened to the original tape of the first song, 'A Certain Girl I Know', but Harold Orton told me one night at a party in his Uxbridge home that he had given it to Mary Ure.

'Why?' I asked.

'She asked for it,' he answered simply. 'Anyway,' he went on, 'you can always make another one.'

'Sure,' I said, but to myself, I wondered, how do you make another Mary Ure? The answer is, you can't.

Instead, you get to know Jeannie Carson. What a lovely person she was, and a good actress too. We were lovers in a kilted fantasy set in Elstree's American idea of Scotland, and 'skedooled' to be shot in a fortnight. A lot of it was shot at night, but I was able to wangle a bit part for Sheila, so I at least had her company in my caravan between shots. However, it was after a day's shooting in the second week that Jeannie Carson came into my life, so to speak. I had been released for the day and was coming along the corridor at Elstree, singing enthusiastically to myself. The upper dressing-room corridors at Boreham Wood had a bathroom propensity that is flattering to even the least musical of voices, and I was giving big licks to something or other when a door in the long corridor suddenly opened and Jeannie's head was asking, 'Was that you singing?'

'Yes. Sorry about that. Just youthful high spirits, you know.'

'It was lovely.'

The head disappeared again. I was in my dressing-room and had just got changed when there was a knock at the door. It was Jeannie again. 'I was thinking of that voice of yours.'

'Was it as bad as that?'

'It was different. That's maybe what I like about it.'

'Jeannie, I never knew you cared.'

'I'm serious. I'd like to speak to Norman about you.'

'Norman?'

'Norman Newall, an A and R man from HMV.'

'A what man?'

'Artists and recording. He's lovely. And he's a good friend of mine. Talk to you later.'

'But Jean – '

Next thing I knew I had a call from Norman Newall himself. He'd never heard of me, but he trusted Jeannie Carson, and for her sake, he would give me a test; what sort of voice had I, and what would I like to sing? I couldn't think of anything, but I said I would get in touch when I did. We left it at that.

162

When I got home I rang Harold Orton and asked his advice. He told me that the sound man who made the recording of Sammy and me had kept a copy. He thought he might be able to get it for me. Well, at least it would give HMV an idea of my voice. Harold got it and I sent it to Norman's office. Next thing, he was on the phone – our very own phone, not long installed – saying that he wanted to record the number on the tape, and did I have any more?

'But you only need one for a test, surely?'

'Not for a test – but as a commercial recording. I'd like to make an EP with you and your accompanist – '

'He's not my accompanist – '

'Well, whoever he is. His guitar isn't brilliant, but we can do something about that, but the vocal blend is lovely. I think we can do something with you both. When can you come in?'

I was completely taken aback. It was all so unexpected. 'I'll have to get in touch with Sammy again. I haven't seen him since Pinewood. He could be – '

'I'll leave that to you. Ring me as soon as you both can come up with, say, six titles; we'll choose four and record.'

'All right,' I replied weakly. 'If you think – '

But he had already rung off.

'What was all that?' asked Sheila.

'I don't know, but a man at HMV wants me to make records.'

'At what – the 5,000 metres?'

Sammy was delighted to hear from me again, and by the time the Abbey Road recording date came up we had the songs ready. HMV gave us a lovely Cockney, Sid Haddon, as a rehearsal pianist and with his help we rehearsed four titles: 'A Certain Girl I Know', 'Two Strangers', 'Alone' and 'Your Trusting Love'. For the actual take we had Ike Isaacs and Bert Weedon on guitars, a bongo player and Geoff Love to conduct. I think we got a good sound. At least it was different. I sent the first pressing, an Extended Play on HMV issued as 7EG 8310, December 1957, to Jeannie Carson in Hollywood. She never replied. Maybe we should have recorded in the dressing-room corridor at Pinewood. 'A Certain Girl' was even released as a pop single. One unexpected side-effect of my new recording career was that Teddie Holmes of Chappell Music offered me a contract as a lyricist. I tried it in my spare time, and even managed to sell a song to Frankie Vaughan, but I had no desire to spend my life up a blind Tin Pan Alley. Anyway, Sheila had just made an advert for Typhoo Tea, so who needed money, Besides, it was time to get to work as an actor.

I reported for my next film, *A Night To Remember*. This was the story of the sinking of the *Titanic*, and starred Kenneth More. I was to play an Irishman who led the steerage passengers in a singsong and also to the lifeboats when the crash came. Most of the shooting was done at Ruislip Lido over several weeks of bitter winter, and for the first shot, several of us were to be discovered standing on an upturned lifeboat. I found myself between Kenny More and David McCallum, as the director, Roy Baker, called out through the megaphone, 'Right, let's have you in!'

Kenny said, 'He surely doesn't mean in the water.'

'No,' I said, 'he means in to land.'

'Oh, no, he doesn't,' said David. 'He means in the water.'

And he did. What amazed me is that no had ever asked me if I could swim, and there I was, standing with big boots on, a tight collar circa 1912, plus a big Irish cloth cap, and now I was being asked to jump into black water at two o'clock in the morning in the middle of winter. Somebody had to make the move first and we all turned to Kenny More.

'You're the star,' said David.

'You must be joking,' said Kenny.

It took an older American actor, Jimmy Dyrenforth, a former dance band pianist, to lead the way. 'Hell, let's go,' he said, and jumped, and in a moment, we all did.

The filmed scene consisted of our efforts to get back on the lifeboat again. I hit the water feet first, and heard the sound of splintering ice as I did so. It was so cold I was convinced it was boiling hot, and as I came up, I discovered I had lost my hat and went back down for it. The director saw this and decided to cover it, which meant I had to do it all over again in close-up. It seemed hours before I got out of that water, but at least there was a large tot of rum waiting and a dry suit of clothes, then it was back into cold water again. Its coldness was such that when Roy told me to shiver, I found I couldn't. I had a frozen jaw!

The end of shooting on *A Night To Remember* coincided with Rank's twenty-first birthday party, and big celebrations were held at the studio. It seemed then that Rank, like the Bank of England, would go on for ever, but in only a few years it was gone, and the great contract star system had crumbled. David McCallum and I were among the first to go. We had dinner together at his place in Warwick Avenue. He and Jill Ireland, his wife, also freed by Rank, had decided to go to America. Sheila and I decided to stay where our mortgage was.

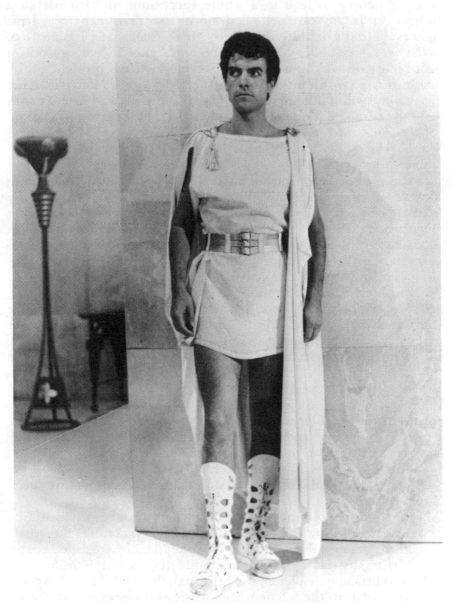

Cleopatra – *Rome 1961*

Luckily, my Titanic Irishman was seen by sufficient London casting people to lead to a whole succession of Irish parts on television. In any case, I looked more Irish than many real Irish actors, perhaps because I was more Irish than many Irish actors. Whatever it was, Ellen McLaughlan's and Agnes O'Neil's grandson got plenty of work as a Paddy. I became a virtual resident of the Irish quarter in Kilburn and Notting Hill Gate, while rehearsing Irish plays with Eddie Byrne and Donal Donnelly and Noel Purcell and the rest. It was one of these TV plays that led to another film, *Shake Hands with the Devil* which was to be directed by Michael Anderson at Bray Studios, near Dublin, and to star no other than James Cagney.

I was pleased to get such a big feature film at this time, because Sheila was pregnant again. We were especially delighted, because she had had a miscarriage not long before. This time we were taking no chances. All the books were brought out, schedules and times considered, diets prepared, relaxation classes attended – all the necessary drill of the cautious and well-intentioned parents-to-be. In case of emergency, we had Dr Spock's instructions on how to deal with a home birth pinned up on the inside of the wardrobe door in the bedroom – not that we would need it, of course. But the day of my departure for the Dublin location of *Shake Hands* was drawing nearer all the time, and still no sign of 'the boy' yet. My departure became so imminent that I asked Sheila if she was sure about her dates.

'Of course,' she said, 'it's about the only thing I'm sure of.'

The baby was due a week before I was to leave. But then the film people brought their shooting dates forward from early October to late September, and I was then in a panic. We got to the day before my departure and still no 'son'.

'What do we do?' I moaned to Sheila.

'Let nature take its course,' she shrugged, 'but I suppose we could hurry it up.'

I spent most of the afternoon walking her up and down the stairs, from hall to landing and back again, trying to encourage the break-ing of the waters. Then, around tea-time, they broke, Sheila went up to the bedroom. I rang the midwife, bathed Jennifer and mopped up the stairs. I then went through the drill as per Dr Spock. I lit the stove in the kitchen, spread several weeks of the *Sunday Times* around the bed, laid out all the implements and articles required by the midwife on the dressing-table, which had been cleared, said Jennifer's prayers with a special one for Mummy and her little 'brother', then I went back to hold Sheila's hand. She was more concerned that I was packed and ready for the morning.

'What time does the car come?' she said.

'I think about half past eight. I've got to be at the airport for nine fifteen.'

'Good,' she said, 'you can drop Jennifer off at the nursery school.'

Ever the practical mother. The evening wore on, but still no sign of either doctor or midwife. I rang again.

'Are you sure it's this month?' said the doctor.

'Plenty of time, dear,' burred the old country midwife in her languid Berkshire drawl.

But there wasn't. Around seven o'clock the pains were coming quicker and faster, and I was getting more and more agitated. Item by item on Dr Spock's timetable was being ticked off, and I was becoming very anxious indeed. I made one last call to the midwife, but there was no reply. She must be on her way. I went back to hold Sheila's hand.

'Is Jennifer all right?'

'Sleeping.'

'Is the stove lit?'

'Yes.'

'Is everything looked out on the table?'

'Yes.'

'Have you checked Dr Spock's – '

Suddenly she broke off with a little puppy squeal. And as we both looked down, a baby slid out. Entangled in tubing, it seemed to me, and of a light blue/grey colour, but there it was. A baby was born. All I had felt was a sudden clenching of my hand, and all I had heard was that little squeal, but lying now on a white towel at the corner of our bed was a baby, a real live person.

'Is it all right?' said Sheila, trying to struggle up.

'If you let my hand go, I'll look.'

I lifted up the little baby. It was beautiful. As I lifted it, it turned from that blue grey to a lovely ruddy pink. Apart from a little scaling around its head, there was not a mark, although I noticed it had the loveliest little Roman nose, quite curved.

'Well?' came Sheila's voice.

I counted the fingers and toes as instructed. They were all there.

Sheila lay back on the bed. 'Thank God!' I heard her sigh.

I then untangled the cord from round the little body. It was a girl. 'It's a girl,' I yelled, 'and she's beautiful.'

Sheila only smiled.

I had the baby on the bed again and the cord tied the appropriate eight inches from Sheila's tummy as per Dr Spock, and was preparing to tie the other end when the midwife came bursting in and ushered me out abruptly, saying, 'This is no place for a man!'

Her Morris Minor had broken down coming from Cookham Dean, and she'd waited for the AA.

'Alcoholics Anonymous?' I shouted gaily through the closed door. I went into the bedroom next door and wakened Jennifer.

'I know,' she said sleepily. 'I've got a little sister.'

She must have been psychic, for I had never mentioned it. Maybe she'd been told in a dream. The innocence connection. I was called back to the bedroom by the midwife, given a bundle wrapped in a newspaper and told to burn it. This was why I had to light the stove, I suppose. I took it down to the kitchen, put it in the stove, then had a very welcome cigarette at the kitchen door, looking up to the autumn stars. It was the 20th night of September, 1958.

Unto us another child is born, and she shall be called . . . Alison Isobel Sarah Cairney.

I repeated the names over again, like a litany, both favourite aunties honoured, and then I sang it out to the dustbins. A new name for a new person. It was really very exciting. We had made a person and I had actually seen her born into the world. Will she grow up to be a singer, perhaps? I could get her a contract at HMV! I was brought out of my reverie by the midwife.

'Everythin' perfectly safe an' natural an' normal, thank the good God,' she said. 'That wife o' your is a good, sensible girl, now don't you go frettin' 'er, mind.'

'No, Nurse.'

'I'll call round tomorrow. Expect you'll be 'ere.'

'No, Nurse, I'll be in Ireland.'

The good woman could hardly believe it. 'Is 'er mother comin' down then?'

'Not that I know of.'

'No womenfolk to attend her then?'

'We've got Jennifer.'

'She's only three!'

'But a good, sensible girl though, Nurse.'

The midwife left shaking her head at our strange ways. It was a problem but Sheila had said she could cope, and Mrs Webber, a friend from the houses opposite, would look in, and our cleaning lady would come in every morning until Sheila was up and about again, and the nursery school would take Jennifer for most of the day. Now that Sheila had given up working we no longer had the au pair girls. Not that they would have been any use in the present situation. They were more for decoration, I think. Oh for a grannie, but both of them were four hundred miles away. I came upstairs again.

I remember shivering, whether with cold or excitement, I'm not sure, but in the bedroom, Sheila was now lying on her usual side of the bed, the papers were all lifted from the floor, all the medical evidence removed, and apart from a slight disinfectant odour, our bedroom was as it always was. Except that in the corner, in the new straw Moses basket, an extra little person was sleeping. I got into our bed at my side, reached for Sheila's right hand, and gave it a little squeeze, 'Well done, darling.'

'Well done, you,' she whispered. 'Did you take the list down?'

'From the wardrobe you mean?'

'Yes.'

'Yes.'

'Good old Dr Spock.'

It was lovely lying there whispering in the silence, with the new baby smell still in the darkness around us, and only a peep of star-light through the Ventian blinds facing us.

'Do you know what I didn't do tonight?' I said.

'What?'

'I never boiled a kettle of water.'

'Why should you do that?'

'John Wayne always does.'

We laughed quietly except that now, tears were on my cheekbones.

'And do you know what else you didn't do?'

'What?' I whispered.

'You never said "good night" to Alison.'

'Good night, Alison,' I called out softly.

And from the little person in the corner, wrapped as tight as a mummy in her Moses basket, came the most delightful little snore!

The Shelbourne Hotel in Dublin looked on to one of that charming city's many green places, and was supposed to be my home for the six weeks of location on *Shake Hands With The Devil*, but I saw little of it. The reason was the Irish proclivity for all-night parties and singsongs, and for the fact that I now had an almost symbiotic rela-tionship with Donal Donnelly, that fine actor, good singer and witty companion who led me gleefully astray amid the bars, shebeens and backrooms of his native Dublin. He and I, with Richard Harris, comprised Mr Cagney's IRA gang in this film about 'The Troubles' and every morning we were picked up from the Shelbourne and brought to the studios at Bray by 'Chalky' White, our English driver. At least, that was the plan, but it was a case of 'first find your actor'. Donal and I were invariably in a working-man's café having bacon and eggs and hot tea after singing the night away somewhere, but Chalky would find us, and then we would go in search of Richard. When we found what was left of the night before, we'd throw him in the back seat and speed for the studios. It was all very stupid of course, but we were young, and it was Dublin. Coming into the warm lights of the make-up room, we would fall asleep right away, only to be waked by a soft voice murmuring, 'Come on, boys, sing me a little song.'

It was Mr Cagney, and we could refuse him nothing – even at 8.00 a.m. I had little to do in the film except react to him, and what a pleasure that was. Here was the man who was the star of the first film I ever saw – *The Fighting 69th* – and now he was sitting in the next make-up chair to me. When I asked him about *The Fighting 69th* he could hardly remember it.

'Was Paddy O'Brien in it?'

'Yes, he was.'

'Then I must have been in it.'

And the Irish eyes would twinkle. Of course, he was quite an old man, as we saw each morning, but once he was ready for the set, and had done his five-minute tap dance in the corner, he came in front of the camera like a forty-year-old. We were in our twenties, but after our Dublin nights, we came in front of the camera like geriatrics! There was a professional lesson there somewhere. I was glad when the location was over and I could go home for a rest!

Months after the film was in the can I had a most warming note from James Cagney, from his home in Martha's Vineyard: 'Johnny boy, you'll find a tape enclosed. Will you and Donal put a few of the old songs on it for your Uncle Jimmy so that he can play it over to himself as the sun goes down . . .?'

I found Donal again in Notting Hill Gate, and we spent a night in front of a tape-recorder, with Dermot his landlord, and other Irish friends, singing all the old ballads, or as many as we could remember. It was like old times, except there was no Chalky White to guide me back to Cookham in the dawn.

I had to pretend to be a British Tommy in *Shake Hands With The*

Devil, but I became a real one in the next film of my Elstree phase. This was *Girls In Arms* starring Donald Sinden and I was enlisted as Private Willie Ross of the Royal Artillery during the Second World War. It was a comedy and I had to sing 'You've Done Something to My Heart' in the dancehall sequence as 'Lieutenant' Donald danced with the ATS girl, Carole Lesley, who was my girl in the film, and was being hailed then as Britain's answer to Marilyn Monroe. The similarity was cruelly apt as poor Carole cut her wrists a few years later. She was a young, joyful girl who was no actress but knew it and was glad to have a good time while it lasted. It didn't last long, I'm afraid. Nor did the film, released the next year as *Operation Bullshine*.

It mattered little to me. Every picture-making experience was invaluable at that time and I was piling up priceless camera experience. I only wish it had made me a better film actor, but the trouble was I would insist on 'acting' instead of 'being' and a kind of dedicated mugging occurred as soon as the lens found my face. Despite working at close range with wonderful artists like Dirk Bogarde, Peter Finch, Kenneth More and Jimmy Cagney, I was still over-earnest and over-rehearsed in everything I tried. I had just enough technique to get by but it was a flimsy cover at best and I wondered if I would ever find that magic ease under the lens which all the 'natural' film actors seem to have – the Spencer Tracys, the Jean Gabins, the Henry Fondas. Never mind, I seemed to have a 'hire-able' face and it had got me six films in a row. Now, with 1959 well under way, I landed number seven. Or eight, if you include the week or two I had at Elstree on *Lucky Jim* for the Boulting Brothers, but that was only a case of filling in time. Still, it was film time, and I was glad of it.

The next film took me to Shepperton, a studio I'd never been to before. They were making *Suddenly Last Summer* on the next sound stage, and I kept passing Montgomery Clift in the corridors. I got a kick from that: he had been a hero of mine. My film was *The Flesh and the Fiends*, a re-make of the Burke and Hare story with Peter Cushing as the doctor. I was his student assistant and I had several scenes with Billie Whitelaw again – including a love scene, in which she had to appear nude. This worried her. Well, it didn't worry her so much, as her mother. One forgets that actresses have mothers! Billie came to my dressing-room just before we had to do the scene and asked what she should do about what she called her 'bare-chest bit'. I told her that in my opinion she should just do it. She was playing a prostitute, wasn't she? Anyway, I would enjoy it. But she wouldn't be kidded, and when we landed in bed to do the

171

scene that afternoon, she had two great lumps of Elastoplast criss-crossed across her nipples! They scarred my chest like razors as we embraced. It must have been murder to remove them after shooting. I hope Billie's mother up north thought it all worthwhile.

John Gilling, the director, shot two versions of the script, one in white pages and one in yellow pages. The white pages were for the UK and America and the yellow pages for the rest of the world. The difference was that when I opened a door in one take and charged into the brothel, all the ladies and gentlemen were in what might be called a state of discreet undress. In the next take, the yellow pages, I charged in on cue, and nobody had a single stitch on! Their mothers obviously didn't mind. My reaction was very natural, I can tell you. I dried stone dead, and the crew laughed their heads off. We took several takes of that scene. I never saw this version of the film, but George Rose, who was playing Burke, said it ran for years in Amsterdam!

I never got to know our star, Peter Cushing, very well, although I worked closely with him. He was a quiet, retiring man and not at all one's idea of a film star, and perhaps all the better for it. However, I became great pals with Renee Houston, who was playing an old character part, and still sexy at seventy. She was great fun, called everybody 'son' and remembered well her beginnings in Shettleston. She was half of a marvellous singing act she had with her sister Billie, before the war. They were really big-time before the war, and Renee still had that mysterious 'star' charisma about her even though she only had a tiny part in the picture. There was always a laugh when she was on. Finlay Currie had the same kind of aura, so had Wilfred Lawson. It's an extra light some people have on their shoulders, and it reflects in their eyes. It doesn't matter how old they are or how far they have slipped down the billing. The evidence of all the good work they've done is all about their personality. I grow more and more convinced that you are in life what you've done in life.

The benefit of being on a feature film is that you don't work every day. This gave me a chance to catch up on the children, take them walks, do some light, ineffective gardening or home decorating, and generally catch up on home life. And letter-writing for instance. We learned from Dad that Jim had moved to Canada to play soccer for the Canadian All-Stars. I understand that he had originally intended to go out to New Zealand to help set up soccer there, but he stopped off in New York to see relatives and friends, and met a pretty dentist's receptionist from London whose family now lived in Toronto. She invited Jim to come and visit, and somehow he stayed on and on. New Zealand seemed to have been forgotten, and Jim's teeth had never been whiter. Since he is by far the handsomer of the Cairney brothers, people often asked him why he didn't go on the stage.

'No, thanks,' said Jim. 'I'll leave that to John. Besides, he couldn't stand the competition. No, it's floodlights, not footlights for me.'

He was always the more sensible too.

I wondered what I'd do about the occasional 'sub' now that Jim was across the Atlantic. I didn't think we'd need it somehow.

The Cairneys were now what would be called upwardly mobile and certainly nothing was going to stop us now! I bought a new car and re-opened negotiations with Heal's for some additional furniture. The arrangement was that as soon as I got any new job, I rang Heal's and gave them the go-ahead to deliver the latest item previously discussed with Sheila. For instance, a new armchair roughly equated to a one-off TV play, but for the whole suite, I'd need at least six weeks on a film, and for the dining-room table we had our eye on I'd need twelve weeks on a film, or two pictures back to back. After a time Heal's knew better than I did what each job was worth in terms of merchandise. It was a practical, working arrangement and it meant that both parties were secured at all times!

That summer I worked one armchair (ironically, it was yet another Armchair Theatre for ABC/TV at the Didsbury Studios in Manchester, this time with Dylis Laye) and I also worked a set of sitting-room curtains for the BBC in a play about Mary Queen of Scots in which I was the ghost of Lord Bothwell. This was one of the first plays to be done from the new BBC television studios at Parkhead. What I knew once as the Black Cat Cinema was now transformed for TV. The very building where I had seen Bebe Daniels singing 'Lullaby of Broadway' and to which I had run after school every Wednesday to see Johnny Mack Brown or Flash Gordon for a penny, now housed a very prestigious group of London actors rehearsing a play for television. Instead of squirming in hard wooden seats I now lounged on a rehearsal couch chatting with Diana Churchill and Catherine Lacey. If my fellow East End kids from the 'penny crush' could see me now!

We extended my working stay in Glasgow to a family holiday in Scotland up to the time when both Sheila and I had to report for rehearsals for the 1959 Edinburgh Festival production of *The Thrie Estaites* at the Assembly Hall. This time, I was to play the young King Humanitie and Sheila was in the crowd. She didn't mind. It allowed us to be together and her wages paid for the petrol. It was great to be with Tony Guthrie again, and all that formidable old gang: Macrae, Macmillan, Keir, Fleming and Gibson. A forward line of class, skill and power as they say on the football pages. But best of all was in being reunited with the ebullient Tony. He hadn't changed a bit: the same nasal drawl, the same clapping hands, the same slippers. This time, I was meeting him for the first time as a lead, and his attitude to me was exactly as it had been when I had been an extra eight years before. He allowed me to do it my way until I wasn't doing it well, or doing too much, then the hands would clap and some witty and merciless comment would halt me in my tracks and then a suggestion here or a thought there: 'Suggest you might . . .' or 'Think perhaps that you should . . .' and we were off down another road. It was stimulating, refreshing and above all, encouraging. Everyone was a star in a Guthrie production, mainly because he was. I loved playing the king. I loved being at the centre of Guthrie's fabulous theatrical machine.

It was wonderful being at the festival again but it was sometimes a problem getting to and from performances. Sheila and I were living with her sister, Lillian, in Dunfermline, and as there was no Forth Bridge at that time, catching the ferry at Inverkeithing was a matter of some importance. We had several near misses and the strain wasn't good for our festival or marital enjoyment. One morning the alarm had failed to go off, and we missed the ferry. As a result we were an hour late for rehearsals, so, late one night, I decided to call the local telephone exchange.

'Hello operator, I would like to make an alarm call, please.'

'Hold on,' she said in her official voice. But then I heard her say to a colleague, 'He sounds in a bad way.'

'Hello,' I said.

'Hold the line, please.'

I held on.

'What number are you speaking from?'

I gave Lillian's number.

'May I have your name, please?'

I told her.

'Thank you, sir, I'll ring you back.'

'Hold on a minute. Look, operator, I just want to make an alarm –'

But she had rung off.

'What's going on?' I said to Sheila.

'Here, let me,' she said. As she went to pick up the phone, it rang. 'Hello – yes,' She handed the phone to me. 'It's for you.'

A lady's voice said, 'Mr Cairney?'

174

'Yes?'

'This is Good Samaritans here. What is your problem?'

'Good Samaritans!' I said.

'Yes, I understand you're in some sort of trouble.'

'Look, the only trouble I have is in catching that ferry in the morning.' And when I explained she put me back to the operator. I could hear her laughing. I must have sounded really agitated. That damned voice of mine again.

I stayed on in Scotland after the festival because of location work on the BBC TV serial *Redgauntlet*. For this we had to report to the Glencaple Hotel near Dumfries. Tom Fleming and I shared the leads, and the love interest was provided by Glasgow's lovely Claire Isbister. My main problem in the shooting was that I had to ride a horse. Of course, like every actor, when asked by the director, 'Do you ride?' I said 'Yes.' But here was I faced with the real thing in no uncertain measure. Ben was a big, black horse, so tall that I thought I would need an oxygen mask rather than a riding helmet, but the script called for me to be in pursuit of Tom Fleming, and therefore I had no option but to get up into that saddle. To my surprise, after a few days, I was riding Big Ben as if I were Roy Rogers.

On one particular day the camera was put on the roof of the camera car, and my job was to canter behind it and then, as the car picked up speed, I was to similarly accelerate, so that Ben and I were at full gallop. I wasn't so sure who was in charge – Kevin the director or Ben the horse, but we got started. It was rather exhilarating riding along the country lanes on the back of that splendid animal, but then as the car speed increased, Ben responded almost before I did, until we were going like an express train along the hedgerows. Then the camera car suddenly turned right, but Ben didn't, and I went hurtling along, completely out of control, but not looking it. The actor part of me kept working as long as the camera kept turning. As it turned abruptly right, it got a wonderful shot of me on the horse almost like a Rowlandson print. I decided that if I couldn't beat it, I would join it, and just tried to stay on. Ben, with ears back and neck glistening, now had the bit between his teeth and hurtled on his way. His mad careering set up the cattle in the field on my right to stampede as well as the sheep on my left and there I was, on top of this immense charger, leading what seemed to be half the animal population of Dumfriesshire towards Galloway. It was quite some time before I finally brought him under control again. We returned to the hotel at a gentlemanly trot. I had found my 'seat' again in *Redgauntlet* and I found that it was sore!

The finished serial was one of the several I did for the BBC around then. They were especially expert at costume drama on television, and fortunately I was very much at home with a cape and a sword, and even on the back of a horse!

Tom Fleming stayed on in London to do another job for the BBC, a play, *McAdam and Eve*. I was asked to join him again. This was the same play I'd done with John Laurie only a few years before. The only difference now was that I got feature billing. Such is progress, but sometimes billing and dressing-room accommodation are the only guide to the actor as to how he is doing in the profession. Even more than the money.

Just before Christmas I returned to Pinewood for a television film series called *Interpol Calling*. It was while filming as an Indian in these that I was first asked to play Robert Burns for Jimmy Logan, but that is a saga that is told elsewhere.

1959 ended with an invitation from Orson Welles to play Feste in his projected production of Shakespeare's *Twelfth Night* in which he was to play Malvolio. I was thrilled to be working with a legend, but ghost would have been a more apt description. After the reading at the Central London YWCA, he got up and lumbered out. We waited, and waited, but he never reappeared and was never seen again. We sat around for a bit, then we all went home. All's Welles that ends . . . well?

My thirtieth birthday present was an offer to leave the British winter and spend a month making a film in the Middle East for the army. A propaganda film in fact, but who cared? It was still under the ABPC banner but in association this time with British-Pathe, and in it, I was to be an army officer. It was called *The Lieutenants*, and I was one of them. The other was a blonde South African actor, Sean Kelly. This time, the location was Aden in the Middle East, and off we all went, by courtesy of the War Office, in virgin officers' wear. Because of the political situation in that area, we had to travel as an army unit, and, to all intents and purposes, we were enlisted 'for the duration' of the film. This had odd repercussions.

The army, in its way, insisted on treating everybody according to his film casting. As a result, the small part actor with a couple of lines as the general had the red carpet treatment, the best hotel room, the best table and all that, while the supposed leads, Kelly and Cairney were down among the odds and ends as befits the most junior of officers. It was a hard lesson on how not only the army, but the world

176

works. In the army, it's rank that talks, and in the world it's money. There wasn't much of the latter in this film, but at least it would be an experience. It certainly was that. In the first place we were billeted in tents in the desert. I could manage this; after all I had been in the Scouts and if you could camp on Loch Lomondside in a Scottish summer you could camp anywhere.

The story of our film concerned itself with the difficulties two young officers had in settling to army life abroad. I was typecast as the 'bolshie' one, not that we got that far into the narrative. For the purposes of army exercise we were given real soldiers to work with, stationed at that time in Aden. This was a detachment of the Yorkshire Light Yeomanry and they showed more than a slight Yorkshire contempt for the imitation officers foisted upon them. Their salutes had all the appearance of thumbs to the nose as far as I could see. Their snarled 'sir' was spelt 'cur'. We tried not to let it bother us. After all, we'd be home in a month while these poor sods had to sweat it out in this hell of a climate for at least six months or more. Not that it hadn't its compensations. To lie outside the tent on an absolutely still night looking up at what seemed a white sky it was so dense with stars, and hear Miles Davis' trumpet come from a hand-wound gramophone two tents away, was to know an almost mystical thrill.

We were lying in the cockpit of the world. No place was older in terms of man, and it made me feel ant-like, crawling about obsessed by my mortgage and my next film part. By the morning, though, I was back in the army and back at work. One of the first sequences called on me to lead a platoon of soldiers up a hill to deal with an 'enemy' compound entrenched at the top. This seemed straightforward enough. A hill was found, a platoon mustered, and the director (acting major) organised the action. I was told to go to a certain tree and blow a whistle, then move up to a marked boulder and fire my pistol, then cut, and they would do the dialogue close-ups back in Elstree. So, like any one of Pavlova's dogs, I went through the described motions with the promise of lunch at the end of it. It was gruelling work. It is very hot in Aden, and a hill is a hill anywhere, and after about three goes at charging up the hill and down again I was feeling like a very laboured Duke of York. Besides, the troops were giving me a hard time with their remarks, particularly about my heterosexuality. I would be glad to get this sequence over. The director consulted with the real army colonel. 'Let's go for a take,' said our director.

All went as rehearsed until I got to the rock, but when I fired my pistol as scripted, a volley of answering fire came from the top of the hill! I was utterly taken aback; this wasn't in the script. I looked up, and there along the rim of the hill, in sculpted silhouette, was a solemn row of immense Arabs pointing their rifles directly at us. I saw the flash from their muzzles, a pinging sound went up under my nose and grit from the rock went in my eye. I was down on the ground in a flash.

'Are you all right, sir?' The voice came from a young corporal who was just behind me. A moment ago he'd been calling me a poof, now he was calling me 'sir'.

We were lying about halfway between the menacing Arabs at the top of the hill and its bottom, where a film director was dancing about doing his nut.

The voice of the real colonel came over the wind on a metallic Tannoy, 'Who is the officer in charge?'

Six pairs of eyes turned on me.

'Listen,' I muttered, 'I'm not in your bloody army, I'm playing a part in a picture – for money. I joined Equity not the Yorkshire Light Yeomanry.'

The Tannoy voice came wisping up the hill again. 'Will the officer take appropriate action?'

'What do you want us to do, sir?' This time it was the little sergeant speaking.

'I don't know,' I exclaimed wildly, 'I tell you, I'm not an officer.'

'Platoon awaits orders, sir,' replied the sergeant impassively.

The young corporal stood up, swearing and lifted his Sten gun to his shoulder. Next moment, he was on his face, blood spurting from his arm, and thigh and knee-cap. He was so shocked he was laughing. Without knowing what I was doing, I knocked him out with my pistol, and he collapsed, blood running down the brown, parched hillside. The other young soldiers only stared.

'Sergeant,' I said. I was very cool, but I was very conscious of acting a part. This had to be a play. It couldn't be real.

'Sir?'

'Get two men to lift the corporal.'

'Sir.'

'Sergeant.'

'Sir?'

'How do we surrender?'

'White flag, sir.'

'Have you got a white flag?'

'No, sir.'

'Then what the hell do we do?'

'Platoon awaits orders, sir.'

I did the only thing I could think of. I took out my khaki hankie and offered it to the sergeant. 'Here, wave that at them.'

'Only officers can conduct a surrender, sir.'

This sergeant was obviously a survivor.

'Bloody hell,' I muttered and I rose up with my right arm held aloft, holding the hankie. I saw the rifles rise again, but this time there was no flash. I could hear the corporal moaning as he was being roughly dragged down the hill by the squaddies.

'Sergeant. Get the men to hell.'

'Sir.'

I stood as tall as I could on the incline, trying to look like a hero but feeling very much like a pansy actor. For no reason at all I suddenly found myself almost enjoying the tension. I turned away wondering what a bullet would feel like in the back. Would it be sore? Or would I feel nothing because of the adrenalin pumping through me? I decided to play safe, however, and said every prayer I knew on the way down. Nothing thudded into my back and as I reached the camera position again, the real colonel came forward and shook me warmly by the hand.

'Well done, young fella.'

My grip on his hand tightened, and I was sick all over his arm!

The picture was cancelled of course. Pity, it was a good part.

I didn't have much luck with the next job either. Christian Simpson, a producer at the BBC, had the idea of highlighting the race mix that was happening in London then, particularly in the Notting Hill Gate area which was rapidly becoming London's Harlem. He had the idea of a musical play contrasting the white rock and roll, as exemplified by the emerging skiffle groups, with the black rhythms of the calypso and West Indian song. I was to play the Scots leader of a folk group which specialised in Scottish traditional melodies and the script concerned my love for a coloured girl. Despite my recent Aden tan I was an acceptable white boy. I was coached to play a banjo, or rather to mime playing a banjo, by Peggy Seegar, Euan McColl's American wife, in their flat at Croydon. I was also rehearsed in a special song he had written for the programme, called 'The First Time Ever I Saw Your Face'.

It was a beautiful song, with a beautiful lyric and I was looking forward to singing on the transmission. Actually it wasn't exactly a

179

transmission, it was to be my first ever pre-recording. We were to telerecord it at the new Riverside Studio at Hammersmith. Rehearsals, however, were in Gower Street and wh.t a joy they were. The largely West Indian cast sang and laughed at every opportunity and the atmosphere was every bit as casual as in the Irish dramas. As the leader of the pop group, I had a fight scene with Cy Grant, the brother of Nadia Catouse, the coloured girl, with whom I had a most delicate love scene by the river bank. It was here I had to sing 'The First Time Ever'. Unfortunately, I had to sing it unaccompanied, and as it had to arise naturally out of our dialogue, there was little chance of my being given an introduction, still less a key. As a result, I started in a key that would have strangled a boy soprano. After a few lines, I broke off – and all hell was let loose in the studio. I hadn't realised that the 'take' had to be continuous just as if, indeed, it were a live transmission. Nobody had told us that. Everybody was a new boy to pre-recording then. So there was nothing for it but to set again as from the top, and go back over it all from the beginning. Understandably, I wasn't the most popular boy in the class that night. What bothered me, though, was that I had to try and carry that key for the song in my head all through the opening numbers, the preceding dialogue scenes, the fight and so on. When I finally came to the moment, I was so relieved that I sang it more like Paul Robeson.

But the biggest crisis was yet to come. It was the delicate matter of my kissing Nadia. In 1960, racial tensions were not so overt, but the Notting Hill riots were of recent memory, and the BBC were nervous about how viewers would accept a black and white embrace. The director was very sympathetic to Nadia's feelings but he had been given his ruling – no kiss. He suggested quietly to me that, perhaps, at the end of the song, I should put my arms around her, and lean in as if to kiss, and he would fade out the picture gradually before any actual labial collision. This had worked well enough in rehearsals, only because Nadia and I both broke off at the crucial moment, out of a mutual embarrassment, but on the take it was a different matter. Since I had 'blown' the song first time round, we had never actually got to this moment, but now, with all eyes on us, especially all those eyes in black faces all round the set, I leaned in to Nadia. I could see in her eyes a full understanding of my quandary, but I could also see she was the lovely girl I was supposed to be in love with, and so I leaned nearer – and nearer – and I kissed her!

Fade to black.

More pandemonium. Nadia gave me a hug. The West Indians were cheering, the floor manager was yelling for silence, and the director was heading angrily for me. But I just held Nadia all the tighter. Needless to say, the recording of *My People and Your People* was never shown, and I never got to make a single of 'The First Time Ever I Saw Your Face' as was planned. But Roberta Flack did some time later.

I was in disgrace all round after this, but I didn't mind. It was worth it, although I've never worked with West Indians since. I had a theatre offer next from Murray Macdonald to play in *The Amorous Prawn* at the Saville Theatre, but I was unable to do it because of a previous contract to do a space serial for ITV in Birmingham. I was annoyed about this because the part in the play was a good one. Stanley Baxter played it instead, while I travelled up and down the new M1 motorway with Frank Finlay to the the ATV Studios where we were to be scientists for the six weeks of the serial. It was hack work, but good hack work, and it's what many professional actors have to do from time to time. Anyway I enjoyed old Frank's company.

Then Joan Geddes of Christopher Mann rang to tell me that I had been offered another television part – BBC this time. I was delighted to be told I would be working with Alastair Sim in *Mr Gillie*. Mr Sim was surprised at my getting co-star billing, but since the director was Jimmy MacTaggart it was perhaps not surprising. Jimmy and I seemed to have come a long way from Duror of Appin, and anyway, he owed me a favour for sacking me from the university dramatic club! I needn't have had any fears about Alastair Sim. He couldn't have been kinder, especially as I agreed to give him a lift in my car to and from his home in Nettlebed each day. He was the very best kind of Scottish actor: highly intelligent, articulate, sincere, unflashy but with an impish twinkle behind the donnish façade that warned you of the unexpected. What a lovely month of June it was. We got on very well, and the car journeys were veritable seminars as he ranged over the whole continent of his wide knowledge of every conceivable subject. I was sorry when the job came to an end. I felt I should have sat an exam!

We went up to Glasgow for the actual transmission, and the final few days were spent once again in the new Springfield Road Studios in Parkhead, no more than fifty yards from my old home in Williamson Street. Knowing I was going to be away for a week in Scotland, and as a surprise for Sheila, on my last night at home, after dinner, I decided to paper the kitchen. That was the sort of daft thing I did then. I was doing the dishes while Sheila was bathing the girls and I looked around the little kitchen. Then I thought, I should really have got round to putting that wallpaper up. After all, we'd bought the paper a while ago, but what with the early starts with Alastair, the long rehearsals at White City, and the long journeys home via Nettlebed, I'd never got round to it. At the weekends there seemed to be so much to catch up with – like sleep for instance. But standing there at the sink, I suddenly thought, why don't I just do it right now? I felt good, rehearsals had gone well, and I was looking forward to Glasgow the next day. Anyway, it would be a nice surprise for Sheila if I could do one wall at least. So I made my plans. I persuaded her to stay upstairs, have a long bath, and read a magazine in bed, rather than come down for television. I would clear up the kitchen, and we could have an early night since I was going off again next day. She agreed, and said she would pack a case for me, while I cleared up in the kitchen.

It was 6.15 a.m. when I finished!

I had worked all through the night, sustained by coffee and music from foreign stations on the radio. I felt good and had a cigarette as the dawn came up. I had only round the stove to do. Like all amateur decorators I kept the hard bits to the last. I took Sheila up a breakfast tray at seven. The bed-light was still on and the bed was covered in *Woman* and *Woman's Own* magazines. I kissed her awake, after I'd cleared the magazines.

'When did you come to bed?' she asked drowsily.

'You were asleep,' I lied glibly, 'I'd better be off.'

I was catching the 7.30 a.m. train from Cookham station – change at Maidenhead for Paddington – Circle Line to Notting Hill Gate – Central to White City and cross the road to Wood Lane. I had done it so often. We would all get the afternoon train from Euston, except Mr Sim who was flying.

'Got everything?' Sheila asked, still half asleep.

'Except my wits about me.'

I went in and wakened the girls and let myself out the back door. The place stank of wallpaper paste, but at least it was still up on the wall and all trace of my all-night efforts had been cleared. I thought it looked pretty good. Nice and bright and country-kitchen. I hoped she liked it. She should. She chose it. Anyway, it'd be an eye opener for her when she came down to start her day. I liked to surprise her from time to time.

I whistled my way down to the station, and felt just as good as I waited for the connection at Maidenhead. It wasn't until I got into

Jonathan at 13

Mother at Southend 1961

*Looking up at
Christopher Lee!
Bray Studios 1963*

the train for Paddington that the trouble started. I don't know whether it was the heat of the summer day, the lack of ventilation in the old-fashioned carriage, or my nocturnal activities catching up with me: whatever it was, I was beginning to feel very dopey. I tried to pull myself together and I think my efforts to do so were worrying the lady opposite me. I caught her eyes staring over her newspaper at me. I gave a kind of cross-eyed smile of reassurance, but the carriage was already swimming about me. I wanted to open the window, but I didn't want to go into all the necessary negotiations. I was beginning to nod. I couldn't stop myself. I would wake with a start, and stare round me as if I'd just fallen through the roof. Everyone else seemed to be intent on their newspapers, but I could tell from their stiff shoulders and set necks that they were only showing that very English reserve. They knew exactly what I was trying to do – to stay awake. But slowly and inevitably I felt myself slipping, letting go, sliding inexorably into the abyss . . .

I was wakened by a gentle tapping on my shoulder. I tried to shrug it off, I was so cosy and comfortable, but the gentle tapping persisted, and I opened my eyes. I was still on the train, still in the carriage, but my head was lying in the lap of the lady who had been sitting opposite. I jerked up my head, almost dislocating my neck, blushing crimson.

'Gosh, I'm so sorry. I – '

'It's quite all right; you must have been very tired,' said the well-dressed lady, brushing her skirt.

'What happened?'

'I noticed you were having some difficulty staying awake. Then you just pitched forward and landed on my lap.'

'Oh, blimey!'

'You looked so peaceful, I hadn't the heart to disturb you. Now I must run. You will excuse me. My daughter will be wondering. Good morning.'

'Good morning.' I rubbed my neck and couldn't help laughing.

Clive Donner, the film director, saw *Mr Gillie*, and asked me to come in and see him at the Anglo-Amalgamated offices in Wardour Street.

'As soon as you walked in I could see the star quality, but as soon as you opened your mouth I could see you were your own worst enemy!'

These were Clive's first words to me, but it didn't stop him hiring me to play the lead in his next film at Merton Park Studios. *Marriage of Convenience* concerned a convict's escape from a registry office to take his revenge on his bride, and I was to play the convict. Larry Wilson was a Cockney, but that didn't worry me unduly. The problem about playing the part was that I had to ride a Vespa scooter, and I'd never been on one in my life. Still, it couldn't be worse than riding Big Ben, so it was arranged by Jack Greenwood, the film's producer, that Merton Park Studios would send me out a brand-new scooter over the weekend, and on Monday morning I would ride it back for shooting in Kingston Market that day. I spent Saturday and Sunday going up and down the lanes around Cookham, and I was sufficiently proficient, if not skilled, to drive the thing to the studios on the Monday morning. By the afternoon, I'd got so cocky on it that I was flying about like Geoff Duke – so much so that when the actual take was under way, Anglo-Amalgamated, not being noted for their largesse, hadn't bothered to pay for police guidance for shooting in a public place. Clive just told me, 'Head off how you like. Harry Corbett will follow in our police car and we'll follow in our camera car. When we get enough footage, we'll signal you to stop.'

Unfortunately, no one told the real police this, and as the chase got underway through Kingston, a real police car interpolated itself between me and our film police car.

Of course, I didn't realise this, except to think isn't Harry Corbett a good driver! I began to think they were taking it all rather seriously – horns tooting, sirens wailing – and no sign at all of the camera car. It wasn't until I turned up an alleyway and ran out of petrol that I stopped, and turned, grinning. 'What kept you, then?'

I was pounced on by two policemen, who were not Equity members, but had me in a half-Nelson against a wall in minutes. Luckily, the film police car came up the alley just in time to stop me from getting a thumping. Clive, being an astute director, had kept his camera running and got an extra realism free, but it was a near thing for me. I have never been lucky with the police.

Somehow, the film got finished, including some delightful location days on the south coast at Wareham. The convict haircut I had for it fortunately grew in again in time, but its severity did me quite well in my next job as a crew-cut jazz man for BBC. I had to play a trumpet in the Zombie night-club for another six-part serial, *Here Lies Miss Sabry*. It was to be directed by Dennis Vance, who by this time had married Claire Isbister, my girlfriend in *Redgauntlet*. Although I was miming to Dizzy Gillespie, I was particularly pleased to kid quite a few people that I could really play the trumpet. A lot of people said it was easy for me because I'd been blowing mine for quite a long time.

I had a call to my home from Callum Mill, the director of the Citizens Theatre, Glasgow. With the candour that is so much part of the man, he said he was in a little bit of a difficulty. Ian Bannen had been asked about being the Citizens' Hamlet, and the first Scot to play the Dane since John Laurie. But they had run into a snag because of Ian's film commitments, and would I, by any chance, be free, and would I like to think of playing Hamlet?

'When do I start?' was my immediate response.

I had to take an overnight train to Glasgow and, lying in the sleeper, I read the Penguin *Hamlet*, making suggested cuts. Callum and I met for breakfast in the Central Hotel next morning and compared cuts. They were virtually identical. I knew it was going to be all right. Callum was a theatre man through and through, as an adjudicator, lecturer, actor and now director. He had no time for fancy theories or psychological imperatives. For him, directing was merely a matter of translating scripts into stage terms and placing the actors so they could be seen and heard. That's all we decided to do with *Hamlet*, let the lines speak for themselves. We were reluctant about the cuts, but we wanted to tell a clean story within three hours and thought that some of the First Folio material might go. Anyway, if we played the full-length version at the Citizens, half the audience would be leaving before the end to get the last trams out of the Gorbals. The only controversial decision taken was to excise much of the political element within the play itself which was to reduce Fortinbras at the end to mere dumb show, but this was on my hint that effectively the play might end, verbally, at least, on Hamlet's line: 'The rest is silence'. So we proceeded in the three weeks left to us to rehearse the great piece for its two-week run. It seemed to me an awful lot of work for such a short run, but I never hesitated. I might never get the opportunity again.

Many actors have different ways of preparing their *Hamlet*. Some make exhaustive research into the history of the times, the medical reason for his apparent procrastination, the psychological basis for his Oedipal attitude to Gertrude and many other well-known Hamlet theories. For me, I humbly acceded to the primacy of the text and set about learning the lines. With my dear father's help, who by now had retired from working, and was retained by Jim and

186

me as our 'press agent', I walked along the banks of the River Clyde, where it is yellow and brown by the Dalmarnock power station, and while he fed me the cues, I tried to put the well-known words into my head. The only trouble with this method was that my father kept reading all the parts, rather than just my cues. When I asked him why, as I grew more irritated, he said, 'Hold it, John, hold it. This is good stuff.'

So with that sort of view from the proletariat, I was happy to continue in my study. Sometimes I would be sitting in the back bedroom working on a soliloquy, while outside in the street there would be a crash of bottles and another Saturday night rammy would be in progress, or else maudlin songs would creep up from a family party in the next close. 'How all occasions do conspire against me!'

The Citizens company were not unduly impressed by me, and I'm quite sure they would have preferred Ian Bannen, so that when we came to the first night on 3 October 1960, I had nothing to lose but my head. So, with a quick sign of the cross in the foyer, I made my entrance through the audience and stepped up on to the stage. Callum had assembled the cast in a semi-circle to face me. I could see them all staring at me fearfully. I felt just as bad as they did, until I noticed Queen Gertrude's cheek twitching, and I suddenly realised, this is just a play, and what is more important, these people are looking to me to lead them through the rest of the night. This is what the term 'leading man' is. It gave me a new courage and I turned round to face the audience myself, at which all my courage fled me:

O! that this too too solid flesh would melt!

but technique prevailed and somehow the words came out.

Everything went by in a haze until the interval, and it wasn't until I said the dreaded 'To be ...' that the first magic moment happened – by accident. In the first rehearsals I had experimented with dropping the knife on to a stool on which I had my foot between 'To be' and 'or not to be', and in one rehearsal, it stuck beautifully, quivering on its point. Callum thought it a wonderful effect, but unfortunately it never ever worked again and by the dress rehearsal we had dropped it as business. But in my first-night nerves, I reverted to the original move and on the line, dropped it, and by the grace of all the gods, it stuck! In my amazement, I inadvertently paused, and heard the audience say audibly in one vast whisper 'or not to be'. I improvised a quick nod of agreement and countered,

187

'That is the question'. The dagger didn't stick every night, and by the end of the first week, I had cut the business again, but during the two-week run, I never ever said, 'or not to be'. The audience said it or willed it every night.

The notices were wonderful. Sir John Martin-Harvey's belt had obviously brought me luck. The houses were packed, especially the school matinees. It was often hard to get a total silence, but we usually managed it by the end, and my last line as the prince in this production was, 'The rest is s . . .'. I faded on the sibilant in order to work the silence for the final mimed action, but in one of the school matinees, a little girl's voice wailed plaintively from the auditorium, 'Oh, don't die!'

There were, of course, the usual production incidents. Like all actors, I fell into a routine, and one nightly practice was to obtain a cigarette from one of the ladies-in-waiting. But one evening the poor girl said she didn't have any cigarettes, but would a Mint Imperial do, Horatio and I politely accepted the alternative and were munching away when our cue came up to go on to the gravediggers. There was no time either to swallow or spit out. We were on.

The stage direction says, 'Hamlet and Horatio enter in grave discourse.' What I was really saying, under my breath and beneath my raised cloak, was, 'What the hell do I do with this damned sweetie?'

'Swallow the damned thing,' answered Horatio, unconcernedly.

I bit and gnashed and I chewed and by the time my cue came up and Yorick's head emerged on the gravedigger's shovel, I had disposed of it. Unfortunately, the debris, still in my larynx, gave an unexpectedly lacrimose effect to the line, 'I knew him well, Horatio.' This produced such a good effect that I resolved to keep the interpretation in, although I dispensed with the Mint Imperial. This is theatrical serendipity.

My visitors were many and varied, but none as unexpected as Tony K. He had lived round the corner from us in Parkhead and from being an amateur ne'er-do-well had graduated *cum laude* as a successful professional. This he told me when he came to the dressing-room one night and wanted to speak to me alone. He had heard on the juice-of-the-grapevine that I had had my car broken into at the stage door and had my transistor radio pinched. I said that was quite right. With that, and with a quick look over his shoulder, he produced no less than half a dozen transistor radios and asked which one I wanted.

'Where did you get all these, Tony?'
'Ask no questions, friend, and you get no shit. Whit yin's yours?'
'None.'
'Right. Whit yin wid ye like tae be yours?'
'That one.'
I pointed to one which was very much superior to the one which had been stolen, and I felt not the slightest twinge of guilt.
'Fine. A' I can tell ye is it came frae a good home.'
'Would you like a drink, Tony?'
'No, thanks. Don't drink. Gets ye intae trouble.'
With that he was at the door. 'I must say, I like yer English patter, John.'
'That's Shakespeare, Tony.'
'S'at a fact?'
Exit Tony Kempton – Glasgow 'gentleman'.
Also exit a fellow Glaswegian – Hamlet the Dane alias John Cairney – carrying one Philips transistor radio!

I didn't go very far as it happened, only from Glasgow to Stirling, or from the ramparts of Elsinore to the battlements of Stirling Castle. John Jacob, the director, said he had wanted a young James Mason, who could sing like Noel Harrison. I was the nearest he could get, so I joined Lee Montague and Julia Arnall in Stirling for night shooting which was to represent the escape sequence from a German schloss. My part, as the English student earning a living as a troubadour in a café who gets mixed up with the resistance, was good, but hardly memorable. However, my night's shoot at Stirling Castle certainly was.

I had finished my bit that night and was waiting for Lee to complete his so that we could go back to the hotel in the car together. Having nothing better to do, I wandered around the historic corridors, fascinated by the military paraphernalia and regimental tartanry. It was the home, after all, of the Argyle and Southern Highlanders, a very famous regiment. Being aware at one point of the call of nature, as they say, I began to look for the appropriate office, but with no luck.

Just then a squaddie came along the corridor towards me, trailing a huge Alsatian. I asked the soldier where the nearest lavatory was, and he pointed behind him, 'Second on the right, mate.' And he and the dog continued on their night patrol.

I thanked him and strolled off in the direction he had indicated.

189

When I came to the area on the right, there were, in fact, three doors. I hesitated, then opted for the centre one. The room was stygian black as I opened the door, and as I was feeling for the light switch on the right-hand side, an officer-voice enquired, 'Can I help you?'

I jumped – 'Sorry' – and immediately closed the door. I tried the other two doors, but both rooms were absolutely empty. By this time, I thought I might as well wait till I got back to the hotel, and started to return along the corridor. I met the squaddie again still on his rounds, and told him that I had blundered in on his CO.

'What are you talking about?' he asked in an English accent. (I am always surprised by how many Englishmen serve in Scottish regiments.)

'I went to the door on the right as you suggested – '

'I didn't say no door on the right, I meant the second corridor.'

'Oh, I thought you meant – '

'Show me.'

I retraced my steps along the corridor and turned into the area where the three doors were, at which the dog stopped dead in its tracks and started to whine. It would not go any further.

The soldier said, 'Do you mean that door there?' pointing to the centre door.

I nodded.

'S'truth,' he said and pulled the dog away, indicating for me to follow.

'What's the matter?' I said.

'There ain't no officer in there.'

'I'm telling you, I heard a voice.'

'Couldn't 'ave, mate. That was the old CO's room – '

'I told you it was an officer,' I broke in.

''E shot hisself two year ago!'

'What?'

I was out of the corridor, and back down into the courtyard within seconds. Lee Montague was waiting with Julia. 'What kept you?' he said.

We returned to London the next day, and I didn't have the heart to tell anyone about my ghost voice. But I told my children when I got home again. They were most impressed.

I was still with large Alsatians in my next job. I had to play a homicidal maniac about to strangle Maureen Beck when she is rescued by a huge dog, which crashes through the roof of a greenhouse on top of me. The film was being shot at Twickenham Studios for television and its star was Louis Hayward, the former Hollywood swashbuckler. By now, he was more buckled than swashed, but he still had that ineffable charm all the old stars had. This was my first villain and I was relishing it. Just as the Devil gets all the best tunes so the baddies get all the best lines! However, they sometimes get some crummy action and this was my feeling as I looked at that greenhouse roof, then at the dripping mouth of the Alsatian, and then at the director, Norman Harrison.

'Norm,' I said.

'Don't worry, John, the handler says he's like a lamb.'

'I'm sure he is,' I said, 'it's his dog I'm worried about.'

'He's on a leash.'

'He's what?'

'It's a long, nylon cord coming down from the roof. The handler's up there with him all the time.'

'But what happens when Rin Tin Tin's down here?'

The debate went on and I wasn't at all convinced. I didn't like the idea of a full-grown Alsatian landing on me from a great height – no matter how strong the nylon cord. I just didn't like Alsatians. Louis Hayward pointed out that Victor Mature had the same worry about lions.

'But this isn't a lion,' said Norman.

'You could have fooled me,' I said.

The upshot was that my stand-in did the shot for an extra tenner. I would have gladly paid him myself. He put on my jacket and, kneeling down, put his hand round Maureen's throat as she lay on the floor of the greenhouse.

On 'action' the brute jumped, the cord broke, Maureen screamed, the stand-in was thrown clear, his arm held fast between the great jaws. It took two men to pull him off. The jacket was ruined, poor guy had a broken arm and needed a row of stitches.

'Vic certainly had a point,' said Mr Hayward.

In my next picture – what a silly phrase – at the start of the year, I was reunited with Dirk Bogarde. *Victim* was not my picture, but the next picture that I was in. It was a thriller with a homosexual theme, which was very daring for the time, in which I played an immemorable policeman. This policeman's lot was not a happy one in that film.

191

Christopher Mann's office then arranged that I should meet Charles Schneer. He was a Columbia producer, seconded to Screen Gems in order to set up a television series, based on *Gulliver's Travels*. Following tests in Twickenham, I was chosen to play Gulliver.

'I'm gonna make you a star!' The voice sounded even more the archetypal American producer, because he rang me at home at seven o'clock in the morning. I remember taking the call sitting up in bed, thinking how uncivilised. But I was delighted to accept his offer, even though negotiations hit a sticky patch at one point. Not only did he make calls before breakfast, but he worked on Saturday mornings. This was really no concern of mine, however, until he asked me to come in for a conference on the Saturday morning of the Wembley game between England and Scotland that year. Brian Maller another Scot, and the film representative at Christopher Mann, was to accompany me in order to work out contract details. I remember, as we talked in that office, I was concerned only about getting away in time to get to Wembley, or at least pick up my ticket from Frank Maguire at the Piccadilly Hotel. But I had to sit and listen to Charlie droning on about what a great series it was going to be and what a big star I was going to become. I was not over-impressed. I never was by film executives. Looking at him behind that big desk, it brought to mind my father's definition of an executive: 'rolls of fat descending in ever-increasing circles'. It's one way to keep a sense of proportion about office display. The bigger the desk the smaller the man. 'Just picture them naked and you'll never be nervous,' my dad had said. Looking at Charlie, it was a horrible thought! I was aware that he was now going on about how he couldn't pay that kind of money for someone he hadn't heard of till I had done the test.

That was too much for me. I stood up, saying, 'Look, "Mr Sneer", I hadn't heard of you till a couple of weeks ago, and now because of this blooming meeting, I'm going to miss my Wembley ticket. So you can stuff your job. I'm off.'

Despite Brian's very proper attempts to restrain me, I went. I did meet Frank at the hotel, we did get to the game – and Scotland were annihilated by England! After the game, Frank and I sat with other ex-St Mungo pupils, staring down into our pints. Did I walk out on a good job for this!

Sure enough, Sunday morning, before breakfast, Schneer was on the phone again. 'We didn't get to conclude our business,' he said. 'What I had in mind was . . .'

A toughie cookie was Charlie Schneer.

My mother had stayed on at Windom's Way so that I could take Sheila on the *Gulliver* location to Spain. We stayed at the Rex Hotel in San Feliu de Guixols, and treated the whole thing like a holiday rather than a working location, although as the star of the series, I certainly had to work. The leading lady was an attractive English model, not an actress at all, and some of the takes were 'extended' to say the least. At one time, we had both to rise, dripping from the water, and embrace sexily. I saw Sheila rise from under her sun umbrella and walk up the beach towards the trailers.

Good, I thought to myself, my wife's jealous.

She said later she was only going back for her sunglasses!

It was lovely being with her again, on her own again, away from the children and domestic matters. I'd almost forgotten what funny company she could be.

'Let's treat it as a second honeymoon,' I had said.

'Why second?' she said. 'We never had a first!'

After dinner with the unit at the hotel in the evenings, we took to wandering round the little Spanish town on our own, but one night we decided to eat out. We strolled about San Feliu looking for a typical Spanish restaurant that wouldn't have film people. One particular bar looked promising. But going in, we saw our wardrobe master sitting in the centre of a group of young Spanish boys. He was a cheerful Londoner, the life and soul of the unit, with a quip for everybody as he whirled around all day in a perspiring circle dealing with everybody's needs and wants on the set. But now, in the late evening, he sat, an inscrutable mandarin figure, in an immaculate white suit, smoking a cigar slowly and carefully, with the boys' hands playing all about him. It was an eerie and frightening spectacle, and we didn't want to know. And we didn't want him to see that we saw him either. That little Spanish place, far from promising, was suddenly quite sinister. We scurried back to the hotel, and had something in our room.

Next morning, he greeted us as cheerfully as ever. 'What did you two get up to last night, then?'

I might have asked him the same, but that was the last thing I wanted to know.

We returned to London with the exteriors safely in the can, and with a couple of weeks of interiors due at the Twickenham Studios. It was a funny business filming the *Gulliver*. I was either looking down at nothing at all, which would later be a tiny Lilliputian, or I was playing the scene with a crick in my neck, staring up at nothing at all, which would later be a giant. It was a tiring process. The effects were to be achieved by a complicated technical procedure, master-minded by animator, Ray Harryhausen, which was part cartoon animation and part live action. For instance, the late Patrick Troughton, playing the Lilliputian mayor, was encouraged to flail his arms about and overact generally, which was no trouble to Patrick, except that he would turn up on the screen later about two inches high. Similarly, I was having to cope with gargantuan sections of tables and chairs, which reduced me to the appropriate pygmy size. No doubt it would look believable, but it made for a long day's work. When the pilot was completed, I was put on standby at a very considerable wage, and told to go home until I heard further from them.

Having been given a large part of the summer free, we moved house, to a very modern bungalow at Maidenhead Court, a select group of houses set in a forest development near Boulter's Lock on the banks of the Thames. We were now among the stockbrokers and lawyers and shady characters who were 'something in the city'. The only difference was I was 'at home' when they were 'in the city'. It was good to be around the house when everyone else was at work. There was a pleasant feeling of truanting. And it let me get on with odd jobs, like filling up holes in the road. It was a mark of high caste in Berkshire to live in an un-made-up road. The local council left heaps of gravel at the end of the road and it was the responsibility of each householder to fill in the holes along his own frontage. One sunny afternoon, I was working happily doing just that with my barrow, rake and spade, banging away at the heaps I was making, when a big car came round the corner and stopped by me. A very haughty female inclined her head at the passenger seat window. An older man was driving.

'My man,' she said.

I supposed she was meaning me. I shuffled over.

'Can you direct us to Bella Vista?'

This was the name of the big house at the end of the drive, on whose grounds our modern homes were built. I told her it was just round the corner, and quickly positioned my barrow so that their car went over the heaps I was working on. That saved me a lot of work with the back of the spade!

Some nights later, the phone rang, and I could tell by Sheila's very English voice that it was somebody we didn't know. It was the new people who'd just moved into Bella Vista. They wanted us to come to dinner.

'But we don't know them,' I said.

'What does that matter, a dinner's a dinner,' said Sheila. 'And anyway I've always wanted to see that house.'

So, we got a babysitter and went to dinner. The new owners turned out to be the couple from the big car.

'Didn't we see you working on the road?' enquired the haughty lady when we introduced each other in the hallway.

'You did,' I replied.

'I thought you worked for the council,' she laughed.

'But I do,' I said solemnly, taking Sheila's hand quickly and disappearing into the crowd of guests.

'What was all that about?' she asked.

'Well, it's the council's gravel I use, isn't it?'

'What are you talking about?'

'Snobs,' I said.

It didn't take long for our haughty host to track me down. 'You naughty boy. I've been checking up on you; you are the actor chap, aren't you? And you making me think you were a workman.'

And she and her husband laughed again. But I didn't. What else is an 'actor chap' but a workman?

Such social hazards had to be faced quite often. As soon as I was in the local *Maidenhead Advertiser*, the invitations started to flow in, and after a few television appearances, I was soon a minor social celebrity. This could be good fun too. Sheila and I were asked to attend a meeting of the local Civic Society at the Ferry Hotel.

'Why are we going?' I asked.

'Just to be civil,' answered Sheila, 'and no doubt they want you to add a little colour to proceedings.'

'A bit of red among the true blue, I suppose.'

I was put on to a panel when we got there and at the end of the meeting questions were invited from the audience. One very earnest young lady from Stanford University, who had a residence at Cliveden asked why her great country of the United States didn't have the equivalent of the Civic Society.

'But you have,' I said.

'We do?'

'Yes – the Mafia.'

I wasn't invited back to the next month's meeting.

Jimmy MacTaggart invited me back to Glasgow to play the lead in a thriller called *Drop Dead*. My father was most impressed watching the location filming up and down Woodlands Road. He still couldn't believe I could drive a car, and was amazed that I could manage to bring the sports car on to the required marks for the take.

I was in Glasgow when I received a telegram. 'Report Twicken-ham. Shooting commences immediately location.' And it was signed Charles H. Schneer. But it wasn't for *Gulliver* as I expected. It was to fly immediately to Rome to begin filming on an epic, *Jason and the Argonauts*.

As Schneer put it when he met me, 'It's not the lead part, but hell, we're paying you anyway, we might as well make you work.'

Beverly Cross and I flew out from London together. He was the writer on the picture and was delivering the final draft. He refused to be parted from it. 'It's worth a year's money, this.'

It was my first time in Italy, and I was thrilled to be in Rome. We had to go on next day to the unit, but now we had most of the day and all of the night before us.

'Where do you want to go?' asked Beverly.

'The Vatican,' I replied without hesitation. 'What about you?'

'Via Veneto.'

'Right,' I said, 'we'll do the Via Veneto first, and then go on to the Vatican.'

Beverly laughed. 'I think a better order would be the opposite way about. Things don't start to happen on the Via Veneto till later on. So let's do your Vatican.'

We got a taxi outside the hotel, and I was most surprised at Bev's Italian. He told me that he didn't speak any Italian, only French. All he did was add an 'o' on to everything. We arrived at Il Vaticano, coming to St Peter's Square among a long line of taxis. We stepped out of the cab on to a red carpet.

'How nice of them,' said Beverly.

With our dark London suits and our pale London faces, and with Bev still carrying his briefcase, we found ourselves being escorted up a flight of steps and into a crowded reception room. It was some sort of function or other. I was still too agog at being in Rome at all, never mind at St Peter's, and here I was in one of the papal apartments. I couldn't help thinking how theatrical all the little red caps looked and all the long, black capes.

'It's just like *The Thrie Estaites*,' I said to my companion.

In no time we had a drink in our hands and were talking to two American priests, but I made the mistake of asking an attendant where the Sistine Chapel was. He replied in a mumble of Italian, then, with a signal, summoned a colleague who asked me in English who I was. I told him proudly I was with Charles Schneer's company in Rome making *Jason and the Argonauts* for Screen Gems. I had my back to a wall in a flash, held there by the pikes of two Swiss Guards. I had always thought they were merely ceremonial, but take it from me they can be effectively utilitarian. I was frogmarched ignominiously out of the room and deposited abruptly in St Peter's Square within two minutes. No red carpet treatment now. I don't suppose I was the first Catholic to be thrown out of the Vatican. Bev followed up in the rear, protesting to one of the lounge-suited officials that he'd been thrown out of better places in his time.

'Where's your briefcase?' I asked.

'My God – the script!'

'Say a quick prayer to St Anthony,' I proffered, trying to be helpful, but he was already running back indoors.

He re-emerged holding it triumphantly like any Chancellor of the Exchequer. 'God, I need a drink,' he said.

By this time, I had a taxi waiting. Bev fell in. 'Via Veneto,' I called to the driver.

We reached the unit next day by train from Rome. Palinuro was a tiny fishing port just north of Salerno. The unit had been there for a week getting things ready for shooting, and Charlie himself came to meet us. He was a different man from the one we knew in Wigmore Street. This was an American tourist – in sunhat, sunglasses and sunburn.

'Welcome, you guys,' he almost shouted. 'Come and have a drink and meet the boys. You got the final draft, Bev?'

Beverly handed it over, with almost tangible relief. I met Don Chaffey, the director and he told me I was to play Hylas, the water carrier on the *Argo*, Jason's galley-ship.

On my first morning in front of the cameras, Don introduced me to Nigel Green who was the Hercules in the film, the character with whom I would be most closely involved in the action.

Big Nigel looked down at me in my little white belted tunic and sandals, my hair newly curled with tongs, and laughed. 'I see they've picked a queer to play a queer.'

'Who's a queer?' I countered angrily.

Mr Green and I are not going to get on, I thought.

Palinuro was a small place and the film unit was a large one. One result of this was that Gary Raymond and I were billeted in a garage of the house taken by the production manager, Johnny Dark, and his Danish girlfriend. The open garage with its Mediterranean views was no real hardship, as all we needed was a place to put our heads at night. Most of the days were spent on the beach or on the deck of the *Argo*, a fantastic recreation of the Grecian galley created for the film. My job was to go up and down the alleyway between the rowers, giving them water from time to time. While doing this, I was often taunted about my skinny figure by the musclemen cast as the rowers. They were constantly flexing their biceps and comparing each others deltoids and trapezoids! They were muscles for show, I'm afraid, not for use as one instance showed.

While filming out in the bay one afternoon, the ship, which was powered by a hidden engine down below, suddenly stopped and we found ourselves becalmed. A grimy, sweaty, unshaven face, under an oily old cap, suddenly popped up from the hatch beneath the actors' feet to announce the Italian equivalent of 'engine failure'. Tod Armstrong, our Hollywood-made leading man playing Jason, was suitably annoyed, but the older hands, like Laurence Naismith and Andrew Faulds, just sought out the shade and had a nap. Everything of course came to a halt, and it was realised that in order to get back at all, the rowers would have to actually row the ship to harbour. The oars were, after all, practical implements.

'No problem,' said the chorus of he-men, and they set about eagerly to their task. For ten minutes. Sure enough, we were moving, but only just. They put up the sail, but there was little wind. 'All hands to the oars!' shouted our director. Gary Raymond and I had particular satisfaction in taking over from two of the huskiest musclemen who collapsed in a faint after half an hour, and it was we, along with the make-up men and hairdressers and sundry stand-ins, who brought the *Argo* to harbour. It was the body-builders who 'ran out of steam!' I was never taunted about my physique again.

I had to die in the film by being crushed to death by the 'monster'. But the monster was once again a technical effect created by Ray Harryhausen, who had done the same kind of work in the *Gulliver* series. Don Chaffey told me just to run along the beach looking back every now and again over my shoulder, and when I got to a particular point, I was just to fall flat, then turn and keep my eye-line on a particular cloud. But the clouds kept moving! I was then to hold it till he said, 'Cut.' I did this, feeling very foolish, but they tell me it is one of the most realistic sequences in the finished film. Children, especially, seem to enjoy it. No one believes that the foot that crushed me to death was painted in six months later.

We moved to the Cinacitta studios in Rome for the interiors. By this time I was walnut brown and, thanks to the running about on location, as fit as I'd ever been in my life. To all intents and purposes I was an Italian. I had just enough superficial hold on the language to get by in every ordinary situation, and I looked more native than many of the young local actors who were desperately dying their hair blond and red in order to get work in the Americano films. This was a period long before the spaghetti westerns. The epics being shot in Rome and Spain at that time were multi-million-dollar projects. Nothing was spared in their pro- duction – except taste perhaps. I was part of the English Circus, as they called it: a coterie of classically trained actors who moved around from epic to epic, playing feature parts and taking the lines, so that the stars were allowed to take the limelight, and the Italian actors the small parts and extras. It was a good working arrange- ment, and fortunes were made on all sides. John Crawford, an actor I met at that time, had never been home for years. He just went from one film to the other throughout the continent, playing his small part effectively and expensively. I suppose it could be said I was doing the same, even though I was under contract to Uncle Charlie at the time.

On my last day, the action called for Hercules and Hylas to find the treasure cave. This meant pushing a supposedly heavy door open and being blinded by the dazzle of the gold and silver within. This was created by a special arc-lamp being focused directly on our faces as we opened the door. I noticed a sort of sizzle sound coming from the uncovered lamp, but since we were in an Italian studio, where everything was dubbed later, nobody worried about extra noises, and we got on with the action. Eventually, the sequence was completed and so were our parts in the film. After a final check, Nigel and I were formally released.

'See you, then,' he said to me gruffly in the dressing-room.

'Sure,' I said, as we politely shook hands, and went our separate ways. I didn't care much if I never saw Nigel again, and I suppose the same held for him. You don't have to love everyone you work with. I had a last stroll around Rome after dinner and sat with Giselle, a French girl, on the Spanish Steps.

Back in the hotel room next morning, I got up after breakfast and started to pack for the flight back to London a few hours later. The room was full of the early morning yellow Rome sun, and when I opened the wardrobe door, it took me a moment to get used to the change of light. I started to put my things on the bed, going backwards and forwards to the wardrobe. As I did so I thought the room was getting darker. It was almost like an eclipse of the sun, but I paid little attention and carried on packing. Then as I turned from the wardrobe again into the room, everything went completely black. I couldn't see a thing. I had the horrifying sensation that it was the end of the world or something. I kept rubbing my eyes. They weren't sore, but I couldn't see. Then, in a panic, I realised I was blind. I let out a yell. A maid came running in and I just stood there, a coathanger in one hand and a pair of shoes in the other, yelling uncontrollably. She took the things from my hands, and pushed me back to sit on the bed.

I kept repeating to myself, meaninglessly, helplessly, 'I'm blind. Oh, God, I'm blind.'

People then came scurrying about me, and in a welter of female voices I found myself undressed again and put to bed. I was now mute with shock, and didn't know what to think. I had an almost nauseous feeling of suffocation. Being claustrophobic by nature, blindness was about the worst condition I could know.

Schneer himself arrived, having been summoned from the studios. 'I just want you to relax, and leave everything to us. We've got a guy coming. He'll attend to everything.'

I kept trying to turn my face away from the onslaught of after-shave and suntan lotion assailing me. The 'guy' he mentioned turned out to be an eye specialist. I could feel his expert fingers gently lift my eyelids.

'Ah,' came the response, and in a glissando of Italian, he told the unit interpreter that I had ultra-violet blindness, caused by long exposure to an open arc-lamp. He said it was a common condition that skiers know, which is why it is often called ski blindness. It is the effect of concentrated radiation which temporarily paralyses the eye function and causes blindness. There was no reason, with proper clinical treatment and rest, I shouldn't be back to normal within the week.

I almost cried with relief, and reached up to take his hand, but he was already gone and other hands put mine down, and helped me to get dressed. The heat of the sun seemed to hit me with the force of a blow as I was assisted down the steps of the hotel and towards the waiting limousine. The inside of the car was almost cold, because of the air-conditioning, and I settled back with relief. The car had hardly moved off when a hand found mine. I jumped in fright, and tried to pull it away, but a voice said, 'That you, mate? We're a right couple of Charlies.'

It was Big Nig. He had been blinded too. Of course, we were in the same sequence. It was that noisy arc. I knew it. Nigel kept a tight grip of my hand, reassuring me all the time. I felt myself warming

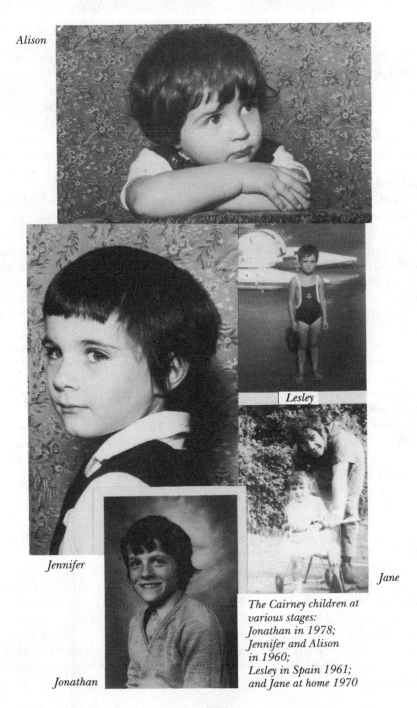

Alison

Lesley

Jennifer

Jane

Jonathan

The Cairney children at
various stages:
Jonathan in 1978;
Jennifer and Alison
in 1960;
Lesley in Spain 1961;
and Jane at home 1970

towards the big man, but all I said was, 'You'd better stop holding my hand, Nigel. People will think we're a couple of queers.'

He let go, laughing, and from that time Nigel Green became a dear friend. We soon found ourselves in another kind of interior, which was not quite hospital, but yet not hotel. The voices were English, and Irish too, and all female. Nigel insisted that we share the same room, and throughout the several days we were there, he never stopped talking. But such good talk. Theatre talk. Of actors, of directors, of theories he had about production and so much that showed him to be a much better mind than his location clowning had indicated. I loved hearing him talk like this.

To our surprise, we received visitors. The first thing we heard was a clink of bottles, and there was Andrew Keir, the Scots actor, who was in Rome on *Cleopatra*, and with him, two Welsh voices, who turned out to be Ivor and Richard Jenkins – the latter better known as Richard Burton. The story had gone all round the English film colony that two actors had had their faces blown off in a studio accident, and, typical of Burton, he had come to find out for himself, bringing a case of good champagne as an introduction. We finished most of it throughout that long evening. Being blindfolded by bandages, Nigel and I were bottle-fed by the two actors while Ivor sang Welsh songs quietly to himself in the background. It transpired that Burton had known Nigel in London in the same way that Andy Keir had known me in Glasgow. Ivor knew neither of us, but was quite oblivious I think. It was a wonderful experience, lying in the dark, my mouth full of champagne, listening to the music of Burton's Welsh voice. I drank in every word. Things got even better when Nigel and Richard got on to comparing Shakespearean ideas and swopping sonnets. Burton asked me about my own *Hamlet*, and I was delighted to tell him that I had unashamedly copied as much as I could remember of his, which I had seen at the Edinburgh Festival in 1951, especially his remarkable stillness.

He chuckled sonorously, as he opened another bottle, 'That's because I never know what to do with my hands.'

The day came when the specialist took off the bandages. Nigel cried out peremptorily, 'Do me first.' So the specialist took the bandages away. I could hear Nigel's immediate exclamation, 'God, you're an ugly bastard!' And when I saw the specialist's stubbled chin and large thick glasses, I thought I'd never seen anything more beautiful in my life. I then looked around me and saw other smiling faces. The voices that had attended us so calmly, and been party to our actors' ribaldry without a murmur, belonged to an order of white-robed nuns! 'Ye Gods!' roared Nigel. 'Get thee to a nunnery.'

We were advised to stay in Rome for a further week to make sure that normalcy was maintained. For some reason, Nigel didn't want to do that, and insisted on flying home to Brighton immediately. Poor Nigel died suddenly only a few years later. I was only too happy to stay on in Rome, especially as Columbia Pictures were paying all expenses. I lay back in a luxury hotel room and telephoned everybody I could think of while sipping expensive white wine. I even phoned my cousin in New York.

'What's wrong?' she exclaimed. 'Nothing,' I beamed into the receiver. 'Absolutely nothing at all.'

During this sybaritic hotel convalescence, I had a visit from Stuart Lyons, a bright young Scottish lawyer, who was now acting as a casting consultant for American films in Europe. We had never met before, but he had seen me at the Citizens and told me he'd been very impressed by my Malayan in *Windom's Way*. Would I like to come and meet Mr Mankiewicz?

'Joe Mankiewicz?'

'Mr Mankiewicz to you.'

'The director of *Cleopatra*?'

'The same. Since you were here I thought it would save us a plane fare bringing you out, so I got Charlie Schneer's permission to use you in Rome pending your *Gulliver* call-up in London. That is, if you're agreeable.

I was very agreeable, and with my hand on Stuart's shoulder, and wearing my dark glasses, I was led on to the set of *Cleopatra* to meet its director, Joseph L. Mankiewicz.

I wondered why he grinned at me. He was not given much to laughing. But he said at once, 'Sure, you'll do if Stu here thinks you can do it.'

'What's the part?'

'Phoebus,' said Stuart.

'He's Cleo's personal boy,' said Mr Mankiewicz.

'And he's blind,' added Stuart.

I almost dropped my sunglasses.

'John's been blind in a Rome clinic for the last two weeks,' Stuart told the famous director.

'Hell, there was no need to go that far!' said old Joe calmly, putting his pipe back in his mouth.

I happily attended Queen Elizabeth Taylor in Rome for several weeks. I wasn't asked to do much, merely to stand about in my little white tunic and sometimes sing to her in my made-up song. Alex North, the composer, came on the set and took it down in notation. He didn't realise I changed the tune on every take. More pleasurably, my main job was to stare sightlessly for hours at the costliest assemblage of pulchritude ever gathered to face a camera. I was glad I was only acting blind! My dialogue scenes were with Rex Harrison, who could certainly never be described as pulchritudinous. I found him as grumpy as Elizabeth was cordial, but given his uneasy position between la belle dame Taylor and Burton at that time, who can blame him for being short-tempered. I made particular friends with twelve-year-old Francesca Annis with whom I had to work, and we couldn't believe that we could be paid so much for doing so little for so long. I couldn't spend all that I got for expenses, so I took to putting it in the bottom of my case in the circular room I now had at the top of the Pensione Shelley in the Corso d'Italia near the Villa Borghese.

When I had enough lira in my suitcase I carried it down to the production office and asked them to convert it into return first-class tickets to bring Sheila and the girls to Rome. The day Sheila arrived with Jennifer and Alison (and Lesley in her tummy), it rained for the first time for months and it didn't stop raining till she left. Not that that spoiled the family enjoyment. On my days off we would do our tourist bit. 'Oh, not another church,' said four-year-old Alison. She was at her very prettiest then, having been a cover girl on a recent issue of *The Nursery World*. Sheila told me she had been inundated with offers for Alison to do commercials. But one actor in the family was enough, it was thought. Jennifer was seven and straight and serious and skinny. She didn't get half the attention that Alison did, but it didn't seem to worry her. She lived quite happily inside herself. Knowing the Italians' love of children, our ruse whenever we went into a crowded restaurant was to push Alison ahead of us. The waiters would so crowd round *la bella ragazza*, that we had a table in no time.

We all crammed into my little round room. It only possessed a single bed, but the signora in charge, understanding my needs, added another single bed and two camp-beds for the children. Showing a little enterprise, I tied our two single beds together with my tie. In the morning all we saw were two little heads peeping down at us from the end of our improvised double bed. In the night, the two singles had drifted apart, and we were lying on the floor.

At the end of a week I swept them all out to the airport in a studio limousine. Ironically, as soon as the plane took off, the sun came out again!

I had been slightly upgraded in the plot, and was given an extra scene to be shot in Alexandria, Egypt, in the New Year, I was delighted. Like many English actors, I was finding that *Cleopatra* was not so much a job as a whole career. Some had been there for as long as nine months, doing very little, and being paid very well. No wonder Twentieth Century Fox went bankrupt. Not that that was any concern of mine. I was living the life of Riley, and was quite unashamed about it. I couldn't stuff any more lira into my jeans and what I couldn't spend I put in my suitcase again for another rainy day. Out of the fees, which went straight to the bank, we bought a fabulous dining-room suite from Heal's and carpeted the house expensively throughout. And with the overtime, I had a guest-room extension built at the back. I can't really say my Rome time was wasted.

Then Miss Taylor invited me to join her party at the Salvaggi Restaurant in the Via Quintino Cella for what she called 'a family Christmas dinner'. But on the day before, I was called to the production office to be told that Charlie Schneer had exercised his option and was calling me back to London for post-synch work on *Jason*. I was furious. Not only because I was missing the extended shooting, and a much better chance of career advancement with Mr Mankiewicz, but I was also going to miss that dinner with Elizabeth Taylor and Richard Burton. I phoned Schneer to explain, but he was adamant I should return, and said he would contact Walter Wanger, *Cleopatra's* producer, directly, if I didn't get on the next plane. I made a very reluctant farewell to Francesca and Liz and was booked to leave Rome airport the next night.

Elizabeth Taylor gave me a long, warm hug. 'I guess we'll see you in Hollywood, Johnny.'

She guessed wrong.

I huffily obliged Screen Gems with a day of post-synching at Twickenham on *Jason*, then, after a stormy interview in his Wigmore Street office, I was told that because of 'technical difficulties', it didn't look likely that the *Gulliver* series would be made after all. I would therefore come out of contract at the end of the year. This didn't worry me as much as it might have done, as I am glad to say I had plenty of work offers around then. The Citizens Theatre in Glasgow gave me regular 'star spots' and I could go to places like the Connaught, Worthing, and play things like *On the Spot*. Peter Hall had also offered me work at Stratford, but it was to play Demetrius in the *Dream* and two others parts 'as cast', so I let it go. That may have been a big mistake. Meantime, I was due to begin 1962 in yet another BBC six-part serial. This was *Barbara in Black* and was to be set in Wales. I was also asked about playing the Errol Flynn role in *The Master of Ballantrae*, but both dates clashed. The director of *Ballantrae*, Pharic McLaren, took the unprecedented step of delaying his shooting so that I could do both jobs.

Cardiff was quite a contrast to *Cleopatra*. I found the Welsh a little less giving than the Italians, though they had the same love of singing. Jack Walters, one of the cast, a full-time actor and part-time millionaire in the scrap business, drove me up the Rhondda Valley one weekend to his Roller to hear the Morrison male voice choir. This was the real Wales. The mining villages were hardly different from what I remembered of Ballieston. What complicated *Barbara in Black* was that I was simultaneously doing fencing pre-rehearsals for *The Master of Ballantrae*. This meant that on many of the weekends I didn't get home. I found a lovely little private hotel in Cardiff run by a young girl who was in the cast. I couldn't help but admire the courage and efficiency of Joy Leman as she managed the hotel, her mother, her sister and rehearsals. I was glad to stay there to help out. I helped to move the furniture around, for instance. We changed the dining-room around one night and next morning there was indignant confusion among the regulars who suddenly found themselves sitting facing a wall instead of a window and vice versa. Some of them wouldn't have it and with much huffing and puffing lifted their chairs back to where they had always sat!

Cardiff had its other little adventures. Coming out of the studio late one evening, I saw a naked girl walking in the rain. Passers-by weren't paying any attention at all, and I thought even only as a matter of chivalry, I should try to help. I had to run to catch up with her, and saw that she was sleep-walking. Two women were coming in the opposite direction, and I tried to tell them, but they pointedly ignored me and turned their heads away. A policeman passing on a bicycle stopped and threw back his cape, only to take out his notebook and ask ponderously for my name and address. By this time, the girl had walked on, almost to the horizon, but as we both looked we saw her turn into a building.

'Where's she gone?' I said.

'That's the Mental 'Ome,' said the policeman.

When the telephone rang in the hotel in the early hours of 10 February, I jumped to answer it. It was Sheila herself to give me the news that on the previous night, with the help of a neighbour, she had given me another girl!

'How did you manage without me?' I asked.

'Easy, she replied. 'When will you be home?'

'Tomorrow.'

I was showered with congratulations from the Welsh cast, though I didn't think I'd done much. They gave me flowers for Sheila: '*Pob Bendith Adym Uniaday Gorau I Lesley Oddiworth Gwmni, Barbara in Black.*'

I took the train to Reading, where I had left my car and drove fast to Maidenhead. Lesley Susan Helen Cairney was in her nursery. She was the first of the Cairney babies to have a nursery, and really lovely it looked. Lesley, herself, however, looked like Andy Stewart, just as Jennifer had done. My old friend, Andy, wasn't doing so badly himself in the children stakes. He and his Sheila also had three, and neither of us had finished yet. Lesley was also the first Cairney baby to have a nanny.

Miss Clare had come to us from the *Lady* magazine, although her mother lived in Twyford, which was a nearby village. Miss Clare (she would never tell us her first name) was in the old tradition of English nannies that had served generations of dukes and duchesses, lords and ladies, and now here she was, working for an actor. Not that Miss Clare minded. We certainly didn't. She was a little surprised, though, in being asked to help out with the washing-up occasionally, or take round the Hoover. That wasn't quite her job. But she adapted to our eccentric family ways, and soon became firmly established in the Cairney circle. She had a lovely relationship with Lesley, and a good one with Sheila, so it didn't matter if it were quite impersonal with me. Since her own home was so near, she didn't live in, but every morning, 8.30 a.m. there she was at the door in her uniform, ready to begin a working day at Fawley.

With the new family settled, I headed for Scotland for studio work on *Ballantrae*. Pharic McLaren, the director, was a young man and an expert fencer himself. He gave John Breslin and me further coaching, as he supervised every detail of that production. He was especially pleased to get John and me together as the twins. We were both so alike physically, and so very unlike in every other way. John was quiet, well mannered, patient and tactful. I was none of these things.

What was sad about *Ballantrae* was that Pharic, so dashing, so lithe and handsome, fell ill with multiple sclerosis and spent the rest of his life in a wheelchair.

As my mother used to say: 'You never know the minute.'

I came back to Maidenhead to open St Joseph's fête, and make an appearance in *Doctor Finlay's Casebook*. I played the tinker who got a village girl pregnant, and there were plans to bring this character back in the series. But the BBC planned instead to make a series round the tinker and I had several sessions with Harry Green, the writer, about it. Needless to say, this series was never done, and I never returned to *Finlay's Casebook*.

Instead I went back to Scotland for a special Edinburgh Festival production of a new play by Robert McLellan, called *Young Auckinlech* based on the life of James Boswell. This was unexpectedly successful at the festival and brought me a whole shoal of offers, one of which was a Royal Command, no less. *Rob Roy*, based on the novel by Walter Scott, was the Victorian vehicle chosen by the Lyceum Company and director, Gerard Slevin (my long ago friend from the Catholic Arts Guild), as the Gala Performance on the occasion of the state visit of King Olaf of Sweden to Edinburgh. This production became something of a truly royal event. A *Rob Royal* one might say.

Preparation around the city and about the theatre were thorough and intensively detailed. The only thing the authorities didn't bother about were the actors and the play itself. Pavements were painted white, windows that were thick with the dust of a century were suddenly scrupulously cleaned, and new curtains hung, dressing-room furniture was replaced, and flowers were everywhere. Just the normal preparations, one might say, for a royal one-night stand, except that the actors were still in the same old sweaty costumes, and backstage was as grotty as it had ever been. So many theatres are palaces in the foyer, and slums at the stage door. The Lyceum was not quite in this category, I must admit, and it certainly put on its best face for the royals.

My mother had something of the same problem. Each of the cast was allowed two seats. Being a state occasion, they were of extreme value and protocol had to be observed at all points. I was required to give the name and address of my two guests as tickets were to be delivered personally. Just as we actors had been literally commanded to appear, so the guests were formally invited. Sheila told me she had her hands full with the three children now that Miss Clare had departed, and suggested that I invite my parents. I gave their names to the gentleman from the Scottish Office and left it at that. Invitations were delivered by hand. I suppose it was a kind of vetting. But I could just imagine the scene as the official black car swept from London Road into Williamson Street, everybody scattering as they had always done. I could just see the bewildered look on that senior civil servant's face as he searched out No 20 and made his tentative foray into the dark close – a place he had probably never gone in his life, carrying in his hand the treasured invitation, and looking to deliver it into the hands of Mr and Mrs Thomas Cairney, if he could find them. Bending to examine every name plate, being followed by the inevitable troupe of urchins, resisting the temptation to post the scroll-like invitation into an outside lavatory, he would eventually find the second floor, and our name on its brass plate. My mother told me it was she who opened the door. When she saw the official-looking gentleman, she thought at first it was a priest. And when he handed over the scroll, she was convinced it was a writ.

He had hardly gone when she was on the telephone right away to me. Not that we had a telephone. Like everyone else in Williamson Street, we made use of the telephone on the wall in Effie Reid's fruit shop on the corner. Her shop was the vortex of local gossip: 'Reid all about it' she was called. Since the only public telephone was on her premises, she was privy to everything that was going on for at least two miles around. On this occasion, there was my mother, yelling at me down the phone, with all the ease of someone who never used one, complaining about this invitation, and telling me she couldn't go.

'You must go, Mother. It's a Command performance.'

'I couldn't – '

'Why not?'

'Because I've nothing to wear.'

'Then go as a nudist, Mother,' I rejoined, jocularly.

'I'm no' goin'.' Her voice was quite determined.

But she reckoned without the neighbours. Word soon got round the street that Mary Cairney was going to see the Queen, and, one by one, the women all came to the door. One would hand in a pair of gloves: 'I've never worn them since our Susie's wedding.' Another handed in a fox fur: 'It was my grannie's.' Another a silk scarf: 'I got it for my birthday from my boy.' There was also a dress coat made in barathea, innumerable shoes and a string of pearls – imitation of course. My mother was bewildered by the choice now laid before her. Nobody bothered to ask what my father might wear.

I was playing the villain of the piece, Rashleigh Osbaldistone, and had a splendid entrance in Act One. I came up steps from the rear on to the stage alone, and had rehearsed a slow walk down to the floats. This was a little slower than rehearsed, because I was taken aback by the 'aurora borealis' that greeted my eyes. Most actors look out into the audience and see it as an overall darkness with just the occasional oasis of light from exit signs and the narrow spill that goes out from the stage on to the first two or three rows of the stalls. But on this special evening, it was as if every lady in the auditorium was wearing a miner's lamp, like Grandfather Cairney. But the light shining around them was in fact the reflection of their jewellery in the stage lighting. It reminded me of that Aden starlight. '*Vidunderlig*,' as King Olaf might have said. At any rate, it was enough to put me right off. What made matters worse is that as I glanced up to the royal box, there indeed was the Queen. What else had I expected? But she looked so small and real and accessible, somehow. Suffice to say, I dried stone dead, and could not remember my first line. It was only as I gazed around, I suddenly thought of my mother. What was she wearing? I suddenly had visions of her sitting in her stalls seat, like an overloaded dromedary, draped in everybody's offers, and with that picture in my mind, my words came flooding back and I delivered my first line.

During the interval, five of us were presented in the royal box – all those who had billing above the title! I lined up to be formally presented behind Archie Duncan, Lennox Milne, Andrew Downie, and Callum Mill. Her Majesty remarked on the splendid pause I held on my first entrance.

I confessed at once, 'That wasn't a pause, Ma'am. I forgot my words.'

She looked quite understanding. 'What a shame. I do that sometimes.'

She asked me what was going to happen in the second part.

I said, 'I have a fight with Rob Roy.'

'Oh, good,' she said. 'Who wins?'

I glanced across at the towering figure of Archie Duncan, and said, 'Who do you think, Ma'am?'

She laughed. 'I see.'

Archie duly won his fight and I was killed, and the play ended to a tumultuous reception. We were ordered back to our dressing-room to await the royal pleasure. Archie and I were sharing No 1 and every now and then a lackey would put his head round the door and yelp excitedly, 'She's coming. Stand by.'

We stood by for quite a long time, being unable to get changed until the royal party had been and gone. We weren't even allowed to smoke, so it was an uncomfortable wait. Then at last we heard noises in the corridor, the door opened again, and the frenzied lackey almost squealed, 'She's on her way *now*!'

We stood up at attention facing our mirrors. Mine had a good view of the door. But it wasn't the Queen who entered. It was the Queen Mother. And just a few steps behind Her Majesty – my mother! I nearly fainted. She scuttled quickly beside me. There was no sign of my father. The Queen Mother was accompanied by the young Prince Charles and two ladies.

Suddenly she was saying to me, 'Your mother tells me that you live in Windsor.'

'No, Ma'am. In Maidenhead. My children go to school in Windsor.'

The Queen Mother smiled in her gracious way. 'Yes, we have a place there.'

As the royal party left, my mother slumped on the couch. 'Oh, my God,' she said. 'I need a fag.'

'What happened, Mother?' I asked incredulously.

After she'd taken a powerful draw at the cigarette, and while Archie was getting changed at the other end of the room, she told me what had happened. 'When youse were taking yer bows, I said to Tom – my God, where is he?'

'It's all right, Mother, we'll find him. Go on.'

'Well, everybody stood up to see the Queen leave her box, and then they all rushed to get out at the front, tae see her again mair like at the front but I said to your father, "If we go through that pass door there, we can get to see John first before a' the palaver, and then we can get away nice in time tae catch that Glasgow bus frae the station,"'

'Don't worry, Mother, I'll take you back. Well . . .?'

'Aye,' she said. 'That'll be handy right enough. Well – we had a helluva joab squeezing through the crowd, because we seemed to be the only wans coming this wey, wi' everybody else goin' that wey. Onywey, we got through the door and up the stairs. And here, did we no' meet these people comin' doon the corridor the other way. So I stands back to let the woman past. It was the Queen.'

'No, Mother, it was the Queen Mother.'

'Well, it wis wan o' them. But, here, did the young man wi' 'er no'

211

make his hand like so.' She indicated a sort of 'After you, madam,' gesture.

This was Prince Charles and no doubt he was politely allowing my mother to pass, but she took it as an invitation to join them, and thus, by accident, found herself in my dressing-room with the royals. I couldn't help laughing. Neither could Archie.

My mother wasn't amused. 'Here's wis I jus tryin' tae catch the last bus,' she said.

By the time I was ready, she was sufficiently calmed down again to accompany me on stage where everyone was assembled and mixing informally. Duncan Macrae was there with his wife, Peggy.

Then I saw my father. He was wearing a dinner jacket and black tie. It was the first time I had ever seen him in this male uniform, and he looked most impressive. He was thinner and paler than I would have liked, but still with that Glasgow chutzpah and thirties charm. He was leaning on a sword. (I thought, God, have they knighted him?) He was talking to gentlemen of the Duke of Edinburgh's party.

When I got near I said to him quietly, 'Where did you get the suit, Dad?'

'From a "menage".' (Pronounced 'minodge'!)

This was uttered in a throwaway Glasgow style, which must have sounded, in its elision, quite incomprehensible to the nearby gentry, one of whom thought Dad was a member of King Olaf's staff. Dad didn't mind. He took it all with his usual sang-froid, and gave me his empty glass for a refill. I walked away as he explained to the toffs how one could purchase articles in Glasgow via a club and a small regular weekly amount – this was known as the 'menage' – from the French, 'to manage'! Dad could really pile it on when he had to.

My mother raised her eyes as she caught my glance. 'Wid he no' gie ye a red face?' she whispered.

By the way, she looked lovely. She wore the simplest of dresses, cream, I think, with golden threads through it. There was a touch of blue rinse in her grey hair, which set off her dark eyes, and round her neck she wore a string of pearls – imitation of course! Yes, for me, on that *Rob Royal* night, we were certainly in the presence of kings and queens – and my mother and father were two of them.

From a Royal Command like that, nearly everything is downhill. I was given a page in the *Scotsman* newspaper to state my hopes for a Scottish national theatre, but it made little difference. I was given the opportunity by Gerard Slevin, the director of *Rob Roy*, of fulfill-ing my long-held ambition to play a one-man Robert Burns, and was strongly considering it. The biggest change of all, however, was that Christopher Mann had retired, and the agency was being reformed. I took this opportunity to throw in my lot with a young agent starting up on his own, a little Jewish dynamo called Barry Krost, who had been with the Fosters Agency. He had written asking me to consider joining him if the opportunity ever arose. So here I was, in the New Year of 1963, having been nurtured all along the way by Christopher Mann since John Cadell's visit to the Bristol Old Vic in 1954, suddenly at a crossroads in my career. And for the first time since I left college, I was out of work. But I reckoned without Barry Krost.

He knew a man who knew a man who knew Disley Jones, whose company, Jade Productions, was putting on a production of *The Rivals* at the Lyric, Hammersmith. A meeting was arranged. This was quite a casting coup if Barry could pull it off. The part was a good one, Captain Absolute, but more important, it would give me my West End baptism, and the cachet that every British professional actor looks for – even if he comes from Glasgow. I got the part, and was even more delighted when I found that my Lydia was to be Claire Isbister, now Nielson and also Mrs Denis Vance. Our stars were Fay Compton as Mrs Malaprop and Laurence Hardy as Sir Anthony. I had seen Mr Hardy often at the Citizens when I was a student. He was the finest type of English professional actor: unassuming and diffi-dent, yet turning in performance after performance of painstaking integrity and effectiveness. Fay was in another world. She was in an even longer line of theatrical eccentrics that can, in a flash of insight, illuminate a whole play. If Laurence Hardy was a steady roll of thunder throughout the production, Fay Compton was its light-ning flash. Brian Murphy was as good a director as he was an actor, and I think we got together a worthwhile revival.

Not that I was helped much by some of my male colleagues. There was a decided locking of horns occasionally. I was being made well aware that I was a newcomer to this West End scene, in much the same way that the Wilson Barrett actors had made me aware I was a newcomer to theatre ten years before. I found Peter Woodthorpe as Bob Acres especially difficult at rehearsal, and was moaning about this to Sheila that night in bed. She told me to just get on with making a good job of my own part, and let others get on with theirs. She suggested I would do better to get some sleep.

I was wakened by the telephone about three o'clock in the

213

morning of 3 April. It was the young priest from Our Lady of Fatima down Springfield Road, ringing to tell me that my father had died in the night. He had wakened saying, 'There's somethin' no' right here.' As my mother switched on the light, he died. As the priest told me this, I was only conscious of a sea of purple. I put my phone down on my study desk, put my head in my hands and bawled my eyes out. Sheila came to me with a large brandy, and together we watched the dawn come up, sitting on the edge of the bed.

I couldn't make up my mind whether to go straight home to Glasgow or to see through the opening night. I rang Barry and told him the news. He told me to have another brandy and he would get back to me. It was decided I should make my West End debut as planned. It would give the company time to prime the understudy and allow me to make travel plans for the next day. I then rang an aunt who had the telephone and asked her to convey that message to my mother.

I don't remember much about the first night, and the wonderful notices seemed as ashes in my mouth. Jim rang me from Canada, and I advised him not to bother coming for the funeral. By the time he reached Glasgow it would be all over. I would see to everything. I did so in a kind of trance. Instead of being in the West End of London, I was suddenly in the East End of Glasgow. Funnily enough, when I was in the former, I could only think of the latter. And now I was home again in Glasgow, I could only think, I should be on stage in London. Perhaps it's nature's way of keeping us from thinking too deeply on anything. If it's too bad to think about, think of something else.

My first glimpse of my father in his coffin was ludicrous. His handsome face was in its death repose, and he looked better than I'd seen him look for years – if you see what I mean. There was a tranquility again, and the lines had gone. But he was wearing a yellow shirt and a preposterous clip-on brown bow-tie. I snatched it off in a fury, and threw it into a corner. My dapper dad, who had been such a natty dresser, would never have been seen dead in a brown clip-on bow-tie! I kissed the marble forehead, then watched as my mother kissed him full and long on the lips. It was an awkward job carrying the coffin down those stairs. It was much easier when he carried down my little sister's in his arms. But it was even more difficult getting out into the street. It was a sea of men, almost like a football pitch – mostly older men, but so many different types. They were all from Dad's many worlds: the worlds of music and pipe bands, Beardmore's, London and Folkstone and Uncle Tom Cobbley and all. You couldn't see the street for men, and from every street window the women were looking down. It took us a long time to walk the coffin down Springfield Road to the church. From there, the undertakers took over and we left him in Dalbeth Cemetery under a plain stone, which said simply, 'Tom Cairney'. There it was, his name carved in stone, in the very month when mine went up in lights. What was the difference? What's in a name but a life?

My life was in the theatre and it was to a theatre I returned. East End – West End. Was there a difference? I was just the same wherever I was and at that time, I was a grieving son. Would the real John Cairney please stand up? Stand up to what? Life? Or work? To me, it was one and the same, so I got on with it.

I made a film at Bray called *Devilship Pirates* and co-starred with Christopher Lee and Andrew Keir.

'You'll be in Hollywood within the year,' said Tony Nelson Keys.

But I wasn't. Instead I was in Edinburgh and thereafter everywhere else as the man who played Robert Burns.

In the meantime, however, the BBC had invited me to play the lead in their proposed series for BBC2, provisionally entitled *Tomorrow's People*, in which I was to play a schoolmaster at a comprehensive school. At first they intended this to be modelled on Holland Park, but when the producer, Peter Graham Scott, flew to see me in Edinburgh, they had changed their minds and set it in Glasgow. The consequence was that I spent two years commuting between Glasgow and London, and becoming what is known in the trade as a 'name'. This was assisted largely by the fact that I played schoolmaster Ian Craig in *This Man Craig*, a series that went out all over the country twice weekly on BBC1 and 2. One result was that I got a massive fan mail.

But the only letter I treasured was one from a young lady in Kendal, who wrote at her mother's insistence. It seems the old lady was a keen follower of *This Man Craig*, but on one occasion, its transmission coincided with her being washed by her daughter at her cottage fireside. The mother insisted on having a towel over her knees as I came on the screen.

'I don't want him to see me like this,' the old lady had protested. 'He's such a nice young man. He would hate to see my knees.'

So her daughter wrote to tell me and in so doing, made me realise the impact of this kind of regular exposure on television. The habit alone can create the star. If it had disadvantages, like the time spent away from home, the inordinate work rate, the publicity strain, and the constant stress and tension, it also had advantages. My credit rating at the bank soared, for, thanks to Barry's managerial skills it was also highly remunerative.

The Cairneys moved to a bigger house, still in Maidenhead, and Sheila got her own car. I didn't buy a Rolls-Royce, but one luxury we could now well afford was another baby. And one duly arrived at the Clevedon Hospital on 25 March 1966. I was at home in Highways, on my own at the time, when the call came. It was Heulwyn Marriott, a dear friend, phoning from the hospital.

'Hello, Daddy,' she said in her lilting Welsh, 'it's another lovely girl you have.'

'Oh,' I said. There was a pause.

'Well, don't go mad,' Heulwyn said dryly. 'Get the champagne out.'

'Is Sheila all right?'

'Lovely.'

'And the baby?'

'Gorgeous. What you going to call her then?'

'Jane. Jane Lillian Heather Cairney.'

'Goodness, there's a mouthful.'

I got out the champagne together with the sign that I had previously made up, awaiting only the name. It was a series of large capital letters, each hanging singly on a thread. Now I was able to hang it all across the front of the garage facing on to the drive and the roadway beyond. It would be the first thing Sheila would see as I drove her in. It said:

'WELCOME HOME, BABY JANE!'

It was 1967. I was in Glasgow, asleep in my little flat off Hyndland Road. I was wakened about one o'clock in the morning by heavy hammering on the door. I sat bolt upright, wondering at first where I was. Then I thought, There must be a fire, and was out of bed like a shot – wondering what I should save first. '*Me*,' I said to myself quickly, and made for the door. The hammering had stopped and I could only hear a fuzzy mumbling from the other side.

'Who's there?' I croaked.

'Me!' was the reply.

'Who's me?' I said, feeling a little silly, even as I said it.

'John Cairney.' This was a little louder.

216

'That's right,' I said.

There was a silence. Then: 'Whit the hell d'ye mean "that's right"?' a voice growled from the other side.

'I'm John Cairney,' I said, putting one bare foot on top of the other. It was draughty in that little hall, and in those days I rarely wore pyjamas.

'*So am I!*' This time it was a bellow.

'What?'

'I'm John Cairney, your wee cousin, ye daft gowk.'

The sense of it gradually filtered through. 'Oh, that John Cairney?'

'Not at all, *this* John Cairney!' came the truculent rejoinder through the letter-box.

I caught the glimpse of a red eye. 'Just a minute.' I pulled on a pair of trousers and opened the door.

There stood the other John Cairney, every inch my cousin, but looking seven feet high in the doorway and swaying dangerously. What made him seem even more lethal was that he had a bottle in each hand. A bottle of Bell's whisky and a bottle of Barr's lemonade.

'John – ' I began, but he was already pushing past me.

He came to a halt in the middle of the little sitting-room. 'It's hardly the Ritz, is it?' he bleered, swaying round to me. He was very drunk.

'The best I can do on BBC money,' I muttered. 'Take a – '

But he'd already come down heavily on the little couch, swamping it, and was now glaring up at me, one of the cushions seeming to come out of his ear. 'I just want you to know something,' he mumbled thickly.

'What's that, John?' I asked, in the padre-patronising tone one adopts when talking to anyone who is drunk, especially when you're sober.

'I hate – ' It was said so vehemently it made him hiccough violently. 'Sorry 'bout that . . . '

I shrugged and took the chair opposite, watching him closely.

'Anyway, as I was saying . . . whit was I sayin?'

'You hate . . . '

'That's right. I hate *you*.' And he pointed one of his bottles.

I instinctively flinched but said nothing. There's nothing much one can say in the face of such a direct and honest statement.

'Here, have ye a glass?'

I brought two tumblers.

'I just need the one,' he said, splashing some lemonade into his whisky. I grimaced. He looked up. 'What's up?'

'Nothing,' I said quickly. Whisky and lemonade must be Glasgow's favourite tipple after rum and bacardi and Irn-bru, but I hate seeing good whisky ruined by additives – even water.

'Have a drink,' he said, passing me over the lemonade bottle.

'Thanks!'

There was a pause for drink and contemplation.

'Ach, it's no that I hate you so much as . . . resent, I suppose.'

'Thank goodness for that,' I said with a very weak laugh.

'No, although I don't fancy your West End ways and a' this Anglo patter. I mean you're an East Ender – an ordinary five-eight – just like the rest o' us.' At that moment, cousin John looked anything but an ordinary five-eight – more ten by twenty as he sprawled massively on that little couch.

'No,' he drawled, 'it's just that I hate being John Cairney. And it's a terrible thing for a man to hate his ain name, is it no'?'

'It must be,' I agreed.

'And it's your fault,' he shouted, struggling to rise.

'Afore you did a' this acting stuff, naebody bothered wi' me; noo it's "Oh here, John Cairney is it – nae relation to *the* John Cairney, I suppose?" – his bloody cousin! And then they don' even believe me.'

This, then, was old John's problem it seemed – my high public profile. He was at that time a student PT teacher at Jordanhill College, and therefore was not so conspicuously in the public eye. Not that he minded, far from it. He just needed time to climb his mountain and run his ten miles a day, and occasionally see Celtic from the 'Jungle' and he was happy enough. But, as he said, he resented *my* intrusion on *his* name! It was an invasion of privacy in his eyes, a dereliction of personal identity. I had known him all my life as Uncle Phil's and Auntie Mary's son, and therefore *my* cousin, but it had never really occurred to me that I was *his* cousin and that he was John Cairney too.

In my career I had taken, almost unwittingly, a stride across my native city – East End–West End – and bridged a gap to that other West End in London, never thinking that I had left so much behind in Glasgow. So much of my past, my family, myself, was his past, his family, his *self*. It was eerie. We talked through both our problems all the way to breakfast-time. By then he was as right as rain and went away at a trot to his first lecture. But I wasn't so hot. I reported to rehearsals at Springfield Road that morning decidedly hung-over. Nobody believed me when I told them it was the lemonade!

At the time of the teachers' strike in Glasgow, John was frequently

218

on television or in the newspapers arguing his colleagues' case against the Education Department. Perhaps his was more a notoriety than a fame, but nevertheless, for a time, he became something of a name. I had occasion to give my name somewhere, and was startled by the reaction.

'John Cairney? I don't suppose you're any relation to *the* John Cairney?'

'I'm his cousin,' I said.

Perhaps all relationships are relative, in a manner of speaking. Mine own immediate family was completed not long after.

AND UNTO US A SON IS BORN

Jennifer, Alison, Lesley and Jane;
Green twigs on our family tree,
Each a potential branch on her own
Stemming from Sheila and me.
Jenny came first in a wonderful burst,
Nine months – and a week – from our wedding;
As fate had directed, completely expected,
Though both of us parenthood dreading.
But with the aplomb of a veteran sire
Who'd done this sort of thing all his life,
Though suspected of shirking,
I carried on working
And left the whole thing to my wife.

Despite all her fears and an ocean of tears
Both she and the baby survived.
They learned from each other
The daughter and mother
And a real satisfaction derived,
From which I was excluded,
But in no sense deluded,
This was a woman's affair.
But I was quite happy as one dirty nappy
Relentlessly followed another
As I saw my young Sheila gently reveal a
Propensity as a good mother.

219

Just as well perhaps,
For despite some mishaps
And a whole day before she was due
I was called to the bed and out popped a head
– and I was father to two!
Blue as the sky she seemed first to my eye,
The most beautiful sight I had seen,
Except for her mother, her labour now done,
Now resting, relieved and serene.

But with Alison set, and just time to forget
All those wearisome months of waiting,
We moved house again, and once more I was told
That Mummy was 'anticipating'.
Little Lesley this was,
And an angel because she happened
So neatly and quick.
I came back from rehearsal and there they were –
Castor Oil had done the trick!

Another few years and the cot reappears,
The Cairneys have done it again.
And sure enough I was carrying home,
A lovely wee bundle called Jane.
Now she's three, nearly four,
Will there be any more?
Well, I really can't say at this minute.
But I notice that Sheila has looked out the pram
There might possibly be something in it!

If there is, well so be it,
Somehow we will cope,
And know once again that same joy.
But something keeps whispering
In a very small voice:
'Surely next time it must be a BOY!'

Jonathan William Thomas Cairney was born in the early hours of
St David's Day on Sunday, 1 March 1970, and I was there at the end
of the bed to see him emerge. If I hadn't been asked by one of the
young nurses to fetch a cardboard cup of cold water, I would have
missed everything. Because, you see, for seven hours I had been up

220

at the top end of the bed trying to help Sheila through what was her longest labour yet. I talked and talked and sang and read from newspapers, women's magazines, some books I'd brought in – even her palm. Anything to keep her mind off the spasms and help her to relax and face the big one when it came. I held one hand and then the other and then both; I wiped her brow; I kissed her cheek; I watched the freckles rise mottled on her flushed cheeks as her time (or rather Jonathan's) drew near. I never loved her more, or treasured her more deeply as I watched her fight her relentless battle with her own body for the life of *my* son.

What a sober remove is the harsh, hard, hospital labour-room from the soft, semi-dark bedroom of the love-making. One never really connects the two: the act and the reaction. Now I was sitting by the bedside like Dr Kildare: my hair covered in a cap, a mask across my face, swathed in an apron and with green gumboots on my feet. You would think I was about to perform a Caesarean myself, but all I could do was to mutter, 'There! There!' to the still attractive girl in the crook of my left arm whose fair hair was wet across her brow and whose short nightie looked preposterous at the foot of the mountain that was her belly. Yet she was excited. We were both excited. This was to be our last child – whatever. Naturally I hoped it might be a boy. It was now or never. Sheila was thirty-five, I was forty. Life was just beginning for us, and it was also just about to begin for that little someone already hammering at the door with his head. I didn't know it was going to be a boy. I should have been a nervous wreck had I known that. Oh, yes, I went through all the expected macho motions of waiting for a boy like Henry the Eighth, but at that hospital bedside in Taplow, through that long weekend, I only wanted my wife to get through it all as naturally and swiftly as possible and that a child be born that had ten fingers and ten toes, two eyes, two ears and all its future senses about it. I hadn't even given much thought to the name. Unlike most wives, Sheila had allowed me to name all our children. We talked about it, naturally, but by and large, she had other priorities and gave me the responsibility of naming our progeny. So I did.

Jonathan should have been John to keep up the family practice but John Cairney Senior and Junior did not appeal, so Jonathan better suggested little John, and anyway, being born on St David's Day, David and Jonathan seemed to fit somehow.

The tumbler of water I had brought for the little black nurse went up in the air like a fountain as we all saw it was a boy. I bellowed

221

like a madman: '*It's a boy!*' The nurses squealed, the young doctor grinned. Sheila kept calling out, 'Is it all right?'

'Of coure he's all right,' I roared. 'He's perfect – he's marvellous – he's wonderful – he's my son, isn't he?'

By this time, those who weren't crying were laughing, and I was doing both, dancing about like a dervish in my gumboots.

They wouldn't let me near Sheila or the child. Instead I was bundled out into a waiting-room while they attended to the more serious matter of the afterbirth. I had to be helped out of my Dr Kildare costume by a nurse, who then very kindly brought me a glass of National Health sherry, with which I there and then 'wetted' young Jonathan's head. And then sat back in the chair feeling myself shiver all over. How must Sheila feel? Relieved? Euphoric? Exhausted? And did the brand-new human being feel anything yet – did he know he was a Cairney? I don't know how long I sat in a stupor before another young nurse took me along to the ward and there they both were. Two people who belonged to me where before there had been one. It was a touching and tender and very private moment. Then it was time for me to go home.

I was numb with fatigue and I was starving. I had been in that hospital for virtually a whole day. And when I got home eventually, I hardly knew where I was. I poured myself a very large whisky which had been primed ready for the occasion, then sat at the telephone for the rest of the night ringing the good news to the world. When I went to our bed, it seemed vast and cold and very empty. I was very tired but very happy.

Next day was a swim of reporters and relatives and little daughters wondering how they were going to cope with a brother.

'He's just like Daddy.'

'You mean all old and hairy?'

'No . . . well, he'll not be like us.'

'What do you mean?'

'Just wait and see for yourself.'

'I don't think I want a brother.'

'But he's just a baby.'

'My best friend Clare's got a brother and he's not a baby!'

Then my own brother Jim rang – not from Toronto, as I had expected – but from Manchester! He'd got the chance of a cheap flight and he'd taken it. Could I meet him? Of course I could. I could do anything. Didn't he know I was the father of a son? (Jim had three sons!) I drove to Manchester in a dream, telling everyone at every traffic light that my wife had a baby boy last night! I found Jim at the airport and we opened his duty-free bottle there and then! We then decided to have a meal before driving south again, and during it we discovered from the Irish waiter that Manchester United were playing Celtic that night at Old Trafford – only twenty minutes away. The temptation was very great.

Meanwhile, that evening, Sheila, now looking smart again and with her hair done, was sitting up in bed holding a noisy Jonathan, who wasn't enjoying his first press call. Photographers, both local and national, were at the bedside to capture in their lenses for tomorrow's editions the proud parents with their first son.

But the proud father was at that moment telling half the grand-stand at Old Trafford that he'd just become the father of a boy and was inviting all those round him to help finish the rest of Jim's duty-free Johnny Walker Black Label. One man gave me a big cigar, and I delightedly starting smoking again.

At that same moment, two hundred miles to the south, smoke was also rising from the fires of Sheila's indignation and embarrassment as she faced the reporters alone with her new baby.

'But where is your husband, Mrs Cairney?'

Then someone mentioned that Celtic were playing Manchester United that night.

'Did you say Celtic?' said Sheila, and suddenly she knew.

The *Evening Standard* next day showed a professionally-smiling Sheila holding a bawling Jonathan. Coincidentally, on the same day Mia Farrow had given twins to André Previn, and there they were, all four, in the companion picture to Sheila and Jonathan.

When I at last made my shame-faced re-entry to the hospital hiding myself and my hangover behind dark glasses and the biggest bunch of roses I could find in Maidenhead, I was forgiven – I think – but I don't think it was ever forgotten. But all I could think of then was that I had a boy at last. A son. And I shall never forget that. As I write, Jonathan, is six feet tall, eighteen years old and a first-year student at King's College, Cambridge. Is he the end of the John Cairney saga – or is he the beginning?

A final note. Only very recently, I was in Glasgow for a television programme, and was waiting to cross at the traffic lights at the top of Byres Road on my way to the Grosvenor Hotel. I was standing beside a lady who was neither young nor old, in the way that some Glasgow women have, and she was standing beside me holding a pram with a big, fat baby in it. I found myself looking at the baby, making silly faces at it, the way one does, and the baby was looking at me with solemn amazement, the way babies do, when I was aware that the woman was also looking at me. I turned and half-smiled at her and was about to say something complimentary about her immense baby, when she said, 'Excuse me, did you used to be John Cairney? If ye're no' ye're awfy like him. Ye know, the man who played Robert Burns?'

Just at that, the lights changed to green and I was glad it was time to go.

L'ENVOI

D'YE MIND!

D'ye mind
When the sun seemed to shine a' day
And nights were story-book long?
And ye made shadow-fancies on the plaster wa' of the bed
Till ye were feart o' your ain imagination!
But ye fell asleep before the big monster got ye
And ye remember nothing till the mornin'.

D'ye mind
How ye woke fresh as toothpaste?
Eager to brush with the day
That stretched ahead like a rimless desert
Dotted with meal-times
Or unexpected oases to steal a smoke
Catch a breather – even a breath!

D'ye mind
When life was so big a thing
Ye never even thought about it?
And if ye did
It was only to giggle about how easy it all was.

Now ye've grown up
And the world has shrunk a wee
Taking its simplicity with it,
Leaving ye to ponder
On the complexity of the wrinkles on its tired old face.

Your eyesight's not so good
Ruined by politic short-sightedness,
The need to see what ye think ye have to see.
Missing everything essential
In your desperation to miss nothing!

D'ye mind
When ye understood nothing?
And ye see now it was a gift
And ye threw it away!

D'ye mind?